Praise for *Diet for a New Life*

"Mariana Bozesan, entrepreneur, global activist, philanthropist, mystic, mother, goddess, intellectual, and sage, has written a seminal book for all people who wish to make a difference in this world and who wish to do that while living a healthy, vibrant life. She herself is the real-life model from which the experience of the book is written. She glows with thriving radiant health, she speaks with elegance and eloquence, and she has deeply researched what makes a healthy life and one that is conscious and committed. Although this appears to be a diet book, it is really a life skills book, rooted in spiritual teaching and inspiring stories. Mariana has put the whole struggle with weight, health, and maintaining fitness in the much larger and more inspiring context of living a life in which you thrive from the integrity of knowing who you are. From there you are inspired and empowered to develop practices and ways of being that fully express your best self.

"This book, if you truly follow it, will catapult you into a whole new expression of yourself. You will not only lose weight, but you will gain confidence, vitality, and profound contentment. I recommend that everyone read it, incorporate it, and live it. Mariana has done us all a great service and opened the door for a level of health that goes beyond even our wildest expectations. Bravo!"

> – Lynne Twist, author of *The Soul of Money*

"Mariana Bozesan is an inspiration to others. To share her story is courageous—to use it to help others is admirable."

> – Anthony Robbins, author of *Unlimited Power* and
> *Awaken the Giant Within*

"*Diet for a New Life* can be an excellent resource for that special breed of men and women who will never settle for less than they can be. It is an extraordinary tool for achieving weight loss and well-being."

> – Camran Nezhat, M.D., clinical professor of surgery,
> Stanford University School of Medicine

"*Diet for a New Life* by Mariana Bozesan is a brilliant blend of science, personal practice, commonsensical advice, and hands-on direction for achieving lasting weight loss, health, and vitality. I will highly recommend this book to my BioSET practitioners as well as BioSET patients throughout the world."

> – Ellen W. Cutler, D.C., author of *The Food Allergy Cure* and *MicroMiracles*

"In *Diet for a New Life*, Mariana Bozesan shows how to re-construct the blueprint of your body so that you can lose weight, enjoy health and higher levels of vitality, and live a life of joy and fulfillment."

> – Deepak Chopra, M.D., author of *Grow Younger, Live Longer* and *Perfect Weight*

"Mariana Bozesan has discovered a secret: that our body has a consciousness of its own and that being fit and healthy means honoring the body's spirit, the body's heart, and the body's needs as you honor your most beloved friend. In *Diet for a New Life* she teaches you how to get it together on all levels in such an attractive way that it is impossible to miss! If you make this book your fitness bible you'll have a perfect body and a perfect life IN NO TIME AT ALL!"

> – Margot Anand, author of *The Art of Everyday Ecstasy*

"Trained and influenced by extraordinary teachers, Mariana Boze-san has created an outstanding, well-researched, practical, and action-oriented guide for weight loss and well-being. Backed up by solid research and animated by a passionate commitment to help and serve, this is a wise book by a woman who speaks from her heart to our deepest yearnings for health and happiness."

> – Riane Eisler, author of *The Chalice and the Blade* and *The Partnership Way*

"Mariana Bozesan is an awesome person! I knew from the moment I met her that this woman has real soul and incredible beauty! I feel honored to recommend her fantastic book *Diet for a New Life*, which accurately captures her energy, enthusiasm, and intel-ligence. Her inspirational book delivers practical advice, and strate-gies to help you lose weight, feel great, and smile. In fact, reading Mariana's book will help you experience the best day ever!"

> – David Wolfe, author of *Eating for Beauty* and *Raw Chocolate*

"In this easy-to-digest book, we are reminded of the multiple ways in which body and mind come together in our relationship to food. As we seek to achieve optimum health, readers will find Mariana's insights welcome, obtainable, and delightfully nutritious. Happy reading; happy eating."

—Marilyn Schlitz, author of *Conscious Healing*

"This book is an enormous source of information, strength, and weight loss wisdom."

– David Morehouse, Ph.D., 1999 Nobel Peace Prize nominee and author of *The Psychic Warrior*

"The material in this book represents a powerful quantum leap forward in the self-help technology of weight loss and well-being. It successfully combines the best knowledge and tools available today and approaches weight loss from a comprehensive perspective—not just the physical but the emotional and spiritual dimensions as well."

– Howard Martin, co-author, *The HeartMath Solution*

"*Diet for a New Life* bursts with astonishing scientific credibility and practical guidelines for concentrating your thoughts, actions, and emotions toward the attainment of your weight loss goals and well-being."

– Fred P. Gallo, Ph.D., author of *Energy Psychology*

"This book will change your life! What an incredible summarization of today's great teachers and sages! Mariana gives you the facts and lets you design the lifestyle you want. This is not a diet book but a guided path to well-being and to being a naturally happy and healthy person. I learned something from every page, but reading the whole book changed my life!"

– Carol Sands, founder of the Angels Forum and winner of the Influential Women in Business Award

"Mariana Bozesan combines her personal odyssey towards optimal health with solid alternative holistic health information. It is informative and most important highly motivational. I would recommend this book to anyone who desires the attainment of well-being."

– Herb Ross, D.C., author of *Sleep Disorders*

"Increased energy, endurance and clearer thinking are some of the first benefits you'll notice from applying *Diet for a New Life*. As you continue to follow this simple plan you'll experience permanent weight loss and a life of meaning and fulfillment."

— John Maguire, Pain Relief expert and author of
Become Pain Free with Touch For Health

"This book has so many helpful concepts and common sense approaches to following a healthy diet and learning about many important areas of well-being, such as cholesterol and healthy fats, immune function and stress, sugar metabolism, and much more. Most importantly, if you wish to trim your body and weigh less while receiving even more nourishment, Mariana has you covered."

- Elson Haas, M.D., author of *Staying Healthy with Nutrition* and *The New Detox Diet*

"Mariana's approach is not about forcing your body to look a certain way according to a shallow and totally external image of beauty. It's about finding within yourself the healing powers you need, and unleashing the totality of your inner forces in the service of your magnificence. At one level, this is a book about losing weight. But more than that, it is a book about love and about life. It is brave and honest. May it guide you to the fulfillment of your greatest purpose in being alive."

— John Robbins, author of *The Food Revolution* and
Healthy at 100

"This is an amazing book. It is not a mere manual for a successful diet, but an inspiring map for an archetypal journey toward Self-discovery."

— Marius Koga, M.D., MPH, Associate Clinical Professor
of International Health, UC Davis School of Medicine

"*Diet for a New Life* is a brilliant synthesis between scientific research and hands-on advice for achieving permanent weight management. Mariana shows not only how food affects the physical body but more importantly our mood and our relationships."

— John Gray, Ph.D., author of *Men are from Mars, Women are from Venus* and *Mars & Venus Diet and Exercise Solution*

MY GIFT TO YOU

INVITATION TO JOIN THE WISDOM CIRCLE

Dear Kindred Sprit:

Through this book, you have acquired the right to join SageEra's Wisdom Circle at no additional cost. An online resource complementary to the book, the Wisdom Circle provides information and insight from weight loss and well-being experts including Deepak Chopra, John Gray, Udo Erasmus, Elson Haas, Ellen Cutler, and many other luminaries.

So please accept my invitation and sign up for the Wisdom Circle at www.SageEra.com/WisdomCircle. It will give you access to expert articles interviews, complete online community privileges, free coupons, and much more.

Let your free membership to the Wisdom Circle be the beginning of a long-term relationship that will help us transform not only our own, but the lives of our families, friends, communities, and our beautiful blue planet. I look forward to meeting you in person one day. Until then, may you continue to

Celebrate Your Life & Make it a Masterpiece!

Much love and light,
Mariana Bozesan

Diet for a New Life

An 8-step Integral Solution to Weight Loss and Well-being

By Mariana Bozesan

Published by SageEra Institute LLC, PO Box 1603, Palo Alto, CA 94302, USA, www.SageEra.com

Book & cover design by Lewis Agrell—www.theagrellgroup.com

SageEra and the SageEra logo are trademarks of SageEra Institute LLC. Many of the designations used by manufacturers and sellers to distinguish their products are claimed as trademarks, whether they are marked as such in this book or not.

Disclaimer:

Bozesan, Mariana

Diet for a New Life – An 8-step Integral Solution to Weight Loss and Well-Being

1. Diet. 2. Weight Loss. 3. Health. 4. Mind and body. 5. Spirituality. 6. Self-Help. 7. Exercise

ISBN 978-0-9746102-1-4 hardcover
ISBN 978-0-9746102-3-8 paperback

Library of Congress Control Number: 2007921736

I slept and dreamt that life was joy.
I awoke and saw that life was service.
I acted, and behold, service was joy.

—Rabindranath Tagore

*With unconditional love to Albert, Tom, Maria, Grigore, and
to all human beings in search of a higher meaning in life.
To those who have found the key to their true nature
and to those who are still seeking.
May your journey be blessed!*

CONTENTS

PART 3 – Creating Lasting Change

Foreword

Human beings come in all shapes and sizes, and this diversity is part of our beauty. Yet modern society can be very cruel to people whose bodies do not fit the cultural ideal. I certainly do not want to add to the suffering that larger people often have to endure in modern culture as a result of their size. No one should ever be ostracized or put down for their weight. We are each of us of infinite value and worthy of respect, regardless of how much we weigh.

But at the same time, we need to start talking about the dire health consequences of obesity. The number of Americans who die prematurely each year as a result of being overweight is rapidly approaching the number of people who die prematurely from cigarette smoking. Obesity contributes nearly as much to chronic illness and healthcare costs as smoking. It's a problem that is increasingly common in modern society. More than half of U.S. physicians are overweight. Liposuction is the leading form of cosmetic surgery in the United States, with nearly half a million operations performed each year.

In 2001, the U.S. Surgeon General declared obesity to be an epidemic, noting that the percentage of U.S. children who are overweight has *tripled* in the past 25 years. According to James Hill, director of the Center for Human Nutrition at the University of Colorado Health Sciences Center, "If these trends continue, within a few generations every American will be overweight."

And the problem is not in the least confined to the United States. Obesity is increasing in every country in the world.

In England, childhood obesity has tripled in the last 20 years. In 2004, a British parliamentary committee examining the obesity epidemic highlighted the death of a three-year-old girl from heart failure brought on by her excess weight. One expert quoted in the report by the House of Commons Health Committee told of children who require ventilator assistance at home for respiratory conditions because of their obesity. The children were "choking on their own fat," said Sheila McKenzie, M.D., a specialist consultant at the Royal London Hospital.

Fad diets, meanwhile, follow one another onto the best-seller list. People flock to any regimen promising quick and dramatic results, and diet gurus have been eager to oblige. Scarsdale, Beverly Hills, Zone, Atkins, South Beach, and on and on it goes.

Mariana Bozesan's book is not another one of these get-thin-quick scams. It makes no preposterous claims. Instead, Mariana gently shares with you her own journey of self-discovery, and how, in the process of learning about herself and the human body, she not only lost the weight she wanted to lose, but gained deeper access to her inner self.

This is a truly holistic book. In it you will find steps you can take to increase your vitality, enhance your joy, and generate fulfillment. With this approach, you lose weight as a by-product of becoming healthier and more alive.

Mariana's approach is not about forcing your body to look a certain way according to a shallow and totally external image of beauty. It's about finding within yourself the healing powers you need, and unleashing the totality of your inner forces in the service of your magnificence.

At one level, this is a book about losing weight. But more than that, it is a book about love and about life. It is brave and honest. May it guide you to the fulfillment of your greatest purpose in being alive.

John Robbins
Author of *Diet for a New America* and *Healthy at 100*

Introduction

Our diet is what we eat, and there are literally millions of them. How we look and how we feel is a result of our life. What we feed ourselves is of key importance. That's why Mariana Bozesan's new book, *Diet for a New Life* is a great contribution to your health and life.

Recently, Mariana and I taught together during a series of audio teleseminars. Throughout our discussions she inspired me with her simple wisdom such as her guideline for a healthy balanced diet. She stated, "If our body is about two-thirds water, our diet should be two-thirds of high-water content foods, primarily as fruits and vegetables." Now, when I look at my plate and my daily diet, do I see a high amount of vegetables and fruits?

There are a great many ideas about what constitutes a healthy diet. Is it high protein, high fiber, vegetarian, or even raw? Each pattern has its own effects, yet can also have limitations. Can we get all the nutrients we need and does it support our health, or our body temperature, and protect us from our local environment? In my first book, *Staying Healthy with the Seasons*, I re-introduced an age-old concept, which to me is great common sense during the beginnings of the 'back-to-nature' movement in Western culture. Eat from your locale what is available from the Earth. I suggest we eat natural foods primarily as Nature provides them, eat seasonally, eat a variety as well, combine them properly for best digestion and assimilation. I go into this even more in my recent nutritional text, *Staying Healthy with Nutrition.*

Most people follow advertising and convenience foods too much, eat too many processed foods, take too many stimulants to keep going during the day, and then sedatives to calm down later. When we don't do live in a balanced way, we get too tired or can't sleep well, which are two key problems that millions of people complain about to their doctors.

Well, all of this can change now if we can follow the wisdom and guidance of Mariana's book. This text has so many helpful concepts and common sense approaches to following a healthy diet and learning about many important areas of well-being, such as cholesterol and healthy fats, immune function and stress, sugar metabolism, and much more. Most importantly, if you wish to trim your body and weigh less while receiving even more nourishment, Mariana has you covered.

This book is very user-friendly and organized to feed you at many levels, not just about food in your mouth. I hope you enjoy it and your good health for the remainder of your life, which can be extended when you live more according to Nature and with a healthy diet. *Diet for a New Life* offers wisdom and guidance on dealing with weight issues, emotions, and just being down on life. So many people in our modern cultures are in a state of struggle, and they do not even know where to begin to feel better. Creating a positive attitude of Love of Self is a crucial step in treating ourselves with grace and care, and eating better, exercising, and all the other aspects of well-being. Let *Diet for a New Life* be your guide to healthy living.

Elson M. Haas, M.D.
Author of *Staying Healthy with Nutrition* and *The New Detox Diet*

Commentary

"We live in a chaos that we may have created in order to hasten our own meeting with ourselves."
—Jean Houston

In *Diet for a New Life*, Mariana Bozesan employs a model of self-transformation similar to Joseph Campbell's legendary Hero's Circular Journey. According to Campbell, the Hero's Journey is a cascade of life-transforming stages. A metaphor for life itself, the Hero's Journey represents both the outer journey and the inner journey. This path can be difficult when a crisis, such as a divorce, diabetes mellitus, a heart attack, or a coronary bypass brought about by obesity, forces hard decisions. However, after the difficulties of life have been faced and overcome, the Heroine gains knowledge, improved circumstances or maturity, and greater self-awareness.

Understanding the Journey's stages and patterns can help us recognize some deeply hidden experiences that shape our lives, and the health crisis we experience as overweight individuals. If we are able to understand the Journey's stages and how they work, we will master our own epic by making the best decisions to solve our eating problems. More importantly, we will begin to recognize our own points of passage and honor the significance they are meant to have for us. The next step is to remove and transcend both the limitations and the handicaps of the obesity curse.

Archetypal psychologist Carol Pearson believes that Western culture is shaped around six main archetypes: the Orphan, the Wanderer, the Warrior, the Altruist, the Innocent, and the Magician. These archetypes not only have the power to modulate our own heroic journeys, they also represent different modalities of journeying and experiencing reality. We can think of archetypes as inner and outer figures, and as role models or end targets for personal transformation. They can be seen as external, sacred powers such as zodiacal signs or angelic entities, which can become magic facilitators for learning.

Having gone through previous dieting journeys as an Orphan, a Wanderer, and a Warrior, Bozesan's heroine is being guided to embark on the Magician's journey. Its plot is "How I changed my world," its structure is "How I changed myself," and its gift is personal transformation.

The mythical correspondences of Bozesan's eight stages toward successful dieting can be easily plotted on Campbell's Hero's Journey. Bozesan's hero has already gone, as most of us readers have, through previous cyclic journeys revolving around losing and regaining weight. The last failure has once again thrown us into the "Call for Adventure" stage.

Steps 1, 2, and 3 indeed correspond to crossing the threshold and doing battle with our enemies: unhealthy eating habits, cellular toxicity, and a sedentary life. We are fiercely tested and we also meet helpers like Ariadne, an experienced peer, a fated event, or the Mentor, like Mariana Bozesan.

Having arrived at the core of the labyrinth, the legendary Theseus is now confronted with the Minotaur, the darkest, scariest side of himself—the Shadow, to use Jungian terms. If you prefer modern mythology, you can instead think of Luke Skywalker's encounter with his "dark father," Darth Vader. This crucial stage is illustrated in Steps 5 and 6 of *Diet for a New Life*, where the hero is challenged to face his higher Self, attain a new, integrated meaning for his life, and acquire emotional mastery.

Campbell's stage of apotheosis is plotted on Bozesan's map in Step 6, "Lasting Weight Success." The elixir of self-knowledge has now become an integral part of the Heroine. In Step 7, Bozesan invites her heroine to escape the inner world of the labyrinth and come out into the world to live according to what has been learned. Yet Bozesan is also aware that the hero's hard-won accountability and self-responsibility may someday slip into relapse. A realist, she prepares her heroine not only to prevent relapse but more importantly to successfully manage it.

In Step 8 of the book, Bozesan paradoxically invites us to celebrate both the victory and the relapse. For if we are ready to manage any relapse crisis that life throws at us, we are prepared to embark again on the Magician's journey and take care of any unfinished business. It is indeed much wiser and healthier to assume future relapse and be prepared for it than to arrest the spontaneous and sometimes unpredictable flow of life with some obsessive-compulsive "preventive" habits such as anorexia or bulimia.

Mariana Bozesan's book is not a mere manual for a successful diet but an inspiring map for an archetypal journey toward Self-discovery. The Journey she proposes is filled with joy. Not because the adventure is devoid of pain—it cannot be so at an ego level—but because Mariana Bozesan's hero is steadily centered in his witness consciousness, the journey becomes the Journey. And as such, the adventure becomes radiantly fun, like a divine play (Lila). The constant flow of the witness-consciousness narrator reorganizes the dieter's emotional life and accepts the changes of day-to-day patterns and the encounter with spiritual perspectives and insights. In such a flexible therapeutic context, recovery from obesity and self-transformation go hand-in-hand and merge beautifully into the joy of Self-discovery.

Marius Koga, M.D., Associate Clinical Professor of International and Public Health, UC Davis School of Medicine

Vedanta Monastery, December 2006

Acknowledgements

This book would not have been possible without the many wonderful people who have contributed with their content, love, and dedication. I wish I could name them all.

I would like to express my deep gratitude to Tom Schulz, my husband, the love of my life, and my friend of three decades. Without you I would never have conceived of writing this book. Your love, curiosity, generosity, and endless support have made this project come to fruition. Thank you for your absolute faith in me.

I also could not have written this book without the unconditional love and support of the best parents in the world, Maria and Grigore Bozesan. You have unconditionally loved, guided, and supported me ever since I can remember. Thank you for being my guardian angels. Endless thanks go also to the best thing I have ever done, my son Albert. Despite your young age, you have given me the love, the room, and the time to write. I love you all beyond measure.

How could I thank you enough, John Robbins, for your unconditional love and endless support? Your friendship and that of your family make such a difference in my life. Your decision to write the foreword to my first book means everything to me, someone who has become a different person after reading your book *Diet for a New America* almost two decades ago. You have made my dream come true. Thank you.

Thank you, Marius Koga for being the first to see and appreciate the integral message of this book. Your wisdom, love, friendship, and unconditional support mean everything to me.

Elson Haas, you have been instrumental in helping me grow beyond myself. I thank you for being who you are and for bringing your gifts into this world.

I am deeply indebted to my dear friend and teacher, Deepak Chopra, M.D., for believing in me and for trusting, supporting, and encouraging me to look beyond the appearance of the day-to-day reality. Your loving presence in my life has long been nectar for my soul.

I also express my gratitude to Tony Robbins, my teacher, inspiration, and guide of the past 17 years. Your personal friendship, deep caring, and tireless support in the last couple of years have been instrumental in giving me the strength and confidence to grow personally so I could eventually write this book. The same is true for you, my dear and most beautiful soul-sister, Sage Robbins. Your compassionate love and endless caring have been the driving inspirational force behind the creation of the SageEra Institute, which I named in your honor. May the two of you be forever blessed!

My deep gratitude goes also to Dr. John Gray, whose unconditional love has changed my life. You have given me everything I've asked for without expecting anything in return. Your positive attitude and sunny personality have changed not only my outlook on life but my marriage forever. Thank you.

I am also forever grateful to dear Ellen Cutler, D.C., whose healing powers gave me back the good health I lost over the past 20 years of my life. How could I ever show you my endless gratitude, dear sister?

My deep thanks go also to you, Ruth Scott, my dear friend and healer. Thank you from the bottom of my heart for keeping me healthy, vital, and in good spirits. Without your loving support and shining presence in my life, I would not have been able to finish this and many other projects during the past few years.

My gratitude goes also to all those extraordinary people who, despite their busy schedules, have been kind enough to endorse and contribute to my book. I am honored to know you and thank you from the depths of my heart.

I do not have enough words to express my love and appreciation to both Nancy and Emery Rogers, Ph.D. For more than 20 years you have treated me like your own child and guided my path through life with the utmost love and compassion. You have shown me the true way toward philanthropy and social entrepreneurship. Thank you both for your presence in my life. Because of you the world is today a better place.

Special thanks go also to Sheldon Breiner, Ph.D., for reminding me of my strengths and talents. Your encouragement made all the difference at a cross-roads in my life.

Thank you to my aunt Kathe Heptner, who showed me early on that there is good in everything bad that happens. Your selfless giving and compassionate caring have taught me some of the greatest lessons in life. The parcels you sent from Canada to Romania during my childhood have brought light and love into the darkest moments in my life. You have been my guardian angel and I will forever be grateful for your loving-kindness.

I would not have come close to becoming a mathematician and a computer scientist without you, Natalia Fotache, my first and best-ever math teacher. Your love and contagious passion for this subject showed me the beauty of science for the first time. Your confidence in my abilities planted the seeds for my lifelong confidence in my talents. Thank you.

For their presence in my life, as well as friendship, encouragement, contributions, endorsements, and ongoing support, I am deeply indebted to His Holiness the Dalai Lama; Ram Dass; Walter Bortz, Ph.D.; Dr. Wayne Dyer; Riane Eisler, J.D.; Udo Erasmus, Ph.D.; Klaus Fischer; Arielle Ford; Fred Gallo, Ph.D.; Vivian Glyck; Louise Hay; Elson Haas, M.D.; Pam Hendrickson; Walter "Shantree" Kacera, Ph.D.; Byron Katie; Birgitta Kumm; Stephen LaBerge, Ph.D.; George Leonard; Cloe Madanes, Ph.D.; John Maguire; Rachel Markowitz; Charles Mardel; Dr. Gilles Marin; Edgar Mitchell, D.Sc.; Stephen Mitchell; Mitzi Mager; Howard Martin; Tammy McClure; Tisha Morgan; Michael Murphy; Professor Camran Nezhat, M.D.; Dean Ornish, M.D.; Herbie Ross, D.C.; Brenda and Tad Schinke; Carol Sands; Annelise Schinzinger; Marilyn Schlitz, Ph.D.; Carrie Schwab-Pomerantz; Ruth Scott; Bernie Siegel, M.D.; Michele Stern; Lynne Twist; Neale Donald Walsch; David Wolfe, J.D.; Robert Young, Ph.D., D.Sc.; Shelley Redford Young; and the many, many others whom space does not permit me to mention.

Last but not least, I would like to express my deep gratitude to both of you dearest Maria and Johann Ernst. Only because of your selfless giving, were we able to leave the darkness of communist Romania and live in the light of the free world. Your are our guardian angels.

Stop Dieting and Begin Living— Why Permanent Weight Loss Goes Beyond Dieting

"Man was made for joy and woe.
And when this we rightly know
Through the world we safely go.
Joy and woe are woven fine
A clothing for the soul to mind!"
—William Blake

The great sage Nasrudin once told a story about a man who had lost his keys and was desperately looking for them under a street lantern in the middle of the night. Several passersby joined him to look for the keys but none could find them. Eventually, someone asked Nasrudin exactly where he had lost his keys. "In my house," the man replied, pointing in the direction of his dwelling, "but there is no light in there."

How often do we search for the solutions to our problems in the outside world, hoping that we will find an answer? How often do we give up the search when we feel overwhelmed, even though we might be very close to the solution? This brings to mind Thomas Edison's observation that many of life's failures occurred when people did not realize how close they were to success when they gave up.

As we learn to use our inner wisdom to restore balance and beauty to our bodies and lives, we may realize that we've had the answer all along. As my dear friend Stephen LaBerge of Stanford University pointed out to me recently, "We don't really need to go outside of our own heart to find the solutions to our problems. We have our inner light as constant guidance, after all." I too believe that even if we start searching in the wrong place, eventually we will arrive at the spot where we find what's right for us. In my view, continuing the search *is* the key we are looking for. In other words, this search is a lifelong process, and while we continue it, we are being transformed.

This emphasis on inner guidance ties into my intention with this book. While I am presenting to you some of the latest scientific knowledge about weight loss and health, I am also encouraging you to use your common sense—to listen to and trust your own heart and body. I want you to realize that you have to take the responsibility for your own body and mind into your own hands. Permanent weight loss, health, and vitality won't come from the outside but from the inside. Yes, you can get information and guidance, but you are the only person who can unleash your own personal power to act upon the knowledge you have.

This is not a book about a new diet and I am not a diet doctor. In fact, I am not a doctor at all but a transpersonal psychologist, a mathematician, a computer scientist, an entrepreneur, a mother, a wife, and most of all, *I am an expert dieter in a female body.* I speak to you from my personal experience of frustration with yo-yo dieting.

This is a book about *no diet* at all in a traditional sense. It is a reference guide presenting an integral approach to permanent weight loss that addresses not only the physical body, including nutrition, exercise, and health challenges, but also the psychology of weight gain and the importance of a healthy emotional and spiritual life. It is a transformative tool that aims to support you in identifying what a life of meaning looks like for you. Through this program you will learn how to condition yourself for permanent success by adopting healthy habits and a daily practice to support the real you. As Louise Hay reminds us, "A healthy body is at its ideal weight, and an unhealthy body is often overweight."

In a society where more than 64 percent of people are overweight or obese, we need information, alternatives, and choices that go beyond crash diets and pills. By now we should know that no single miracle pill, physical routine, or magic potion contains the solution to weight loss and good health. The results of the past decades are obvious. American society has become not only the heaviest in the world but also the unhealthiest, with 50 percent of us dying of coronary heart disease, 30 percent dying of cancer, and record numbers suffering from often debilitating ailments like diabetes and allergies. As we advance through the information age, which gives us great access to various kinds of knowledge, we are facing great difficulties in distinguishing good solutions from less ideal ones.

These days we drown in information and we starve for true wisdom.

Diet for a New Life was born out of the need to fill this gap. It has been written as a unifying vehicle to share the knowledge and advice of some of the best weight loss and health experts in the world. In my own pursuit of my ideal weight, healing, and personal growth, I have been blessed to learn from and spend time with some of the most extraordinary sages of our era. Thus, the wisdom I am sharing with you is not wholly mine. It is knowledge I have acquired over many years of intense study. However, my greatest teacher has been my life itself—in particular, my pain.

As a university student, I became very ill and was forced to find a way to regain my health and, more importantly, how to maintain it. I soon found out how significant exercise, good nutrition, and detoxification were for a healthy body. I began watching my diet, swimming regularly, and fasting twice a year. As a result, I felt more energized and healthy than ever. But that was more than 25 years ago. As life led me into a career, marriage, and childbearing, I stopped fasting regularly and thought that dieting continually, living a mostly vegetarian lifestyle, eating fish once in a while, taking supplements, and exercising on occasion was a ticket to good health.

One day I woke up and noticed that I had actually gained more than 38 pounds. Although I was only in my late thirties, I thought that having cellulite and varicose veins was an inevitable part of getting older. I did not know that my hormonal system was out of balance; that I was host to four types of parasites; that my adrenal glands were working less than optimally; that my thyroid levels were critically low; that I had common digestive problems such as leaky gut syndrome and irritable bowel syndrome, which were both due to many years of the wrong diet; and that my body was totally depleted of several vitamins including B_{12}, whose reserves in the body should normally last for five years. As a result, I was often ill, felt miserable about my appearance, and was unfulfilled in my life despite having a successful career and a beautiful family.

Like everyone else I knew, I was going on diet after diet. I even thought of joining my friends who were having liposuction to become thin very quickly. Eventually, I did lose weight, but it didn't last. I realized that being thin did not change my life. I noticed that even though when I looked in the mirror I saw a starved-down version of my ideal self, I still *felt* fat. I ended up gaining the weight back because in my *mind* I was still overweight. To make matters worse, I was hungry most of the time.

It took me an additional five years to learn that being slim and healthy required not only my physical but more importantly my mental, emotional, and spiritual participation. The ability to maintain my ideal weight came at the moment I realized I would need to take my body *slowly* through a gradual lifestyle change that would affect every area of my life including my relationships, my spirituality, my career, and my financial well-being. These days, I no longer attempt to be slim but rather strive to be vibrantly healthy and live a life of purpose. The athletic body I have today is a positive by-product of my new attitude to life, not my main objective.

Being part of an extraordinarily complex universe, our bodies are miraculous universes in themselves. As a result, the process of healing the body-mind is equally as multifaceted and takes time. It is important to realize that losing weight is not about dieting, calories, carbohydrates, protein, cholesterol, body fat, food charts, food ladders, or portion control. It is about vibrant health, energy, extraordinary psychology, and above all, living a life of meaning. It involves restoring harmony at all levels of your being—physical, mental, emotional, spiritual, and financial, as well as with the world around you.

The truth is that we all deserve to be healthy and to live in a body of perfect weight. In Ayurveda, the traditional medicine of India, it is said that "desire is pure potentiality seeking manifestation." This means that just by having the wish to achieve something, you will be guided toward the manifestation of your desire. The word *desire* comes from the Latin *de sire*, which means "of the Lord." In other words, the whole universe conspires to support you on your quest for a fit body and healthy bodymind. All that is needed is your own participation.

If you are truly committed, this book could be the beginning of a wonderful voyage back to your beautiful and vital self. T.S. Eliot expresses this so beautifully in his exquisite verse: "We shall not cease from exploration, and the end of all our exploring will be to arrive where we started and know the place for the first time." It might have been your own drive for self-exploration that made you buy this book. I am inviting you to set free the amazing intelligence of your bodymind as the supreme source of your ideal weight, health, and vitality.

Diet for a New Life does not provide a magic pill, but you can turn it into a magic journey. It can be *your* journey to *your* ideal body and to *your* perfect health. It proposes not a revolution but an *evolution*, a process that honors your own uniqueness and supports you not only in restoring your ideal weight but in identifying and pursuing your life's purpose.

Diet for a New Life is based on three principles: (1) that combining proven scientific data about the nutritional and exercise needs of the body with the experiential benefits of regular cleansing and detoxification will lead to weight loss and vitality, (2) that if we are to sustain our weight loss and our increased vitality, we need to understand and harness the forces that drive our behavior—lest our gains disappear as our stubborn habits take over, and (3) that any successful plan for weight loss and well-being needs to be tested, reaffirmed, and integrated in the real world of friends, family, and associates.

Figure 1: Diet for a New Life: 8 Steps to Weight Loss and Well-Being

Part 1: What We Need to Know

The first three steps of the 8-step program of *Diet for a New Life* involve informational aspects of weight loss. Step 1 deals with nutrition, Step 2 with exercise, and Step 3 with cleansing and detoxification. In the chapters on nutrition and exercise, you will learn what the body needs and how to develop eating and exercise plans that meet these needs and lead to weight loss and vitality. The nutrition discussion focuses in particular on righting the body's alkaline-acid balance for permanent weight loss and health maintenance. Overacidity, to which the body responds by gaining weight and losing energy, is the state of most people today. It is fostered by fast food, typical American eating habits, and even some well-known diets for weight loss. The nutrition section describes the foods that restore appropriate and necessary alkaline levels, which in turn lead to weight loss and increased energy. The exercise chapter focuses on the significance of regular exercise for keeping healthy and happy at the same time. The discussion on cleansing and detoxification in Step 3 shows how and why cleansing on a regular basis leads to lifelong health and vitality. This third step is the point where the book departs from existing literature and takes a quantum leap into permanent weight success. It goes beyond nutrition and exercise to help create health and vitality at the cellular level—the secret to having extraordinary energy throughout the day.

Part 2: Why We Act As We Do

But information alone cannot promise sustained weight loss and well-being. If it could, we would not live in a society with such weight and health problems. This is why the second part of the book looks at the hidden determinants of human conditioning. It demonstrates how you can shape and control your behavior to achieve lasting weight loss as well as health and vitality. Step 4 shows how to bring awareness to your current systems of beliefs and values, which often prevent lasting weight-loss success. The discussion focuses on the most important driving force in our lives—the significance of living a life of meaning. The question is, *Do you live a life of meaning?* By analyzing your personal beliefs and values, you can make sure that they serve rather than hinder you in achieving your goals. Living in line with your natural physical identity, which is thin and healthy, then becomes a natural by-product of a life well lived. Just as knowledge alone is insufficient to sustain a program of weight loss, so is the analysis of beliefs and values. Step 5 presents the challenge of gaining emotional mastery. We all know that we can set the best and most thoughtful goals possible, only to forget about our good intentions as soon as strong emotions "hit" us. We seem to become victims of some kind of automatic, thoughtless response over which we seem to have no control—often leading us directly to the cookie jar! This is why this section of the book sets out the techniques that enable you to take responsibility for your thoughts and thus master your emotions for lasting weight success.

Part 3: Creating Lasting Change

The third and final section of the book moves you into the real world and teaches you how to give yourself credit where credit is due. Under the premise that pain is part of life but suffering is a choice, Step 6 illustrates how to use what you have learned so far to develop a life plan and daily rituals for permanent weight loss. The result is an easy-to-apply action map for every day. Step 7 shows how to keep on track for lasting change and test the plan in the laboratory of real life. It lays out principles that allow you to *stay on the lifelong path* of your ideal weight. It leads toward accountable, measurable, and consistent action. Step 8 teaches how to handle relapse, celebrate, and reward successes. It illustrates how to let go of self-blame and criticism and how to connect with inner wisdom, self-love, and joie de vivre. This step is based on the premise that associating profound pleasure with achieving and maintaining the ideal weight is the single most important method of psychologically reinforcing and sustaining weight-loss success.

In summary, *Diet for a New Life* is a program that will guide you how to lose weight *without going on a diet*. It gives you an elective system for health and vitality with fewer prescriptions and more options. It is an integral, holistic, and compassionate system for *losing weight and gaining life*. It presents a *path* for achieving sustainable weight loss, health, and vitality through personal commitment to well-being, life, and self-love. It helps you achieve change through a *1-percent-a-day shift* in lifestyle.

Unfortunately, as good as the advice in this book is, neither buying nor reading the book will be enough to make you lose weight and keep it off. You will have to commit to and implement the recommendations herein in order to be successful. Once you decide to pursue the path of honoring the beauty of who you are as a human being deep down in your soul, regardless of how you look on the outside, you will discover that building your health from the inside out is the key to manifesting your ideal weight and beauty. It will happen naturally and almost effortlessly the moment you decide to honor and trust yourself.

One more thing: you have to promise to have fun in the process. This is the most important component of the program. Instead of making every step a difficult *should*, make it fun and encourage your brain to associate pleasure with losing weight and pain with keeping it on. By creating enjoyment and a sense of playfulness along the way, your brain will create the necessary chemicals to support you in breaking patterns and habits that are not working for you. As you condition your new healthy habits through daily practice, they will become second nature. You will begin to feel better, healthier, more energetic, more vital, and more beautiful. Before you know it, you will have created a new life for yourself that is much more in line with your true nature.

As Theodore Roosevelt famously said, "Do what you can, with what you have, where you are." By pursuing this program you have already begun to apply TR's advice, and I deeply honor your courage to free yourself from the prison of being overweight and unhealthy. I admire your willingness to take charge and overcome the numerous causes of your weight gain. Furthermore, I congratulate you for your motivation to conquer the unknown forces that control you. You are now ready to reclaim your authentic power, learn how to overcome the psychology of emotional eating, heal metabolic disorders, and develop coping skills and healthy eating habits for lasting change. By deciding to throw guilt and frustration forever out of your life, you can now empower yourself with the necessary knowledge and tools to ensure your freedom from the unwanted. You can now achieve your perfect weight by creating a new body and a new life that accurately reflect who you are at your core.

By taking charge of your own well-being, you are supporting all of us in building a critical mass of people who believe in and cultivate love rather than fear, who take responsibility rather than blame others, and who are working to replace ignorance with knowing, scarcity with abundance, despair with hope, turbulence with peace, and sadness with joy and laughter.

Welcome to the miracle that is *you*. Welcome home!

Mariana Bozesan
Palo Alto, California
January 2007

PART 1
What We Need to Know

Losing Weight without Going on a Diet – Why Crash Diets Fail

"The significant problems we face cannot be solved by the level of thinking that created them."
—Albert Einstein

It was on a rainy day in the fall of 1999 that I came across the above quote by Albert Einstein. Its depth and truth stopped me in my tracks and I began thinking about my life. Two years earlier, I had given birth to my son Albert after leaving corporate America to start my own business. While my life was more positive and abundant than ever, I had never weighed more, I lacked energy and vitality, I was exhausted and stressed, and I was having a hard time enjoying the beauty of my life. Einstein's quote brought to my attention first that I had a significant weight and health problem and second that I had tried to solve it by repeatedly going on fashionable diets. I was no different from the fly that throws itself desperately against the window hoping to get out, not realizing that it will eventually die of exhaustion. Later I learned that this is the definition of insanity: doing the same thing over and over again, hoping to get a different result.

However, on that memorable day in 1999 I had had it. I was sick and tired of being sick and fat and was ready to make a change. Right then and there I embarked on a journey that not only saved but changed my life forever. I stopped dieting and began taking back control of my own body. I started by analyzing why fad diets don't work and why less than 2 percent of dieters succeed.[1] Here is what I found out.

1. Fad Diets Put Your Health at Risk

Fad diets often fly in the face of sound nutritional and medical research. The World Health Organization, the American Heart Association, the American Cancer

Society, the American Dietetic Association, the office of the Surgeon General of the United States, and the American Institute for Cancer Research are all highly opposed to the currently popular high-protein, high-fat, low-carbohydrate diets.[2]

Why?

....

Weight loss secret:
Fad diets often do not provide the nutrients the human body needs to function properly in the long term.

....

The human body is composed of 70 percent water, 1–2 percent vitamins and minerals, 0.5–1 percent sugar, 20 percent fat, and 7 percent protein.[3] To function properly, we need to take in a balanced proportion of these nutrients during the day: 70 percent water-rich alkalizing fruits and vegetables, 1–2 percent vitamins and minerals, 0.5–1 percent sugar, 20 percent fat, and 7 percent protein.[4]

This formula, however, is not what popular fad diets prescribe. Many of them recommend prepackaged and processed foods, which are lacking in essential nutrients. In addition, the Atkins, Zone, and Eat Right for Your Type[5] diets recommend taking in a dangerously high percentage of daily protein—more than 30 percent of total intake, which is up to three times higher than the daily recommended allowance.[6] Studies have shown that health problems such as nausea, fatigue,[7] impaired mental functioning,[8] and augmented risk for heart attacks may arise after 12 weeks of the Atkins diet.[9] This is due to increased levels of bad cholesterol (LDL) and reduced good cholesterol (HDL).

Also, according to the American Institute for Cancer Research, it is the overacidity of the Atkins diet, which is based mostly on acid-forming foods, that presents a health challenge for dieters. People lose weight on the Atkins diet because of calorie restriction and because the body enters a state of ketosis, which is caused by an imbalance in fat metabolism. Eventually, due to a lack of proper minerals and other critical nutrients, the body begins to metabolize muscle tissue instead of fat. This leads in the long run to muscle breakdown, nausea, dehydration, bad breath, and even heart disease or cancer.[10]

Dean Ornish, M.D., professor of medicine at the University of California, San Francisco, and founder and president of the Preventive Medicine Research Institute, considers diets like Atkins that promote eating primarily meat "irresponsible and dangerous for people who follow this advice.... The problem with high-animal-protein diets is that even if you lose weight, you're mortgaging your health in the process."[11]

2. Most Dieters Lack Ongoing Support

Dieters rarely have direct access to advice from the person who developed the diet, either in person, by phone, or via email. Most diet books do not provide organizational support, such as weight management, life coaching programs, or access to a buddy system or expert diet representatives who are available for consultation. If support groups do exist, they often develop among the dieters themselves and lack a clinically sound emotional and psychological program for times of crisis. To be effective, a diet must be more than a list of foods or behaviors. It must be an eating and lifestyle program with interactive support.

3. Fad Diets Are Boring

Most crash diets are based on restrictive food groups—high-protein, high-fat, or low-carbohydrate. They do not honor the fact that humans need a large variety of foods, tastes, smells, and colors in their diet. People eventually tire of a narrow food regimen. They often abandon fad diets simply because they are dull.

4. Fad Diets Are Too Rigid and Often Too Complicated

The primary reason why diets fail is because they are too rigid and far too complicated for people to follow. They are very hard to live with because they seem to not address the whole person. Instead they look mostly at the digestive tract and metabolism and introduce far too many rules, which dieters cannot keep to in the long run. As a result, dieters begin breaking those rules one by one until they are off the diet, never to return.

5. Crash Diets Are Not Individualized

Most crash diets are one-size-fits-all. They do not address individual needs or honor human diversity. We all have different blood types, skin colors, fingerprints, DNA, body builds, and other traits. Our nutritional differences, it seems, stem from our ancestral heritage. Over many thousands of years of evolutionary improvement, humans around the world have developed very specific dietary requirements in order to adjust to unique habitats, geography, vegetation, climates, and food supply.

The Chinese have eaten rice for centuries; would it make sense for a Chinese person to embark on a low-carb diet? In Iceland, fat is a necessary part of the diet; would a low-fat or vegetarian regimen work for an Icelander whose ancestors consumed animal fat daily? These evolutionary requirements, which are unique to each of us, need to be identified and reflected upon as part of any individualized weight loss program.

6. Fad Diets Lack a Holistic Approach

Fad diets usually promise a quick fix in a short period of time. They seem to ignore the fact that maintaining ideal body weight comes from true health and a lifestyle that honors and supports the whole person—the body, emotions, spirituality, relationships, meaningful work, and authentic happiness.

A healthy body is at its perfect weight. An unhealthy body is often overweight. Ultimately, we should not have to worry about our weight or our looks at all. When we are fulfilled in our lives, the ideal weight, health, and beauty occur naturally, from within and without effort.

....

Weight loss secret:
You are not only your body but also your mind and emotions.

Treat yourself holistically and address all areas of your life in order to succeed at losing weight.

....

7. Fad Diets Do Not Factor In Unique Mind and Body Types

Standardized nutritional approaches fail to honor not only our unique genetic imprints but also our metabolic individualities. We are all very different from one another, both in our psyches and on a biochemical/metabolic level.

According to the U.S. Surgeon General, Dr. Richard H. Carmona, "Each individual body weight is a combination of genetic, metabolic, behavioral, environmental, cultural, and socioeconomic influences."

A successful diet must address all these areas. The only way to do this is to become aware of our behavioral and lifestyle patterns. We need to observe and become skilled at handling our own physical and emotional reactions to not only food but our immediate environment. Most important, we need to learn to listen to our bodies and trust what they tell us. Professor Emeritus Walter Bortz of Stanford University suggested in a personal interview that our genetic imprint contributes less than 15 percent to our weight problems.

Fat is not fated. But weight loss requires paying attention to the many factors that affect our biochemical/metabolic makeup. Fad diets rarely touch upon this aspect of long-term weight control.

8. Fad Diets Address the Symptoms of Excess Weight but Not Their Causes

Achieving lasting health and vitality is sometimes a side effect, but not the main concern, of most crash diets. Why? Because crash diets do not focus on identifying and eliminating the reasons why people become overweight in the first place. These reasons can be as complex as the dieters' personalities, and often involve nutrition, quality and/or quantity of food, lack of emotional balance, stress, unhealthy habits, lifestyle, and social environment. All of these factors need to be included in a weight loss program.

9. Fad Diets Perpetuate the Yo-Yo Effect

Many crash diets prescribe a daily caloric intake that is well below what the body needs. That's why such regimens may work initially but are not sustainable in the long run. Instead, they create the "roller-coaster" or "yo-yo" effect. When the body is deprived of nutrients, it goes into survival mode. The body slows down its metabolism and actually uses up fewer calories to prevent what it perceives as starvation.

Eventually dieters go back to eating more calories. And because their crash diets did not teach them how to eat better or condition them to live a healthier lifestyle, dieters gain back the weight they lost and often a few extra pounds as well. Not only did the fad diet fail, it put the overall health of the body at risk due to a lack of necessary nutrients, vitamins, minerals, and protective phytochemicals as well as carbohydrates and fiber.

Weight loss secret:
To succeed long-term you must address the reason why you gained weight and compromised your health in the first place.

Dealing with merely the symptoms of the problem will not get you where you want to be long-term.

10. Crash Diets Neglect the Detoxification of the Body

Regular detoxification needs to become part of a healthy lifestyle and good metabolic balance for anyone who wants to stay healthy and keep their ideal weight. While crash dieters may experience some level of detoxification while losing weight, they rarely, if ever, are introduced to the concept of cleansing as a regular component of a healthy lifestyle.

11. Fad Diets Neglect the Power of the Acid-Alkaline Balance

After breathing and keeping the heart beating, the most important physiological function our bodies perform is maintaining a balanced pH level. The human body operates optimally at a pH of 7.3. Barring accidents and genetic factors, pH levels can get out of balance through emotional turmoil, smoking, absorption of chemicals, and consumption of acid-forming foods such as meat, sugar, saturated fats, caffeine, refined carbohydrates, alcohol, and dairy products. These factors force the body to use up vital electrolytes (minerals) to buffer the acidic environment.

Once the body's electrolyte levels are depleted, health begins to seriously deteriorate, because we cannot survive if the overall pH of our body is acidic. Therefore, the body responds by retaining fat to neutralize the acid. Ultimately, *being overweight turns out to be a life saver.*

12. Fad Diets Neglect the Role of Essential Fats in Weight Loss

Fad diets have waged a war on fats for the past few decades, making us believe that fats are the main culprit when it comes to gaining weight. Yet it's now clear that two-thirds of people in the Western world have become fatter on the low-fat approach.

The reality is that the human body needs fats, especially the essential ones, in order to survive. Fat molecules are a rich and lasting source of energy for the body and are crucial for losing weight[12] and establishing health. Essential fats are the critical building blocks of our cells and ultimately our organs. However, the body cannot synthesize all of them, so it has to get them from food. Thus, essential fats have to be an integral part of every successful weight loss diet.

13. Fad Diets Often Ignore the Importance of the Glycemic Index and Fiber

As we have become increasingly afraid of fats, the main diets of the industrialized world within the past 20 years have begun successfully promulgating low-fat/low-cholesterol approaches. Consequently, there has never been a society that has consumed more processed carbohydrates. The result is overweight and obesity of epidemic proportions.

One significant reason for this is that neither the importance of fiber nor the glycemic index (GI) are addressed by most crash diets, although these concepts have been quite well known within the medical community from studies of diabetes. The GI is a means of measuring the effect a food has on blood sugar levels.

••

Weight loss secret:
You must become the expert.

You must know how your nutrition, affects your weight, your health, and your emotions in order to know how to   regain your health and vitality.

••

The consumption of refined carbohydrates (white bread, white rice, white pasta) and high GI foods causes a rapid spike in blood sugar. This draws extra insulin into the blood. The high insulin, in turn, makes the blood sugar level crash and suppresses the fat stores as well. As a result, we get that famished feeling that leads to overeating. This is caused by the fact that over time the body becomes inefficient in manufacturing simple sugars from complex carbohydrates, protein, or fats.

Thus, the body shuts down its proper functioning, the blood glucose levels drop, and we become addicted to sugars. The vicious cycle has begun. These swings in blood sugar create terrible addictions, and we "must" have our candy bars, cakes, and breads.

14. Fad Diets Do Not Address "False Fat" Created by Food Reactions and Food Allergies

According to Dr. Elson Haas, an estimated 80 to 90 percent of overweight people have food allergies[13] and food sensitivities, and correcting these helps return the body to normal weight.[14]

Food reactions are triggered by the inability of our bodies to completely digest the foods we eat because of age, stress, unhealthy eating habits, or lack of proper enzymes. As a result, the body declares that the food is an enemy, much like bacteria, viruses, or parasites, and treats it as such. When these partially digested food macromolecules enter the bloodstream, the immune system attacks them just like it would any allergen. This is called food reaction, food sensitivity, or food allergy.

The results of food reactions and sensitivities are often metabolic disorders such as overweight, obesity, fatigue, severe hormone imbalances including immune disorders, bloating and swelling (called "false fat" by Dr. Haas), water retention, and food cravings. Addressing the biological imbalances caused by food reactions is key to the permanent success of any weight loss program. Crash diets rarely, if ever, recognize or address this issue.

15. Fad Diets Overlook the Role of Enzymes in Permanent Weight Loss

Most of the foods consumed in our industrialized world are processed and contain few nutrients, if any. In addition, these highly altered foods often contain too much salt, too many refined sugars, the wrong fats, and a variety of toxins including herbicides, pesticides, antibiotics, hormones, and preservatives. Most importantly, these foods are not live foods and therefore lack enzymes that are destroyed through heating.

However, the reality is that we cannot live without enzymes. Enzymes are proteins that operate as catalysts for essential chemical processes in the body. They participate in every part of our bodies, from our immune system to single organs including the heart, lungs, liver, and brain. They enable the immune system to fight bacteria and viruses. If we don't have enough enzymes, we gain weight and our bodies cannot work optimally, eventually breaking down.

However, we can turn this situation around by taking digestive enzymes. Through them, our bodies can absorb the nutrients from the foods we eat, we get rid of food cravings, allergies, and food reactions, and we begin losing weight.[15]

The sad part about most fad diets is that they offer prepackaged and processed meals as part of their programs, seeming to ignore the importance of enzymes. These foods, which are no different from fast food, lack the necessary enzymes and essential nutrients for successful long-term weight management.

16. Fad Diets Do Not Offer Lasting Solutions to Food Cravings

Scientists tell us that food cravings are true addictions, just like smoking, alcohol, and drugs. Cravings are often much harder to resist than real hunger and are the main reason most diets don't work.

The good news is that most food cravings are caused by food sensitivities,[14] which can be healed. As we begin eliminating the reactive foods from our system, the body at first resists and experiences discomfort, as in the case of a smoker in withdrawal. Once the food that creates the craving leaves the body, we begin to heal within less than 48 hours. When the food cravings subside, a natural weight loss process begins.

We can overcome long-term food cravings and other eating addictions through taking enzymes, cleansing, kinesiology, energy psychology, and other emotional support techniques. Unfortunately, most fad diets do not offer such tools for long-term elimination of food cravings or food addictions.

17. Fad Diets Fail to Emphasize Healthy Habits

While most diets focus on some kind of nutritional plan, most of them fail to educate dieters about healthy habits that guarantee permanent weight success, such as exercise, proper food combining, and regular cleansing. For instance, many fad diets treat exercise as an afterthought rather than as a daily habit and an integral part of life.

18. Crash Diets Do Not Prepare Dieters for Permanent Weight Loss Conditioning

Most crash diets fail because they do not offer the tools and strategies needed to create permanent weight loss. Instead, they present artificially created food plans, menus, and changes in lifestyle that people cannot sustain in the long run.

Permanent weight loss requires a more complete, long-term approach. First, a successful weight loss program promotes and develops healthy habits. For a behavior to turn into a habit, it has to be specific, measurable, and, in the beginning, constantly reinforced. Creating a habit usually takes a minimum of eight weeks of daily conditioning. In addition, it requires dieters to identify personal motives and *leverage* factors that will help develop and reinforce good weight control habits. A good program also provides a framework, such as communities, a buddy system, and coaches, to hold people accountable for their lifestyle changes.

Secondly, a successful program has to offer a wide variety of tools that are fun and playful to encourage dieters to make lasting shifts in their lifestyles. This way permanent weight loss becomes what it needs to be—an evolution, not a revolution.

Weight loss secret:
You must develop a lifelong strategy for your health and nutrition.

Knowing what to do is not enough to get you where you want to be. You must develop a plan to get there and do anything it takes to ensure your success.

19. Crash Diets Overlook Metabolic Disorders and Immune Deficiencies

Improper digestion and food reactions lead to significant metabolic disorders in the body. As the indigested food macromolecules leak into the blood vessels, the immune system becomes stimulated and begins fighting. At that point, the entire endocrine (hormonal) system gets activated and eventually becomes exhausted, leading to immune deficiency. Furthermore, an imbalance may manifest in the disturbed function of the thyroid and adrenal glands. This in turn can lead to the inability of the body to burn fat properly, which leads to a state of being overweight.

Some people maintain proper function of the thyroid or adrenal glands, but their insulin levels get out of balance. Food energy then gets converted into fat and may contribute to low sugar levels or hypoglycemia, a condition that can also lead to weight gain.

Other metabolic disorders caused by food reactions can lead to low serotonin levels that manifest as bad moods, depression, lack of energy, migraines, insomnia, and other physical and mental disturbances. These conditions create a state of low energy and a lack of physical movement, which contribute to weight gain.

20. Fad Diets Neglect Physical Pain and Other Physical Trauma

Most fad diets fail to address physical ailments such as migraines, fatigue, irritable bowel syndrome, allergy-caused pain, and heartburn. As a result, dieters who suffer from such ailments often abandon the diet before achieving any weight loss success, much less sustained weight management. Fad diets essentially eliminate a huge portion of the population from the outset by not offering solutions to physical problems. However, physical pain can often be alleviated by acupuncture, kinesiology, energy psychology, yoga, Pilates, and other healing practices.

21. Fad Diets Fail to Address Food Quality

One of the reasons people gain weight is because the food they eat is of terrible quality. Few people seem to know that two-thirds of the food sold in U.S. supermarkets is genetically engineered, irradiated, and treated with hormones, pesticides, and herbicides. This makes the food actually dangerous for human consumption.[15] Learning about this phenomenon helps create enormous motivation to change unhealthy habits. In addition, when the body stops being poisoned, it finally gets a chance to detoxify and go back to its ideal weight.

22. Fad Diets Lack Emotional Support for Dieters

Research tells us that less than 2 percent of dieters are able to maintain their weight loss for more than two years.[16] Most dieters regain all their weight as well as a few more pounds after each dieting attempt. Science has proven that emotional mastery plays the largest role in achieving happiness and fulfillment in life. Therefore, the lack of emotional support may be the main reason why so many crash diets fail in the long run.

Yet most diets offer little or no psychological or emotional support to dieters. They often provide no techniques for dealing with common issues such as stress management, depression, and job dissatisfaction. They also lack tools for creating new habits through which dieters can learn to associate great pleasure with achieving and maintaining the desired weight.

• •

Weight loss secret:
You can know everything and have the best plan, but if you are not motivated to do it, you will not succeed.

Motivation is key. Knowing why you want to be thin and how good being thin will make you feel will be the key to your success.

• •

23. Fad Dieters Often Lack Spiritual Support

Most crash diets fail to offer spiritual support to their dieters. They fail to guide people to connect with their inner souls, with what is most precious in a human life, with what it means to live a life of meaning where we lose weight naturally because we are aligned with who we really are as human beings. These diets fail to help us use the power of attention and intention to achieve and maintain our target weight. Techniques such as meditation, yoga, prayer, and contemplation, as well as learning how to practice gratitude and forgiveness on a daily basis, are rarely included in a weight loss plan. Through the power of a focused mind and guided by our inner knowing, we are all able to unleash the power within us to support ourselves when we face life's challenges. Only when we do that do we learn to appreciate our bodies as the miracle that they truly are and stop treating ourselves as a garbage can for junk food and negative thoughts.

• •

Weight loss secret:
Losing weight and keeping it off is not just about eating right; it's about living a life of meaning, health, and vitality.

Research[17] shows that most fad diets fail in the long run for one major reason: they do not address the whole person—physically, socially, mentally, emotionally, or spiritually.

• •

In other words, to be successful, a weight loss program must encompass and address all of the significant dimensions of life and so must you. The following chapters will guide you through these steps. Have fun with it and continue to celebrate your life!

Focus on Your Health—
Your Perfect Weight Will Follow

"Putting off an easy thing makes it hard.
Putting off a hard thing makes it impossible."
—Charles E. Wilson

Before reading on, I would like you to answer the following question:

**Would you want to be one of two people in our society who—
statistically—will die of cardiovascular disease? Or would you
rather be one of four people who will die of cancer?**

I cannot hear your answer but I imagine you might be shocked by these bold
questions—and you should be. But I do not exaggerate. The American
Heart Association maintains in its 2005 update paper on heart disease statistics that one in two (actually 2.6) people are currently dying of cardiovascular
(i.e., heart) disease.[18] Furthermore, according to a study performed in 2002 by
the U.S. Department of Health and Human Services, the Centers for Disease
Control, and the National Cancer Institute, one in four people are currently
dying of cancer.[19]

If that isn't scary enough, the U.S. Surgeon General tells us that for people
struggling with overweight and obesity, the risk of death increases significantly
in the following ways:[20]

1. **Heart disease**. Overweight or obese people—those with a body mass
   index[21] (BMI) higher than 25—have a greater risk of heart problems, including twice the likelihood of high blood pressure, than people with a
   healthy weight. The American Heart Association has proven that obesity is
   also associated with elevated levels of bad cholesterol (LDL) and decreased

levels of good cholesterol (HDL), a scenario that is a leading cause of heart problems.

2. **Cancer**. Clinical studies performed by the National Cancer Institute show that overweight and obesity may be associated with increased risk of colon, gallbladder, kidney, prostate, and postmenopausal breast cancer.

3. **Diabetes**. More than 80 percent of people with diabetes are overweight or obese. The likelihood that a person who is 15 pounds (6.8 kg) overweight will develop Type 2 diabetes is twice that of a person who is of normal weight, the above studies show.

4. **Premature death.** The U.S. Surgeon General estimates that approximately 300,000 people die per year in the United States due to obesity. The risk of death increases with weight gain, because even a moderate weight excess of 15 pounds puts a person of average height at risk. People with a BMI higher than 30 increase their risk of premature death by 50 to 100 percent compared with individuals of a healthy weight.[22]

Other health problems that tend to plague overweight or obese people are sleep apnea (interrupted breathing during sleep), asthma, arthritis, and reproductive complications. In the same paper mentioned above, the Surgeon General points out the social, academic, and workplace discrimination that may occur due to overweight or obesity.

Did you know that women risk more?

According to the U.S. National Center for Chronic Disease Prevention and Health Promotion, **women seem to double their risk of postmenopausal cancer if they gain more than 20 pounds (9 kg) from age 18 to midlife** compared to women whose weight remains stable.[23]

According to the National Heart, Blood, and Lung Institute, "In 1999, almost 108 million adult Americans were overweight or obese. If you are overweight or obese, carrying this extra weight puts you at risk for developing many diseases, especially heart disease, stroke, diabetes, and cancer. Losing this weight helps to prevent and control these diseases."[24]

The U.S. Surgeon General points out that 64 percent of U.S. adults were already overweight or obese in 2000.[25] Also, 15 percent of children (ages 6–11) and 15 percent of adolescents (ages 12–19) were overweight in 2000. "Obesity is reaching epidemic proportions in America, and could soon cause as much preventable disease and death as cigarette smoking," the health official claims. Tragically, 30 percent of U.S. adults are considered obese according to the scientific definition of obesity. Since 1970, class 3 obesity—comprising those who are called "morbidly obese"—has increased by 370 percent.[25]

The problem of overweight and obesity cuts across all ages, races, and ethnic groups as well as both genders. It is estimated that this dramatic health crisis will cost the U.S. economy $100 billion in 2005 and is growing fast.[26]

Most reports on obesity focus on the health challenges related to the physical body. What is left out and what I personally believe to be extremely significant is the emotional devastation and the loss of self-love and self-respect that many overweight or obese people face as a result of their struggle with losing weight. I can personally attest to this.

Did you know?

"On average, overweight **American women say they would sacrifice five years off their life span to be thin**," Dr. Elson Haas writes in his book *The False Fat Diet*.

What I consider to be even more tragic is the fact that 95 percent of all women perceive themselves to be more overweight than they really are. As a result, half of them diet frequently and are obsessed with their weight, Dr. Haas says.

And yet, there is hope. There is a lot of hope. I know because I have been there. And because I wasn't willing to give up, I found out that there are hundreds of thousands of people who have successfully found not one but several ways to lose weight, regain their health, and leave the fear of overweight and chronic disease forever behind them. Today I am here to share their secrets with all of you who are sick and tired of being sick and fat. Let's see how they did it.

The Six Secret Pillars of Ideal Weight, Health, and Vitality

"You may have a fresh start at any moment you choose, for this thing that we call 'failure' is not the falling down, but the staying down."
—Mary Pickford

As a psychologist, I can tell you that without exception, successful people have found that the most important secret in excelling at anything in life, including permanent weight loss, is your psychology.

If you want to succeed, you *must* want it badly enough. You must decide today to do anything it takes to lose weight and be healthy for the rest of your life. You must commit yourself to be the best you can be and leave nothing out that may take you off your path. This book will show you how you do that. As you have seen from the above statistics, the alternative is not an option.

••

Top weight loss secret #1:
Decide and commit to yourself.

Become conscious of the beautiful and powerful person that you are. You must *want* to lose weight permanently and be as healthy and vital as you can be. Otherwise you will continue on the yo-yo path.

••

If you don't decide and commit to yourself, you will not be able to join the people who succeed. Instead you will join the majority of people who fail and the 90 percent of people who buy books and don't read them let alone use them to their advantage. You can take this route, of course, but you should know that the only person who will be cheated is you. You will have paid all this money and invested all this time without achieving what you deserve to have: your ideal weight and a healthy body full of vitality and life force. It is your choice.

. . . .

Top weight loss secret #2:
Be inspired and totally motivated to succeed.

Increase your awareness about the extraordinary potential within you and identify with your true self. In order to achieve your weight loss and health goals you must know why you want them.

. . . .

Even more important than deciding and committing to your goal is to know *why* you want to have your ideal body and be healthy and vital. Knowing why will give you the passion and drive that are crucial to help you get there.

As you read these lines, think of all the reasons why you want to be thin. How would you feel once you are thin? What would you gain, how would you look, how would you feel when other people admire you? What else could you do with the additional energy, motivation, self-confidence, and self-esteem? Who else could you help, guide, and support, and what difference could you make in your family, among your friends, and in the world with your newly acquired knowledge? This is what being inspired means— it means to be "in spirit"; it means to unleash the power of your beautiful spirit to guide and support you in the process of being the best and the most beautiful you can be.

. . . .

Top weight loss secret #3:
Have a plan to achieve your goal.

Having a plan means to know how to get from where you are to where you want to be. You must have a plan and know what to do every day to get closer to your goal.

. . . .

Top weight loss secret #4:
Become the expert – learn everything there is to learn on weight loss and well-being.

A couple of hundred years ago, people believed that the world is flat. Then we learned that it is round. Furthermore, people believed that the sun gravitates around the earth and now we know that exactly the opposite is the case. The same is true for everything in life, including diet. Therefore, stay informed and become the expert yourself. Follow the science and more importantly listen to your body—it knows best.

Top Weight loss secret #5:
Stay flexible and make changes until you achieve the desired results because you are what you think you are.

Let go of the beliefs and thoughts about your identity that haven't served you, and let go of what you don't want so you are open to receive what you actually want. Realize that you are not your body and you are not your thoughts. You are that which thinks the thoughts. So begin to be very careful of what you allow to enter your mind.

How often do you know what to do but don't do what you know?

Top weight loss secret #6:
Get a mentor and join a supportive community.

We all know the old adage that says "Show me who you hang out with and I'll tell you who you are" or a variation thereof that goes like "If you hang out with dogs you come up with fleas." There is a lot in truth to those idioms and you can use that to your advantage to achieve your weight loss and well-being goals. Get a mentor and chose people who support you in your new endeavor. If you do not know where to start, join SageEra's Wisdom Circle and contact my office at www.sageera.com.

The reason for this dilemma may be manifold, but again, the most important tool you have to get yourself to do what's needed is your psychology. That means if you want something badly enough you will not give up until you get it. That means furthermore that you must be willing to make adjustments along the way and change your approach until you finally achieve your goal. Just like a child who begins walking and doesn't give up until she knows how to walk, you too must develop the flexibility, open-mindedness, and positive attitude to go out of your way until you succeed and beyond. This is the Diet for a New Life. This is the diet you develop for yourself in order to be, do, and become the most fulfilled and the best you can be for the rest of your life.

The sky's the limit. Are you ready? If so, then let's get started.

Step 1: Eating Without Dieting

"The road to excess leads to the palace of wisdom."
– William Blake

If you have gotten this far in the book, I'm assuming you have already embraced the most important in the program, which is to *decide* and to *commit* to doing everything it takes to achieve and maintain your ideal weight and health. This also means you know exactly *why* you want to lose weight and are very clear on *how you will feel* once you have achieved that goal. I'm assuming you know the extent to which your own psychology and emotional association with your final success are crucial to keeping you on track and guiding you through the process of achieving your goal.

Did you know?

People **have reportedly lost up to 50 pounds** and lowered their cholesterol levels from 420 to 250 **in less than four weeks of beginning to alkalize their bodies and consume essential oils.**[27]

Now you are ready to discover the secrets of top experts and successful dieters. By knowing their techniques you can begin to mirror their efforts and achieve the same results. Let's begin with the following testimonial.

"My name is Mitzi Mager. After a lifetime of poor choices I found myself at Innerlight.[28] In November of 2001, not only was I tipping the scales at around 240 (my highest weight was 252), I was experiencing symptoms that kept me bedridden for about two months (vomiting, extreme vertigo, migraines, blacking out). During that time, my sister brought me a tape about the acid-alkaline balance and it just made sense to me! I studied more about this in about 30 different books but kept coming back to Dr. Robert Young's *Sick and Tired?: Reclaim Your Inner Terrain*. By the time

January 2002 came around, I was ready to start anew. I threw away everything in my cabinets that was considered acidic and began drinking five to six green drinks a day. I also began a 10-day cleanse, which, although highly uncomfortable, was apparently necessary. During that time, I had some live blood analysis tests done by a holistic doctor. At the beginning of the process, the tests showed that I had a severe hypothyroid

Figure 2: Mitzi Mager before and after alkalizing her body

condition that would require medication for the rest of my life. I refused medication, knowing my body would heal if I let it. I also had digestive stress, adrenal stress, liver stress, pancreatitis (my entire life), skin problems (rashes, acne, etc.), and bad migraines. The more greens I drank, and every day that I didn't reintroduce acidic foods (and thoughts), I could feel myself getting stronger and stronger. The extreme vertigo passed, the migraines went away, the thrush on my tongue disappeared, and I knew this was working. I am thrilled to say that during this time, *I lost 90 pounds in the first 90 days.* When I went to the gym to start training for a marathon, they measured my body fat at only 18 percent with no previous exercise. Not only that, but a year later, I had *no signs of thyroid imbalance* at all, or any stress on my system, and I no longer needed my contact lenses. It is now several years later and I remain at a size 4/6 and love the simplicity of this program that keeps me at this size and state of health. My mission is clear: to help as many people who want to be helped realize their dream of a better quality of life. Through Dr. Young's pH Miracle Plan, these products, and their commitment, people can reclaim their inner terrain!"

Here is how you can achieve the same results.

Top Weight Loss Secrets of Successful Dieters

1. **SECRET #1: Establishing the Acid-Alkaline Balance in your body**: Research performed over the course of 20 years by Dr. Robert Young29 and many other researchers around the world, shows the significance of the acid-alkaline balance for weight loss and health.[30]

2. **SECRET #2: Being Energized.** A healthy body is at its perfect weight and full of energy. To lose weight and keep it off, your system requires a

lot of energy. You can support your body in this process by helping it optimize all of its metabolic processes so it can use its energy to help you achieve your weight loss goals, heal, and detoxify.[31]

3.   **SECRET #3: Massive Supplementation.** The third secret to permanent weight loss is to support your body in regaining health, preventing disease, and building new cells and tissues by refilling its stores through aggressive supplementation[32] with vitamins, minerals, essential fats, and essential amino acids (protein).

These three principles represent the nutritional foundation on which the world's top health experts and successful dieters stand. Successful dieters are those who have been overweight, lost their extra pounds, and maintained their ideal weight for more than five years.

The scientific research presented in this program and the successful dieters I have studied suggest that if you observe these guidelines every day, you will not only lose significant weight, never to gain it back again, but you will begin to enjoy a health and vitality that you may have rarely enjoyed before. However, don't take my word for it, because I am only one messenger out of the hundreds of thousands of scientists around the world who are advancing our knowledge in the area of obesity, health, and well-being. Instead, use your common sense and allow your body to guide you through the process.

In this chapter, you will get a detailed explanation of the above principles. You will learn how food affects your body's weight and health. You will learn about foods that heal and foods that kill, find out how to combine foods to alkalize and give energy to your body, and learn how digestion works and how you can optimize your metabolism to lose weight. In addition, you will see what causes bloating, false fat, and food cravings. You will know how to address these conditions and how to nourish and replenish your body so you can lose weight and regain your health and vitality permanently.

Why Is the Acid-Alkaline Balance So Important for Losing Weight Permanently?

> *"To each of us, at certain points of our lives, there come opportunities to rearrange our formulas and assumptions—not necessarily to be rid of the old, but more to profit from adding something new."*
> – Leo Buscaglia

Just as the body's temperature has to stay constant in order to ensure health, your blood's acid-alkaline balance, also called its pH level, has to stay between 7.35 and 7.45, which is slightly alkaline.[33] The regular elimination processes in your body, including digestion, respiration, metabolism, and aging, create acidity. Under normal circumstances the body can get rid of these acids by buffering and eliminating them.

Unfortunately, our contemporary lifestyle adds significant acidity to our systems through food, drink, stress, and negative thinking. Therefore, most of us end up living in an acidic body all the time, as Dr. Young has proven through his microbiological research over the past 20 years.[34]

Did you know?

One glass of cola could kill you instantly if your body did nothing to neutralize the acid produced by it.[35]

One of the major culprits of acidity is the Western diet, claims the *American Journal of Clinical Nutrition*. This type of diet leads to a series of health challenges, including inflammation, kidney dysfunction, loss of bone density, loss of muscle mass, and several other diseases, the journal reports.[36] It doesn't stop there. According to a study performed in 2003 by the Institute of Preventive Medicine in Belgrade, Serbia, there is even a correlation between an acidic diet and cancer cells, which seem to thrive in an acidic environment.[37]

Weight loss secret:
Avoid inflammation at any price.

You can do this by sticking to a mostly alkaline diet that is high in leafy green vegetables, by taking daily walks in nature, and by avoiding stress.

If you are wondering about the connection between body acidity and weight gain, here is your explanation. According to Dr. Young, "The body protects itself against the acids as best as it can by binding them up with fat and storing them away. We pile on the extra pounds, feel the aches and pains inevitably associated with acidity, and become vulnerable to sickness and fatigue."[38]

So what does food have to do with it? In one word, ***everything***. An acidic diet contains more than 70 percent meat, processed carbohydrates (pasta, rice, and white bread), eggs, dairy products, sugary foods, caffeine, soft drinks such as cola, and alcohol. Doesn't this sound like what most of us eat on a regular basis?

When faced with such foods, the body rallies to neutralize the acidic environment with alkaline blood buffers, because it has to keep its pH level constant. To eliminate these acids, the body uses up calcium, potassium, and other minerals, also called electrolytes, and holds on to fat. Once the storage of minerals (electrolytes) in the body is depleted, the health begins to seriously deteriorate.[39] The human body cannot survive if its overall pH is acidic. This is truly a question of life and death.[40]

"We should thank our fat because without it we would be dead."[41]
—**Dr. Robert Young**

To provide further proof, Dr. Young analyzed fat tissues obtained from liposuction. In a personal conversation with him and his wife, Shelley Redford Young, Shelley shared with me that the fat tissues collected were overly acidic. Exemplifying how nature finds ways to protect itself and life, the body wraps the acid with fat and stores it away in order to protect vital organs.

To test your own body's acidity level you can measure the pH of your first urine in the morning. Test the urine with pH paper, which you can purchase at any pharmacy or online through Micro Essential Laboratory. Ideally, the pH of the urine should be between 6.8 and 7.2. If it's below 6.8 then you *must* begin to alkalize aggressively, because a slight deviation in your body's acid-alkaline balance presents not only a major threat to your health but prevents you from losing weight and keeping it off.

Did you know?

Alkalizing is a very intense chemical process for your body. **It takes 20 parts of an alkaline solution to neutralize one part of acid.** For example, you would need 32 glasses of alkaline water with a pH of 10 to neutralize a glass of cola, which has a pH level of 2.5 (very acidic). A pH of 10 is pretty high compared to the pH level contained in regular tap water, which—depending on its provenance—has an average pH level below 7.42 *Therefore, preventing is better than reversing!*

There Is Hope

> *"Life is about not knowing, having to change, taking the moment and making the best of it, without knowing what's going to happen next."*
> —Gilda Radner

The good news is that the human body is very forgiving. You can reverse overacidity within 12 to 16 weeks through an alkalizing diet of dark green salads, legumes, vegetables, and low-sugar fruits. This is how much time your blood, the river of life, needs to regenerate.[43] The pH test of your first urine in the morning will show you that you are on the right track. Once your blood is and continues to stay alkaline, your body begins to heal naturally and you resume your ideal weight.

Scientific research confirms that an alkaline diet enables the body to heal and get back in balance.[44] As a result, you lose weight permanently, because the body no longer needs the fat to neutralize the acidic load.

In the latest controlled research published in their book *The pH Miracle for Weight Loss*, the Youngs report that the 27 participants in their study lost an average of 50 pounds per person in less than 12 weeks. Furthermore, their patients decreased their body fat, increased muscle mass, lowered cholesterol and blood pressure, and eliminated heartburn, indigestion, and even depression and chronic pain.[45]

An additional benefit of alkalinization is detoxification, whereby the body rids itself of toxins accumulated over many years. As a result, you lose additional weight in a natural way, and most importantly, you heal.

HOW TO ALKALIZE

The fastest way to alkalize your body to lose weight permanently is through the consumption of:

- **Alkaline foods:** Eat dark green leafy vegetables, salads, and legumes. These foods should represent approximately 70 percent of each meal. Fresh, organic, uncooked, and unaltered greens are the most important nutrients for the body. They provide all the essential protein, starch, oxygen, water, fiber, enzymes, vitamins, and minerals/electrolytes in an easily absorbable form.[46] They are your greatest source of antioxidants and phytonutrients, nature's healing medicines.
- **Super foods and green drinks:** Green foods are best if consumed freshly harvested from your own garden, but this is often an unrealistic scenario in our fast-paced industrialized world. So-called super foods or green drinks are the next best thing. Green drinks are made out of greens (stems, leaves, and grasses such as kamut grass, barley grass, straw grass, and wheat grass) that are dried at low temperatures.[47] When mixed with purified water[48] and consumed three times per day or throughout the day as green water, they are just as beneficial to your body as fresh greens. A green drink is made by mixing one quart (1 liter) of purified water—regular tap water is not good enough—with one teaspoon of greens. Numerous green food products

exist. Choosing one is a matter of taste. The taste is neutra
good nor bad. In our family, we consume three different
greens because each one of us prefers a different taste. The best-qual-
ity greens, which I would recommend in no particular order, are
David Wolfe's, Nature's First Food, Dr. Udo Erasmus's Green Blend,
and Dr. Robert Young's Super Greens.

- **Baking soda:** In the absence of green drinks, you can alkalize your
  body for a couple of days by drinking ½ teaspoon of baking soda
  (sodium bicarbonate) in a small glass of water three times per day,
  preferably with each meal. The baking soda neutralizes acid quickly,
  the baking soda burp indicating the antacid is working (the burp is
  caused by release of carbon dioxide gas, which occurs when the antacid
  neutralizes the acid). Although baking soda may provide a short-term
  solution to overacidity, I need to caution you that too much bicarbonate can wreak havoc with your body's acid-base balance and lead
  to metabolic alkalosis. The high sodium content may also cause problems for people with heart failure or high blood pressure.
- **Essential fatty acids:** Increase your intake of essential fatty acids such
  as olive oil, flaxseed oil, and fish oil.

In addition:

- **Reduce** your intake of **acid-forming foods** such as **meat, eggs, and
  dairy products** to less than 10 percent of each meal.
- **Reduce** significantly your consumption of **sugar, sugary desserts,
  and refined carbohydrates.**
- **Avoid** indigestible acids found in **sodas (especially cola), alcohol,
  and caffeine**—all of which produce acids in your body and prevent
  you from losing weight and keeping it off.

Why Is Energy Significant for Weight Loss and Healing?

"The hardest work of all is to do nothing."
—Proverb

Energy is life. Unfortunately, there is only a limited amount of energy available in the body at any one time. In all metabolic processes, especially those related
to weight loss and the correlated detoxification, there is a delicate balance of gain-

ing and using energy. As we grow older we get accustomed to having a reduced amount of energy. Based on our social conditioning, we often think that having less energy than we had as a child is part of the normal process of aging.

However, science tells us that it doesn't have to be this way and that there are many methods of raising our energy level. With respect to the correlation between energy and obesity, we learn from Bradford Lowell and his co-researcher Bruce Spiegelman that energy "is influenced by environmental temperature and diet" and that "obesity results when energy intake exceeds energy expenditure."[49]

To lose weight you need to reverse this process and make sure you have plenty of energy to support the elimination processes.

In order to know what you can do to gain energy to lose weight and keep it off, let's take a look at what deprives the body of energy.

What Robs You of Your Energy?

- **The process of digestion.** Acid-forming foods such as soft drinks, alcohol, and drugs are particularly taxing on the digestive system. This is why more than 44 percent of Americans take antacids.[50]
- **Dealing with poisons.** What we eat and drink as well as our environment are mostly contaminated with parasites, bacteria, antibiotics, hormones, herbicides, pesticides, electromagnetic pollution, heavy metals, and other toxic chemicals, which are difficult for the body to withstand and eliminate.[51]
- **Lack of appropriate ways to cleanse and detoxify the body.** If we ingest more than the body can cope with, it is not able to get rid of accumulated wastes, which in turn requires additional energy expenditure for detoxification. More importantly, it causes the deterioration of health and premature aging.[52]
- **Extensive strenuous physical activity.** Hard physical work, extreme sports, injuries, and accidents[53] all deprive the body of energy.
- **Health imbalances and disease.** Healing processes require significant amounts of energy and have top priority in the human body. This is the reason we are not hungry when we are sick and all other body functions are slowed down, requiring us to stay in bed.[54]
- **Stress, worries, negative emotions, and mental turmoil.** Stress sends the body into a state of anxiety, which uses tremendous levels of energy. We are being prepared to respond to challenges and go to "war" if needed.[55]
- **Lack of meaning in life.** The absence of a spiritual (but not necessarily religious) life, a life without purpose, which disregards the im-

portance of human relationships, culture, and social responsibility, drains us of energy and life force.[56]

Listen to your body and you will soon find out what to do to have more energy. Let go of everything that depletes you of energy.

The human body derives energy from food but also uses energy for digestion. In a healthy body at rest, digestion takes up more energy than any other physical process. To lose weight and keep it off, your digestion needs to be as efficient as possible. The intention is to gain maximum energy from food while using as little energy as possible in the process. The body can then use the leftover energy to lose weight and detoxify.

All these measures help us create a life that gives us more energy than it takes. As we learn to take better care of ourselves by honoring the miracle that is our body, *we not only lose weight—we gain life.* As we begin to appreciate and love ourselves, we find joy and fulfillment in every moment. We begin to live in the now, for this is all there is and all that will ever be: now.

If you feel groggy after a meal, your body is telling you to go to sleep because it needs the energy to digest the food and drink you just had.

When you are sick, you are usually not hungry, right? Why? Because the body contains only a limited amount of energy, and when that energy is needed to heal, the digestive process slows down.

••

WEIGHT LOSS SECRET:
ENERGIZE.

You can energize your body to lose weight, detoxify, and heal in the following ways:

- **Get adequate oxygen and light.** We could live for only a couple of minutes without oxygen. In fact, scientists tell us that cancer cells thrive in an oxygen-poor environment.
- **Drink pure water.** The human body contains between 70 and 80 percent water. We could live for months without food but we would not survive for more than a couple of days without water.
- **Eat live foods.** Full of the sun's energy, live foods such as dark green salads, unaltered vegetables, legumes, and essential fatty acids provide the main sources of energy to the human body.
- **Exercise regularly.** We were made to run, play, and use our beautiful body. Moderate exercise increases

metabolism and gives us energy long after we've stopped exercising.

- **Get adequate sleep.** Adults need an average of seven hours of sleep per night in order to recharge the body and mind. Taking regular vacations provides extra stores of mental, emotional, and physical energy.[57]
- **Live in balance.** Humans are multidimensional beings that require all areas of life to be in balance in order to be fulfilled and happy. These areas include physical, emotional, and spiritual life, as well as relationships and work. By distributing our attention in an equal way between work and play we begin to have a sense of balance and control over our own destiny.[58]
- **Live a life of purpose and service.** Once we fulfill our basic human needs, we want our lives to be meaningful and useful to mankind. It is from contributing to the well-being of others that we draw true fulfillment and satisfaction from life. It is this sense of love and connection with all life in the universe that gives us endless energy and keeps us mentally alert.[59]

To lose weight, you need to conserve your energy for shedding pounds and detoxifying. You can do that by:

- Active breathing. Make sure your body gets enough oxygen by doing active breathing exercises three times a day.
- Superhydration and alkalization.
- Eating foods that give rather than deplete energy. These foods are alive, unaltered fresh vegetables and legumes, dark green salads, and fruits.
- Combining foods properly to optimize the digestive process. For instance, never mix animal protein (meat or fish) with carbohydrates (starches such as potatoes, rice, or pasta) in the same meal.
- Taking enzymes to facilitate and improve digestion.
- Exercising regularly and moderately in any possible way—walking, biking, swimming, etc.—to increase metabolism. This will enable you to use up calories even while sitting or sleeping.
- Eating the right fats help you lose fat. These are essential oils found in extra virgin and cold-pressed flaxseed oil, borage oil, safflower oil, and primrose oil. Olive oil contains some essential fats.

How can we give the body the energy it needs to lose weight?

1. By nourishing it with life-giving foods
2. By increasing metabolism through exercise
3. By streamlining the digestive process through proper food combining and enzymes
4. By dealing with and mastering emotions
5. By calming the mind
6. By living a life of purpose and service to ourselves and mankind, which brings meaning and happiness to life
7. By making a habit of healthy living
8. By celebrating and enjoying life

You Are What You Eat

When we want to lose weight, the first thing most of us think about is food, and the first thought we have is that we'll have to go on a diet. However, as I said earlier, this is not a diet book and I do not recommend going on a diet. Instead, I want to empower you to make your own decisions about what to eat by giving you information about what your body needs to be healthy. I'll also explain how food affects your physical body as well as your mental and emotional states.

Scientific research[60] shows that, in addition to light, water, and oxygen, **the human body needs about 50 essential components (45 of which are essential nutrients) in order to be healthy.** These components are called essential because the body is unable to produce them and thus must get them from the outside world. These nutrients comprise 21 minerals, 13 vitamins, eight proteins (amino acids), two essential fatty acids, fiber, friendly bacteria to maintain a healthy digestive tract, hydrochloric acid, bile, and enzymes for proper digestion.

Let's take a look at these basic building blocks in more detail and see why they are crucial for a healthy body. We'll also learn where they come from and how they affect us—especially when we want to lose weight and keep it off.

Fats That Heal and Fats That Kill

In March of 2002, I had the great privilege of meeting one of the world's foremost authorities on fats and oils, Dr. Udo Erasmus. In 1980, Dr. Erasmus earned a Ph.D. in nutrition after being diagnosed with severe pesticide poisoning, which if not treated would have almost certainly led to cancer. At that point,

Dr. Erasmus began a desperate quest for health that culminated in his first book, *Oils and Fats*. Not only did he not die of cancer, but at age 60+ he looks no more than 45. Moreover, as a result of his own ordeal he has changed the lives of hundreds of thousands of people for the better. Through his books and publications, he has revolutionized the world of nutrition and brought to our attention how important the right fats are, not only for weight loss but more importantly for our vitality and our health.

Essential fats, also called essential fatty acids, are, in fact, essential for the body to survive. However, research has shown that more than 90 percent of people in the West do not derive an adequate amount of fatty acids from their diet, Dr. Erasmus told me in a personal conversation. This is the main reason we face such challenging health problems, he said.

....

Weight loss secret:
The right fat helps you lose weight.

Fat molecules are a rich and lasting source of energy and are crucial for losing weight.[12] Fats provide the building blocks of our cells and ultimately our organs. Many kinds of fats exist, but only two are essential, and you must get adequate amounts of them:

- **Omega 3**, which is found in leafy green vegetables, flaxseed oil, and cold-water fish
- **Omega 6**, found in nuts and seeds, especially sesame and sunflower seeds, and land-animal flesh

We can consume these essential oils in food or through oil blends such as Udo's Choice Perfected Oil Blend,[61] primrose oil, flaxseed oil, and other oil blends available in the refrigerated section of health food stores.

....

Scientific research[62] has shown the following additional benefits of essential fatty acids:
- Slowed aging
- Increased energy and stamina
- Reduced inflammation, for less risk of cancer
- Stronger immune system
- Less risk of cardiovascular disease
- Improved brain function
- Regulate the optimal functioning of organs and glands
- Improved digestion
- Strong bones, beautiful skin, and speedy recovery and healing

•••

Weight loss secret:
Boost the level of good cholesterol (HDL) in your body and decrease the level of LDL, and your additional weight will vanish naturally.

- **Increase your intake of essential fatty acids such as avocados and soaked nuts and seeds.** The process of soaking nuts and seeds for more than eight hours removes the natural enzyme inhibitors from the food and makes essential enzymes available to the body. The enzyme inhibitors prevent the nuts and seeds from growing into a plant. We want and need those enzymes to digest the nuts, which otherwise would be very difficult to digest. Consuming nuts and seeds, such as almonds and flaxseeds, provides the body with essential fats to build cell membrane, support the production of vital hormones, neutralize acids in the body, and increase metabolism.
- Significantly reduce your consumption of processed fats and oils (cheese, milk, egg yolk, butter, margarine, red meat, and shellfish). Such fats cause inflammation and create an overly acidic environment in the body, possibly leading to coronary heart disease, overweight and obesity, high blood pressure, poor blood circulation, and even cancer.

•••

What Is Cholesterol, Anyway?

Cholesterol is a waxy fat that is naturally present in the human body. Two sources contribute to the production of cholesterol in the human body:

- The liver manufactures about 80 percent of it.
- We consume it by eating animal products such as meat, eggs, and dairy products.

Cholesterol is carried through the bloodstream by certain proteins. There are four kinds of cholesterol but we are focusing only on three in this context: HDL (high-density lipoprotein), LDL (low-density lipoprotein), and triglycerides. Total cholesterol measures the combination of HDL and LDL, along with several other factors. The level of "fats" in the blood—total cholesterol, HDL ("good cholesterol"), LDL ("bad cholesterol"), and triglycerides—has been used for years to predict the risk of heart disease. Higher LDL and triglycerides and/or low

HDL have been associated with increased risk of heart disease. Thus our intention is to have higher levels of HDL and lower levels of LDL.

Total cholesterol levels less than 200 are desirable. Total cholesterol between 200 and 239 is borderline high. HDL levels should be 40 or above and LDL levels should optimally be less than 100. LDL levels greater than 129 are considered borderline high, and levels greater than 159 are considered high.

Good Carbs, Bad Carbs

In his 2002 article "Is dietary carbohydrate essential for human nutrition?" published in the *American Journal for Clinical Nutrition*, researcher Eric Westman tells us that we do not need to eat foods containing carbohydrates. However, can you imagine the Italians without their pasta, the Germans without their bread, or the Chinese without their rice? I can't. In fact, the most common foods consumed on our planet today are carbohydrates, and these are mostly in the form of bread, potatoes, pastries, candy, rice, and spaghetti.

Yet, this would be OK—as it was for centuries before we began facing the health challenges we have today—if those carbohydrates were whole and unprocessed. But they aren't. In the industrialized world, we tend to consume mass quantities of *refined* carbohydrates (white rice, white pasta, corn starch, processed cereals, and so on). The body turns these refined carbohydrates mostly into fat. These carbohydrates are devoid of fiber, which is crucial for healthy digestion. Fiber keeps the digestive tract, especially the colon, healthy. Starches from whole grains, which contain more minerals, vitamins, and fiber, are digested more slowly and are therefore healthier.

Sugars

Simple sugars are another important aspect of carbohydrate intake.

If you are tired much of the time, have trouble sleeping and concentrating at work, and are often irritable, then you may be suffering from the metabolic syndrome. That is another word for the body's inability to process sugar properly.

Did you know?

The average American consumes more than 149 pounds (68 kg) of sugar per year.[64]

To function properly, a healthy body needs only two teaspoons of blood sugar at any one time. The body can synthesize this sugar easily from unrefined carbohydrates, fats, or protein. If we ingest more sugars than needed through improper nutrition, we throw off our body chemistry, compromise our health, and, of course, sacrifice the way we look. The worst consequences come from an excess in sugars—from refined carbohydrates.

Potatoes, yams, and sweet fruits contain sugars. The body processes these sugars quickly and absorbs them as saturated fatty acids. When eaten in large quantities, these foods can be an impediment to losing weight.

The Glycemic Index and the Importance of Fiber

Have you ever wondered why you feel hungry only a few hours after eating a big meal? Chances are you've eaten refined carbohydrate–containing foods that caused a rapid spike in your blood sugar. This in turn draws extra insulin into the blood to keep the sugar under control. The high insulin, in turn, suppresses fat burning and encourages the storage of fats while inducing the cellular metabolism to produce inflammatory chemicals. In addition, insulin makes blood sugar levels drop. As a result, you get that famished feeling that leads to overeating.

Over time, the body becomes inefficient in manufacturing simple sugars from complex/unrefined carbohydrates, proteins, or fats. So the body shuts down its proper functioning, the blood glucose levels drop, and we become addicted to sugars. The vicious cycle has begun. Swings in blood sugar create terrible addictions that make us crave candy bars, cakes, breads, and the like. We might feel better for the moment by indulging our cravings, but the body chemistry is still upset and off balance. The body has now received its sugars but is very short on nutrients, so we are hungry again.

> **Sugar initiates the production of insulin that encourages the storage of fats, while the body is starving for nutrients. This is how we keep gaining weight.**

By addressing our intake of simple-sugar foods (refined carbohydrates such as pasta, potatoes, white bread, and cake), we can become very successful in losing weight. In fact, this is the main philosophy behind the popular South Beach Diet: significant reduction of refined carbohydrates in the diet by sticking to foods that are low to medium on the glycemic index.

> **The glycemic index is a means of measuring the effect a food has on blood sugar levels.**

Some foods that contain a high amount of sugar, such as maple and corn syrups, honey, and candy, as well as starchy foods, such as bananas, carrots, potatoes, and breakfast cereals, are rated high on the glycemic index. When eaten, these foods create a rapid rise in blood sugar levels. Other foods, especially those high in fiber, such as whole grains, are rated low on the glycemic index because they do not produce a rapid rise in blood sugar. Stick to those to lose weight fast.

The following is a thumbnail guide to the glycemic index of foods:

EAT MORE Good Carbohydrates/Low Glycemic Index Foods: asparagus, kiwi, bean sprouts, beet greens, broccoli, cabbage, cantaloupe, cauliflower, celery, cucumber, endive lettuce, mustard greens, dried beans, lima beans, radishes, rhubarb, spinach, Swiss chard, watercress.

Medium Glycemic Index Foods: apples, fresh apricots, bananas, blackberries, cherries, cranberries, grapefruit, guava, kiwi, lemons, limes, oranges, papayas, peaches, plums, raspberries, strawberries, tangerines, tomatoes, eggplant, beets, Brussels sprouts, chives, collards, dandelion greens, kale, kohlrabi, leeks, okra, onions, parsley, peas, peppers, pimento, pumpkin, green beans, turnips.

EAT LESS Bad Carbohydrates/High Glycemic Index Foods: dried fruit, blueberries, figs, grapes, kumquats, loganberries, mangoes, mulberries, pears, pineapple, pomegranates, prunes, artichokes, carrots, corn, corn flakes and other processed cereals (with added sugars), honey, white rice, white bread, table sugar, oatmeal, oyster plant, parsnips, potatoes, squash, sweet potatoes, yams.

• •

Weight loss secret:
Reduce your consumption of carbohydrates.

To lose weight, significantly reduce your intake of processed sugars and refined carbohydrates (e.g., white flour–based products). If you must eat carbohydrates, choose wholesome complex carbohydrates such as whole grains, brown rice, and wild rice. These starches can become a problem only if you eat too much of them and live a sedentary lifestyle. Dr. Robert Young states that overweight and obesity is not a fat problem. It's an acid problem. Sugar is a huge culprit in producing acid in our body. By drinking one gallon (4 liters) of green drink per day, you can neutralize the acids produced by sugars and allow the body to let go of the extra pounds in a natural way.

• •

Enzymes Are the Source of Life

Enzymes are catalysts or facilitators of important chemical processes in the body. Enzymes are essential to the human body, especially in the digestion process.

Without enzymes we could not exist.

Our bodies operate on different kinds of enzymes, including:

* **Digestive enzymes,** produced by the stomach, pancreas, and small intestine.
* **Metabolic enzymes,** which help other systems of the body work optimally, including the immune system and the circulatory system.
* **Food enzymes** that are normally in all raw, uncooked, and unprocessed foods, such as fruits and vegetables. If we eat enough raw food and chew it well on a daily basis, we should get enough food enzymes (as long as we are not allergic to the foods we eat).

The human body makes and uses more than 3,000 types of enzymes. These substances participate in every part of the body, from the whole immune system to single organs such as the heart, lungs, liver, and brain.

Enzymes support the immune system in fighting bacteria and viruses.

In the industrialized world, we often become overweight and obese due to the consumption of overly processed and cooked foods. These contain no enzymes, no minerals, no vitamins, too much salt, too many refined sugars, the wrong fats, too many processed carbohydrates, too much protein, and all kinds of toxins (herbicides, pesticides, antibiotics, hormones, preservatives, and irradiation, to name a few).[66]

It has been scientifically proven that cooked food has no enzymes left in it.[67]

Without enough enzymes, the body won't work optimally and will eventually get sick. All foods are made from the same building blocks— proteins (amino acids), fats (fatty acids), carbohydrates (glucose), vitamins, and minerals. These components require different enzymes to be processed. Protease breaks down protein, lipase digests fats, amylase digests starch, and so on.

Food that has been heated to over 108°F (42°C) has zero enzymes. This is why I highly encourage the consumption of mostly raw green vegetables and legumes[68] that should be very well chewed. In addition, I am a big supporter of taking enzymes as a complement to healthy nutrition. Enzymes can be purchased in every health food store or online. However, not all enzymes are alike and of top quality. I personally take Dr. Ellen Cutler's, and I also highly recommend Dr. Udo Erasmus's enzymes.

. . . .

Weight loss secret:
Take digestive enzyme supplements with every meal.

Enzymes aid in weight loss by contributing to proper digestion; helping to eliminate of food cravings; reducing heartburn, gas, and bloating; encouraging high assimilation of nutrients, leading to an early sense of satiation; and increasing metabolism. Enzymes also foster good health by providing the basic nutritional building blocks of healthy cells, healing allergies and inflammation, slowing down the aging process, and aiding the immune system.

. . . .

How Much Protein Do We Actually Need?

Protein, and how much of it we need daily, is one of the most controversial topics in the area of nutrition. Conventional wisdom tells us we must eat meat to get the protein we need.

> **Yet I wonder: where do some of the strongest animals on the planet, such as elephants, gorillas and giraffes, get their protein if all they eat are vegetables?**

I have a natural aversion to meat and stopped eating it in 1992. But we are all different, and a person living in, say, the Arctic eats differently from a person living in Africa. So I encourage you to listen to your body. Furthermore, I would like to continue to share with you what the scientific community tells us about protein (amino acids) and how it affects our health so you can make your own decisions.

Use Your Common Sense

A normal human baby almost triples his or her weight during the first year of life. The baby does that by feeding on mother's milk alone. And yet, scientists[69] tell us that human breast milk contains around 8 percent protein. The adult human body contains and requires a maximum of 7 percent, or only 1 gram, of most essential amino acids or protein per day.[70]

However, research shows that in the industrialized world our daily diet consists of 30 to 50 percent protein. This would not be so bad if we ate more vegetable protein, such as broccoli, which contains 45 percent protein and zero cholesterol.[71] But instead the scales are tipped toward animal protein, a source of a tremendous amount of saturated fats/bad cholesterol, which has been associated with numerous conditions including in-sulin resistance,[72] heart disease, stroke, breast and colon can-cer, osteoporosis, and kidney disease.[73]

If a baby in its fastest growth period is being given by nature less than 8 percent protein and the human body contains less than 8 percent protein, use your common sense and ask your-self, how much protein do you as a grown-up adult need per day? Follow your own advice.

In a 2002 article published in the *International Journal of Obesity-Related Metabolic Disorders* titled "Markers of chronic inflammation and obesity: a prospective study on the reversibility of this association in middle-aged women undergoing weight loss by surgical intervention," Laimer et al. show a clear as-sociation between acid-forming foods of animal source as well as inflammation and its consequences for overweight and disease.

....

Weight loss secret:
Significantly reduce your intake of animal protein.

To lose weight and increase your health, level of energy, and vitality, eat less animal protein. The high content of cholesterol in animal protein (for instance, in meat, egg yolk, and shellfish) has been associated in clinical studies with increased inflammation in the body, leading to high levels of LDL, overweight, obesity, and even cancer. These acid-form-ing foods force your body to hold onto fat in order to neutralize acids.

....

You Are What You Digest: The Power of Food Combining

> *"Nothing will benefit human health and increase the chances for survival on earth as much as the evolution to a vegetarian diet."*
> —Albert Einstein

The most common habit we have in the industrialized world is to mix protein (from animal sources such as meat or fish) and carbohydrates (potatoes, bread, or rice) in one meal. If we eat like this over a long period of time, we'll eventually gain weight.

Why? Because to digest protein, the stomach must secrete hydrochloric acid. To digest carbohydrates, we need an alkaline (base) stomach juice. As you may remember from chemistry class, the acid and the base neutralize each other and nothing gets digested despite the body's efforts. This is energy that we don't have in abundance. This is why we feel tired after a meal.

After sitting in the stomach for a couple of hours, the undigested food begins to ferment and putrefy and starts producing heartburn and gas. The stomach gives up trying to digest, and the food finds its way into the small intestine. No digestion has taken place and therefore not many nutrients have been absorbed through the intestinal walls.

What can happen in addition to the fermentation, gas building, putrefaction, and lack of nutrient absorption is that undigested food macromolecules may enter the bloodstream. As a result, the immune system gets activated and begins to attack the undigested particles. This is how food reactions, food sensitivities, and even food allergies come about in addition to poor digestion.

So to support efficient digestion and speed up the weight loss process, it is a good idea to combine your food properly.

To lose weight, we need to make sure we have lots of energy all the time but especially after eating a meal.

Weight loss secret:
Eat protein and carbohydrates separately.

You can do this by deciding before you begin eating your meal if you would like to have more protein or more carbohydrates in that particular meal. If you want more protein, such as meat or fish, then eat the protein food with vegetables like broccoli, carrots, or salad (but not potatoes!). If you feel like eating carbohydrates during the meal, then eat your noodles, rice, or bread with vegetables like broccoli, carrots, or salad—and save your meat or fish for a different meal.

By eating simple natural foods and combining the food in an energy-giving way, we make it easy for the body to digest the food. The body can then put its leftover energy toward losing weight and detoxifying. Through the detoxification process, we also get a free ticket to a healthy body and more energy.

Food combining can be a real science, and if you want to dive into the topic further, I highly recommend the best-selling books *Alkalize and Energize for Life* by Shelley Redford Young with Robert Young, and *Fit for Life* by Marilyn and Harvey Diamond.

It is not necessary to become an expert on food combining to lose weight. Based on my personal experience, I would recommend observing only three simple guidelines.

Figure 3: Food Combining Chart

Weight loss secret:
Combine foods properly.

1. **Separate protein from carbohydrates.** If you are not veg-
    etarian, decide before your meal what you want to eat:
    protein (fish or meat) or carbohydrates (pasta or rice).
    Then eat either one or the other in one meal. Never eat
    animal protein with starch, sweet fruits, or oils. Eat your
    fish or meat with salad and vegetables (except starchy
    vegetables such as potatoes or corn) and leave out the
    pasta, potatoes, and rice. Eat your pasta or rice with
    salad or legumes.

2. **Drink liquids alone.** Always drink liquids alone and al-
    ways before but never during or within less than an hour
    after a meal. That includes water or any kind of juice.
    Liquids dilute the digestive enzymes in the stomach and
    prolong the digestion process when solid foods are in
    the stomach.

3. Eat fruits alone. Eat fruits alone. It takes the stomach be-
    tween 20 and 60 minutes to process fruits. If a fruit is
    eaten with or after a meal, it cannot be processed in time
    and starts putrefying and fermenting, thereby producing
    gas and bloating. Eat melons alone and one variety at a
    time. Do not combine acid fruits (orange, pineapple,
    etc.) with sweet fruits (bananas, dates, etc.). Eat fruit at
    least 20 minutes before a meal and never after a meal.

Cleaning Up the Mess: Food Quality and the Environment

Few people seem to know that most of the food produced in the industrialized world should not be consumed by humans.

> **Over two-thirds of the food sold in U.S. supermarkets is genetically engineered, irradiated, and treated with hormones, pesticides, and herbicides, and is therefore very dangerous for human consumption.[2]**

Here are just a few of the facts:

1. **Radiation, pesticides, herbicides, hormones, toxic chemicals.** In his book *The Food Revolution*, John Robbins[2] shows staggering scientific evidence of the prevalence of "persistent organic pollutants," or POPs, a group of highly toxic and long-lived chemicals we ingest into our bodies through our food.

Did you know?

a.   About 95 percent of human exposure to dioxin, one of the most carcinogenic chemicals in the world, comes from red meat, fish, and dairy products.

b.   Approximately 70 percent of American chickens and 90 percent of American turkeys are so contaminated with campylobacter bacteria, they can easily cause disease.

c.   To promote growth, more than 90 percent of U.S. beef cattle receive hormone implants that have been proven to cause cancer in humans.

d.   U.S. livestock consumes more than 24.6 million pounds of antibiotics per year.

---

2. **Milk** is a common source of the herbicide atrazine (a known endocrine/hormonal disrupter) and the genetically engineered growth hormone BGH. In addition, more than 80 percent of all cows are pregnant. Thus, we get those sexual hormones in high concentration, too.

3. **Eggs** are typically produced in factory farms where the hens live in crowded, cruel, and unhygienic conditions. This may be one of the reasons salmonella bacteria contaminates more than 2 million eggs per year, resulting in more than 650,000 Americans sickened and

600 killed every year from eating salmonella-tainted eggs.[2] Factory farm eggs also may be lower in nutrients than organic ones, and they don't taste as good as farm-fresh eggs from free-range chickens that are not fed antibiotics.

4. **Wheat** is high in vitamins, minerals, and fiber. However, in a recent review of pesticide residues, 91 percent of the wheat sampled by the FDA contained pesticide residues. Wheat can be one of the most heavily treated grains, because it is stockpiled as a basic commodity and fumigated periodically to keep down pest levels. When it is milled, its outer coating—the bran included in whole wheat bread and cereals—is the portion that receives the most chemical treatment. The bran and germ portions of the wheat also retain the most residues. It has been suggested that some forms of so-called wheat allergy, which has been associated with learning problems and difficulty concentrating, may actually be a neurotoxic reaction to the pesticide residues in the grain. These pesticides are, by definition, neurotoxins.

• •

Weight loss secret:
Eat only organic foods and avoid chemical pollutants in the water, earth, and air.

As shown in these six points, the list of environmental pollutants is very long, and the scientific evidence is mind-boggling. Within the context of overweight and obesity, we need to keep in mind that anything we put into our system that is contaminated prevents us from losing extra pounds and from living a life full of health and vitality. This is because the human body ends up using its energy to fight and eliminate unnatural invaders and poisonous substances instead of detoxifying and healing. This knowledge helps us make intelligent choices and supports our goals instead of sabotaging them.

• •

5. **Corn** contains most B vitamins, especially niacin, and adds helpful fiber to the diet. A primary staple in the American diet, corn is, however, typically heavily treated. Locally grown fresh corn tends to be treated less, so sweet corn on the cob is likely safer than corn by-products, which may contain more contaminants. However, corn is still heavily treated with the herbicide atrazine and is typically sprayed after harvesting.

6. **Parasites and fungi.** Because we eat too much, too often, and do not digest our food properly, we create a splendid breeding ground for parasites, bacteria, and fungi that live off our internal organs and intestines.

The result is disease, a body out of balance, and overweight due to cravings that may not even be our own but may come from those creatures living inside us such as *Candida albicans*. Statistics say that 70 percent of Americans are infected with *Candida*. Much of the bloating and swelling we sense in our system may come from this terrible fungus.

You Are Also What You Breathe and Drink

Air and Water

One of the most wonderful and welcoming gestures in American society is to be served ice water the moment one sits down in a restaurant. Next to oxygen, pure water is the most important factor for our survival. A normal adult should drink at least eight 12-ounce glasses, or 3 liters, of water per day.

Yet we don't usually consume that much water, and we don't seem to care about the quality of the water we do drink. We don't even seem to notice how bad the tap water usually tastes let alone how contaminated the water is with pathogenic microorganisms and toxic chemicals (www.epa.gov./ogwdw/dwh/health.html). More importantly, waterborne chemicals and toxic additives have been linked in clinical studies[75] to cancer, liver, kidney, and other health problems.

· ·

Weight loss secret:
Avoid toxic chemicals in the water and air.

The tap water in most regions of the Western world is polluted with toxic chemicals such as chlorine, fluoride, herbicides, pesticides, radioactive elements, toxic minerals such as arsenic, and other pathogenic microbial organisms that have been shown to poison the body[76] and should be avoided at any price. Also, stay away from contaminated air[77] and use air filters in your home and office.

· ·

In their amazing book, *Water: The Shocking Truth That Can Save Your Life*, Patricia and Paul Bragg, both Ph.D.s in health and aging, reveal among many other truths that fluoride is a deadly poison. They remind us that 11 health-related associations, including the American Heart Association, the American Cancer Society, and the American Psychiatric Association, stopped endorsing water fluoridation in 1996.

Yet in many regions in the United States the water is still being fluoridated. For this and all of the above reasons we need to be very selective about the water we drink and make sure it's purified, both at home and in restaurants, before consuming it.

Another important concern with respect to weight loss is the temperature of the water we drink.

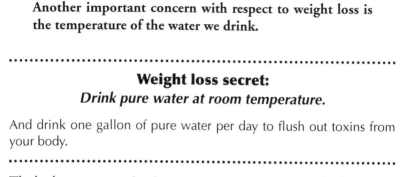

....

Weight loss secret:
Drink pure water at room temperature.

And drink one gallon of pure water per day to flush out toxins from your body.

....

The body wants to maintain a constant temperature. By drinking ice water, iced tea, and other cold drinks, we force the body to heat up the drink to body temperature. This is wasted energy. We need to become more conscious about the way we handle energy reserves. Otherwise, our bodies will not have enough fuel to eliminate waste and toxins that aid in our weight loss efforts.

Alcohol and Coffee

Both alcohol and coffee are poisons to the body in high quantities. Alcohol, for one, is a product of fermentation and ultimately decay. After nicotine, alcohol accounts for more than 100,000 deaths in the United States alone and is a major cause for heart disease causing severe liver damage, gastrointestinal disorders, cancer, hypertension, and brain damage.

If consumed in high quantities, both coffee and alcohol destroy our health by causing inflammation, require huge amounts of energy to be eliminated from the body, and increase our caloric intake (especially coffee, when drunk with milk and sugar), preventing us from losing weight.

Scientific studies performed with 50,000 men at Harvard University[79] show that one or two glasses of red wine per day contributed to a 26 percent reduction in the risk of heart disease as compared to those who didn't drink alcohol. Higher levels of alcohol, however, were shown to have harmful health effects.

Pure water and high-water-content foods are the only hydration needed by the body.

Soft Drinks

If you are concerned with your weight, you need to significantly reduce your intake of soft drinks.

One can of soft drink contains 10 teaspoons of sugar!

Research[80] shows that school-age children in our society consume on average more than one soft drink per day, or a minimum of 365 soft drinks per year. The statistics on adults are even more frightening. **Adults consume an average of 565 cans per year or an equivalent of 124 pounds (56 kg) of pure sugar per year just from soft drinks alone.**

Switching to sugar-free alternatives containing artificial sweeteners actually adds to the problem. We are then ingesting poisonous chemicals that create an overly acidic body that, in turn, can cause autoimmune diseases, high blood pressure, memory loss, cancer, obesity, and other conditions.

Milk

Milk—which is a food, not a drink—has been a very controversial topic for a long time in the industrialized world. Let's look at the scientific evidence. In his book The Food Revolution, best-selling author John Robbins relates that more than **10 percent of people of Caucasian** descent, **90 percent of adults of Asian** descent, and **50 percent of people of other ethnicities are actually lactose (milk sugar) intolerant and experience gastrointestinal reactions to milk.**

• •

Weight loss secret:
Significantly reduce your intake of alcohol, caffeine, soft drinks, milk, and other acid-producing liquids.

1.   In order to lose weight successfully, you must make sure to provide your body with plenty of energy so it can get rid of excess fat. In addition to adding calories and producing an acidic environment that deprives you of vitamins and minerals, alcohol and coffee have a diuretic effect. This causes the body to lose water, causing dehydration, whereas you think you are actually hydrating the body by drinking them.
2.   Drink one large glass of purified water at room temperature before a meal or one hour after a meal to hydrate your body.

• •

In addition, the claim that people who drink milk lower their risk of osteoporosis could not be sustained in clinical studies. Actually, **the opposite is the case.** A 12-year Nurses Health Study involving 78,000 women "found no evidence of…reduced osteoporosis or bone fracture incidence. In fact, the study found that the relative risk of hip fracture for women who drink two glasses of milk per day was 1.45 times higher than for those who drink one glass or less per week."[2]

Another factor to consider regarding milk consumption is that milk contains the "bad cholesterol" found in animal-based foods. Bad cholesterol has been associated with conditions such as prostate and ovarian cancer, diabetes, obesity, and heart disease.[82] Not only that, the mucus produced by milk impedes absorption of nutrients.

Why Is Proper Digestion Crucial for Permanent Weight Loss and Health?

Have you experienced bloating, irritable bowel syndrome, functional constipation, functional abdominal pain, or food reactions and allergies?

Then you belong to the 69 percent of Americans who suffer from such food-related ailments, according to a 1993 study published by the *Digestive Diseases and Sciences Journal*. Further studies show that 44 percent of Americans use antacids to help relieve such conditions. However, this is only addressing the symptom and not the cause of the indigestion.[83]

The fact that we are alive and survive the attacks of billions of bacteria and viruses every second of our lives is attributed to our incredibly efficient immune system. Unfortunately, eating healthy food is not enough to stay healthy and have good digestion. Even the healthiest food can turn into a poison if we can't digest it. If we eat a food that we can't digest, the undigested food can seep into the bloodstream. The immune system can't recognize it as a nutrient, declares it a toxin, and attacks it like an allergen. This condition is known as an allergen antibody complex, also called an immune complex response.

These immune complexes circulate through the body. Over time, they lodge themselves in different parts of the body and actually turn off components of the immune system. Meanwhile, they encourage immune mediators to attack the body's tissues, and we develop an autoimmune disease.[84] When the immune system is compromised, it is unable to fight bacteria and viruses. As a result, we often become ill, and digestive disturbances are often the beginning and a sign of that illness.

> **According to Elson Haas, M.D., an estimated 80 to 90 percent of overweight people have food sensitivities[13] that, when corrected, can lead to normal weight.[14]**

Food allergies, in a classical sense, are more acute than food sensitivities, but only 2 percent of the population seems to get them, according to Ellen Cutler, author of *MicroMiracles: Discover the Healing Power of Enzymes*. Food sensitivities, also called food reactions, are much more common, subtle, and easy to heal.

> **Food reactions are triggered by the inability of the body to completely digest food due to lack of enzymes.**

Enzyme deficiency can be caused by stress, age, and the foods we eat, which are often devoid of enzymes. In addition, many packaged or processed foods contain high amounts of allergy-causing substances such as wheat, milk, eggs, sugar, preservatives, MSG, and other toxic chemicals.

The consequences of food reactions for overall health can be tremendous and can result in:

- metabolic disorders such as fatigue
- hormone imbalances
- bloating and swelling
- water retention
- food cravings
- gas
- heartburn
- irritable bowel syndrome
- nasal congestion

....

Weight loss secret:
Eliminate food reactions and food sensitivities.

To be successful in any weight loss program, you first need to address the biological imbalances caused by food reactions. Do this by

- identifying foods that cause sensitivities
- eliminating foods that cause the sensitivities until is the reaction is gone
- cleansing and detoxifying to back up the body's metabolism

Supported by appropriate enzymes,[85] supplements, and a desensitizing process, the healthy reactive foods can gradually be reintroduced. Step 3 of this program will show how this process takes place.

....

The beauty about healing food reactions is that within days you can lose between 5 and 10 pounds of "false fat," as Dr. Haas calls it. This is basically accumulated water coming from chronic swelling, or edema, of the cells and tissues due to an allergic reaction to certain foods. If these foods are eliminated, so is unnecessary weight. The real (adipose) fat follows easily as soon as the body is back into both physical and emotional balance and new habits are in place.

Food sensitivities also create severe biochemical and hormonal imbalances in the body, including lower levels of serotonin, the so-called "happy hormone." When we heal our food reactions, the amino acid tryptophan (the nutritional building block that produces serotonin) increases, leading to overall well-being and healing. Hormonal interactions in the body are extremely complex and difficult to address through drugs. Permitting the intelligence of nature to heal itself through proper nutrition and absorption provides much higher chances of lasting success. Our goal should be to allow our own body to be the ultimate source for healing and well-being.

All inner organs, including the brain, heart, liver, lungs, kidneys, and hormonal glands—in other words, all 75 trillion cells in our body—are totally dependent upon a well-functioning digestive system.

....

Weight loss secret:
Proper digestion is key to permanent weight loss.

Eating organic fruits, vegetables, and legumes is the first step toward healthy digestion. However, only by taking digestive enzymes with your food can you help break it down. Enzymes help fight immune complexes, reduce inflammation, and support autoimmune mediators bolster the immune system so it works optimally and protects us from disease.

....

Furthermore, the intestinal tract is the hub of the entire body. It is the place where the nutrients in the food we eat are extracted into the bloodstream and transported to every cell in the body. Therefore, cellular health, which is the foundation of our health, is entirely dependent upon our nutrition, digestive tract, and bloodstream. Thus, it is essential to maintain a steady, oxygenated flow.

....

Weight loss secret:
Clean bowels are your ticket to ideal weight as well as health and vitality.

If your bowel is clogged with waste, the blood becomes badly contaminated. As a result, you end up bathing in your own junk. According to Dr. Jensen,[86] 90 percent of people in our society have polluted their bowels with unimaginable filth and have weakened their digestive function. In such an environment, even good food can become toxic. As long as this waste remains within, the body grows weaker and we become more prone to deficiencies and more susceptible to disease. Make sure to eat a diet rich in fiber and to detoxify and cleanse your bowels regularly.

....

Food Cravings

Scientists tell us that food cravings are addictions just like smoking, alcohol, and drugs. Cravings are often much harder to resist than real hunger and are the main reason why most diets don't work. The good news is, however, that we now know that food cravings are mostly caused by food sensitivities that can be healed. As we begin eliminating the reactive foods from our system through cleansing and detoxifying, the body resists and experiences discomfort similar to that of a smoker in withdrawal. America's Detox Doc™, Elson Haas, M.D., tells us that within less than 48 hours of the reactive food leaving the body, we begin to heal, the food cravings subside, and a natural weight loss process begins.

••

Weight loss secret:
Eliminate food cravings.

The best way to eliminate food cravings is through:

- **Alkalizing the body** by consuming one gallon (four liters) of green drink per day.

- **Regularly cleansing and detoxifying** for a minimum of seven days.

- **Taking enzymes.** Through enzymes we begin digesting the healthy food we eat, and the body becomes well nourished and stops craving.

- **Taking supplements.** By replenishing the body's stores of vitamins and minerals, supplements stop cravings.

As the body becomes more alkaline and detoxified, it assumes a state of health and balance and the cravings subside.

••

Food Shopping

Procuring healthy, whole, and organically grown foods can be quite difficult given the polluted state of much of our environment. However, we must make it a priority to consume organic produce if we want to achieve not only permanent weight loss but overall health and vitality.

....

Weight loss secret:
*Uncompromised nutrition – consume only organic
food and drink:*

1. Take advantage of Internet sources.
2. Grow a garden.
3. Join the local farmers' community.
4. Request organic foods at the local market.
5. Take advantage of farmers' markets.
6. Make it a habit to read labels before buying anything.
7. Do not buy foods that contain indecipherable chemicals and are prepackaged.
8. Watch for sugar, salts, and fats.
9. Consume only whole-grain and other whole products in addition to replacing refined everything (carbohydrates, sugars, rice, etc.) with their whole-grain versions.

....

Uncompromised Supplementation

"You must want to fly so much that you are willing to give up being a caterpillar."
—Trina Paulus

In the article "Are vitamin and mineral deficiencies a major cancer risk?" published in the September 2002 issue of *Nature Reviews Cancer*, Ames and Wakimoto conclude that deficiencies in minerals such as iron and zinc, as well as folic acid and vitamins C, B6, and B12, can make us susceptible to cancer.

As stated earlier within the context of the acid-alkaline balance, inflammation is known to be the cause of various diseases including Alzheimer's disease,[87] cardiovascular disease,[88] diabetes, and cancer, as well as overweight and obesity.[89] Additional studies reported on the December 2003 issue of the *American Journal of Medicine*[90] indicate that inflammation can be reduced by 32 percent if patients take a multiple vitamin on a daily basis.

Although human beings have evolved for millions of years on earth without consuming supplements, in our society we need to shore up our food intake with vitamins and minerals for two reasons: the food we eat is often depleted of essential vitamins, and our bodies have become increasingly unable to absorb nutrients due to lack of enzymes.

Vitamins and Minerals

Vitamins and minerals are organic substances required in minuscule amounts to sustain health, yet according to the June 2002 issue of *Journal of the American Medical Association*, "most people do not consume an optimal amount of all vitamins by diet alone." Vitamins and minerals are crucial for our health, and supplementation has become a significant factor in regaining health and vitality and in losing weight.

....

Weight loss secret:
Take your mineral and vitamin supplements daily.

It is essential that you supplement your organic diet with vitamin and mineral supplements to replenish your cells and increase your health and vitality. Vitamins and minerals buffer the acids caused by acidic foods, soft drinks, and alcohol, prevent the depletion of vitamin and mineral deposits in the body, and allow the body to get back into balance and let go of fat.

....

The human body cannot manufacture vitamins or minerals on its own. Therefore, they must be provided from outside sources, preferably food. Vitamins are classified by the fluid in which they can be dissolved:

- **water-soluble vitamins** (all the B vitamins and vitamin C)
- **fat-soluble vitamins** (vitamins A, D, and K), which must be taken with meals in order to be absorbed

Vitamin A is a fat-soluble vitamin that protects hair and vision as well as the respiratory and digestive systems. It heals severe acne and other skin problems; supports immune function; increases resistance to infections, heart disease, and cancer; and plays a major role in the health of bones and teeth. Vitamin A is found in carrots, squash, peppers, apricots, papayas, and dairy products.

Beta-carotene is an antioxidant that helps promote a healthy immune system. It is the precursor of vitamin A. When taken in higher doses it is converted into vitamin A in the body without causing toxicity. Beta-carotene is found in orange and green vegetables such as pumpkins, carrots, sweet potatoes, broccoli, romaine lettuce, and spinach.

B-complex is a prime defender of our nervous system, keeping us healthy and giving us a beautiful complexion. It also increases metabolism of essential proteins, carbohydrates, fatty acids, and amino acids, and helps in the maturation of red blood cells and other vital processes in the body. B-complex supplements are water-soluble, so the body's supply needs to be replenished regularly. Several vitamins make up a B-complex supplement:

- **Thiamine (B1)** defends against fatigue, heart conditions, and neurological disorders. B1 directly helps in the metabolic function of carbohydrates, fats, and proteins. Thiamine is in whole grains such as wheat germ as well as in dried beans, soybeans, nuts, and lean meats.
- **Riboflavin (B2)** assists in protecting the nervous system. It also promotes skin and eye health. Another huge benefit of B_2 is that it provides for perpetual energy production through the generation of adenosine triphosphate (ATP). It also metabolizes the essential fatty acids and amino acids that are the prime catalysts of regenerative elements. Foods high in B_2 are dairy, leafy green vegetables, fish, and liver.
- **Niacin (B3)** helps keep the digestive tract healthy through its metabolic capabilities to process carbohydrates, proteins, and fats. It is found in dairy, lean meats, and whole grains.
- **Pantothenic acid (B5)** is a B-complex that mitigates digestive disturbances in addition to fatigue and nerve problems. It also enables neurotransmitters to function properly. The most widely known sources of B_5 are dairy products, whole grains, nuts, dates, legumes, fish, and lean meats.
- **Pyridoxine (B6)** provides vital support to the neurotransmitters and assists in the metabolism of amino acids. It also helps to ease digestive problems and fatigue. B_6 is found in beans, cheese, nuts, dates, whole grains, fish, and lean meats.
- **Cobalamin (B12)** is a natural calming agent for the nervous system. Hydrochloric acid releases B_{12} in the stomach through the digestion of protein, specifically meat. B_{12} also defends against anemia and fatigue. B_{12} nutrients are prevalent in animal products such as meat, fish, poultry, and dairy.

Folic acid plays a fundamental role in the prevention of cardiovascular disease, colon cancer, and breast cancer. Foods enriched with folic acid include dark leafy greens, whole grains, and legumes such as peas and lima beans.

Biotin is a coenzyme that contributes to the metabolism of protein, fat, and carbohydrates. It bolsters the immune system to reduce the occurrence of anemia and fatigue and helps to alleviate symptoms caused by heart conditions. Excellent sources of these digestive enablers are soy, barley, brewer's yeast, Royal jelly, nuts, and raw egg whites. Biotin is synthesized by bacteria, yeast, algae, and certain plant species. In fact, the healthy flora of the large intestine appear to contribute in large part to the biotin requirements of the human body.

PABA is a catalyst for folic acid. It helps to slow the aging process in that it can reduce the speed at which hair grays prematurely. Good sources of PABA are grains and animal products.

Vitamin C is the gatekeeper to a healthy immune system. It is the main antioxidant that helps prevent illness. Like B vitamins, vitamin C is water-soluble. It is principally found in fresh fruits and vegetables. Citrus products such as oranges are a well-known source of this essential nutrient.

Vitamin D is fat-soluble and aids in the production of strong bones. The main source of Vitamin D is exposure to sunlight, which helps produce vitamin D in the skin. A small source of vitamin D comes from dairy products.

Vitamin E is fat-soluble and essential for promoting healthy skin and nails and preventing heart disease, sunburn, and possibly even cancer. Most importantly, it regulates blood cells, enabling healing throughout the nervous system as well as the reproductive system. Vegetable and seed oils, whole grains, dark leafy greens, and foods high in fat such as butter, egg yolks, and nuts are valuable sources of vitamin E.

Vitamin K is fat-soluble and enables the blood to flow synchronously without serious obstructions to any of the vital organs. It reduces clotting and prolonged bleeding. Eat broccoli and dark leafy greens like kale, chard, and romaine lettuce to help you meet the necessary daily requirements.

Bioflavonoids are water-soluble antioxidants that act as blood thinners and have anti-inflammation qualities. Quercetin is a common bioflavonoid derivative, and a key ally in protecting the body from the damage done by LDL (bad cholesterol). These healing agents are found in many types of alkalizing foods such as citrus fruits and vegetables, as well as in acidic foods like tea and onions.

Calcium is essential for strong teeth and bones. It promotes normal blood clotting and supports the contractions of muscles including the heart. To be effective in the body, calcium should be taken with ample amounts of vitamin D and magnesium. Calcium works with magnesium to prevent osteoporosis. Vegetables such as broccoli, dark leafy greens, and fish oils are excellent sources of calcium. **The calcium-phosphorus balance needs to be 2:1**, or twice as much calcium as phosphorus. If this ratio is upset, neither one of the minerals gets absorbed properly, leading to health problems such as osteoporosis, kidney stones, and cardiovascular disease, which is caused by mineral deposits in many organs including veins and arteries.

Copper is a lesser known mineral but nonetheless has important enzymatic qualities that help to maintain an overall healthy immune system. It plays a pivotal role in the growth of healthy connective tissue and skin. Foods rich in copper are avocados, legumes, and oysters and other shellfish.

Iodine is extremely significant in treating an overactive thyroid gland. It is effective in the metabolism of energy and is said to enhance weight loss as well as boost deficient energy levels. This healing agent can be found in seaweed, algae, and kelp.

Iron is the means by which blood cells carry oxygen to other cells for growth, resulting in sustained energy. It helps to defend against osteoporosis and other bone diseases. Foods rich in iron are lean red meats, legumes, and spinach. However, in their book *Toxic Metal Syndrome*, Casdorph and Walker suggest that too much iron, especially that ingested by additional supplementation, may be linked with heart disease, diabetes, cancer, increased risk of infection, and arthritis. The reason for this could be that the body cannot rid itself easily of excess iron.

Magnesium is a universal curative agent in that it works to improve bone mass, energy levels, and fatty acid formation. It has been known to help with calcium deficiencies, hypertension in children, and problems associated with chronic fatigue syndrome. The largest dietary sources of this nutrient are nuts, dark leafy greens, whole grains, fish, and meat. **Magnesium is, like calcium, a very important mineral that acts as a carrier for delivering calcium to the bones. To function properly, the body must have the right proportion of magnesium to calcium, 2:1**, or twice as much magnesium as calcium.

Molybdenum is an antioxidant that has been linked to cancer prevention. Although enough is not currently known about the direct benefits of this mineral, it is considered to have healing powers necessary for overall good health. This vital element is found in grains, beans, dark green vegetables, organ meats, and dairy.

Sulfur (MSM) is an anti-inflammatory used predominantly to treat joint and muscle pain. A variety of natural products contain MSM, including sunflower seeds, garlic, lentils, soybeans, and yogurt.

Silicon assists in maintaining strong connective tissue and healthy bones. To benefit from its nutrients, one must eat a balanced diet rich in whole grains, fruits, and vegetables.

Trace Minerals

Trace minerals are critical to good health but are present in foods in extremely small quantities. Large amounts can be toxic. Here are the most important trace minerals for weight loss:

- **Chromium** is a fast-fat-burning trace mineral that acts as an insulin regulator and helps prevent inflammation.
- **Selenium** is an antioxidant used as a preventative measure against cancer and heart disease. It helps boost the immune system and is needed to produce glutathione peroxidase, one of the most important antioxidants. Selenium helps neutralize toxins such as cadmium, arsenic,

and mercury. A minimal amount of this nutrient is required to provide its highest potency. Common food sources are Brazil nuts, dairy products, breads, any plant food, and fish.

- **Zinc** is vital to the efficient function of the immune system, bone development, and metabolism. It enables the body to regenerate quickly after injury. It is important to take in adequate zinc during pregnancy in order to minimize deficiencies that may occur during the embryo's development. Seafood, especially oysters, provides a great source of zinc, as do nuts, whole grains, legumes, and some dairy products.

Other Important Supplements

Alpha lipoic acid is a super antioxidant that is about 400 times stronger than vitamins C and E and raises the levels of these two vitamins in the body. Alpha lipoic acid prevents inflammatory reactions and the sugar damage (glycation) in protein-building molecules, helps regulate blood sugars, and slows the onset of several illnesses such as heart disease, arthritis, and Alzheimer's disease.

L-amino acids are the building blocks of protein. They serve the body through protecting the immune system, allowing for defense against viruses and bacteria. These proteins are obtainable through eating dark green vegetables and lean meats.

L-cysteine is an amino acid that in recent studies has been shown to have anti-inflammatory properties for illnesses related to osteoarthritis and rheumatoid arthritis. It helps the body detoxify chemicals and heavy metals. Yogurt, broccoli, and poultry contain a rich concentration of this nutrient.

Gamma-linolenic acid (GLA) is an essential fatty acid derived from the omega-6 group—one of the main vital oils needed for the body. This essential fatty acid is mainly required for reproductive sustainability and for normal development of the neurological system. These nutrients cannot be produced in the body. They must be ingested from an external supply. Oils are the main provider of GLA, boric oil being the most widely used.

Lactobacillus (probiotics) is a key mechanism for proper digestion. This friendly bacterium increases the acidity in the intestines to destroy harmful microorganisms. In turn, it boosts the immune system to help fight viruses and diseases. Common sources are whole grains and dairy products.

Coenzyme Q10 (CoQ10) is an extremely important antioxidant that is most easily depleted through sun exposure. CoQ10 is essential for a healthy heart and skin, protects cells from free-radical damage, assists enzymes in functioning properly, and guards against cancer and other immunodeficiency diseases. Spinach, broccoli, peanuts, and whole grains provide its healing strength.

Digestive enzymes help to break down proteins, carbohydrates, fats, and dietary fiber so that they are correctly filtered throughout the body. Enzymes enable nutrients to be carried into the bloodstream, providing us with our life force. Although we generate enzymes internally, they are vastly depleted when we don't eat the right foods. Dark leafy green vegetables and green drinks provide a plentiful source of enzymes. **Like vitamins and minerals, enzymes should be taken on a continual basis.**

Bromelain is a digestive enzyme used primarily as an anti-inflammatory aid. It also has antihistamine proponents in that it has been associated with minimizing sinus infections. Pineapple is a chief source of this nutrient.

Lithium orotate[91] sounds more like a wonder drug than a regular supplement. It has been shown in clinical studies[92] to help with low white blood cell counts, migraines, constant headaches, alcoholism, and liver disorders. Also, it has been successfully applied in the treatment of depression,[93] unipolar and bipolar disorders,[94] nearsightedness, and glaucoma.[95] However, lithium should not be used by pregnant women and breast-feeding mothers or by individuals with kidney problems, cardiovascular diseases, sodium depletion, severe debilitation, or dehydration, or by individuals who are taking diuretics or ACE inhibitors. Consult your physician if you are taking anti-inflammatory, anti-hypertensive, or analgesic drugs, or insulin.

Omega 3/Omega 6 essential fatty acids (EFAs) (2:1 ratio) are essential fats for proper cell building and functioning. In addition, EFAs are crucial for losing weight. They neutralize acids in the body and operate as anti-inflammation agents. The best way to take EFAs is as a ready-to-consume mix of essential oils that can be found in the refrigerated section of most health food stores.

• •

WEIGHT LOSS SECRETS:

1. TAKE RESPONSIBILITY for your own health.
2. GET TESTED REGULARLY by your doctor so you always know your levels of vitamins, minerals, cholesterol, etc.
3. STAY INFORMED ABOUT SCIENTIFIC RESEARCH by joining a group of people you trust to be well informed and making sure you apply present knowledge to the best of ability to your own life. Note that there are contradictory messages and notice how your own body responds. It can tell you if something is for you by the way you feel.
4. TAKE DAILY SUPPLEMENTS to boost the positive effects of healthy nutrition, mental health, and physical exercise.

• •

Supplements & Supernutrients Summary of Recommendations	Daily Recommended Amounts (consult your physician for specific dosages)
Vitamin A	5,000 IU
Beta-Carotene	10,000–20,000 IU
Vitamin D	400 IU
Vitamin E	400–800 IU
Vitamin K	90–120 mcg
Thiamin (B_1)	50 mg
Riboflavin (B_2)	50 mg
Niacin (B_2)	100 mg
Niacinamide (B_3)	50–100 mg
Pantothenic acid (B_5)	250–500 mg
Pyridoxine (B_6)	50–100 mg
Cobalamin (B_{12})	10–20 mcg
Folic acid	400–800 mg
Biotin	500–1,000 mcg
PABA	75–150 mg
Vitamin C	500–2,000 mg
Bioflavonoids	250–750 mg
Quercetin	300–600 mg
Calcium	600–1,500 mg
Chromium	120–200 mcg
Copper	2–3 mg
Iodine	150 mg
Iron	15 or 0 mg (ask your physician)

Supplements & Supernutrients Summary of Recommendations	Daily Recommended Amounts (consult your physician for specific dosages)
Magnesium	300–600 mg
Molybdenum	250–500 mct
Manganese	2–5 mg
Selenium	200–300 mcg
Sulphur (MSM)	500–1,500 mg
Silicon	50–100 mg
Zinc	30–60 mg
Chromium	200 mcg
Selenium	200 mcg or less per day
Alpha lipoic acid	50–100 mg 2/day
L-amino acids	750–1,500 mg
L-cysteine	250–500 mg
Gamma-linolenic acid (GLA)	240–480 mg
Garlic Extract (heart & blood pressure)	1,600 mg
Arginine (heart & blood pressure)	6,000–9,000 mg
Lactobacillus (probiotics)	1–2 billion friendly microrganisms
Coenzyme Q10	30–100 mg 2/day
Grapeseed extract	50–100 mg 2/day
Digestive enzymes (with each meal)	3–6 tablets
Bromelain (between meals)	100 mg
Omega-30mega-6 EFAs	2:1 ratio 2000/1000 mg
Vinpocetine (memory)	10–20 mg
Lutein (eye health)	6 mg

Dr. John Gray's Mars Venus Wellness Solution

Early in 2006, John Gray, the world-famous author of *Men Are from Mars, Women Are from Venus,* brought to market his own wellness formula called John Gray's Mars Venus Wellness Solution.

I have achieved outstanding success with this product both personally and with my clients and I highly recommend it.

Dr. Gray's solution is a well-rounded cleansing and supplementation system that includes an extraordinary composition of the highest-quality minerals, vitamins, antioxidants, and nutritional supplements available on the market. This product tastes great and is simple to use, making it very appealing for a busy lifestyle. Users report not only steady weight loss and easy weight maintenance, but more importantly a feeling of well-being, nutritional life balance, and increased joy and happiness.

Dr. Gray's Mars Venus Wellness Solution can be ordered on-line through a company called Isagenix at http://mbozesan. isagenix.com/nutrition_marsprog.dhtml. The product set comes with an audio CD featuring Dr. Gray, who introduces the philosophy behind his products that "help create the brain chemistry for health, happiness, and lasting romance." For more information, please refer also to Dr. Gray's book *The Mars and Venus Diet and Exercise Solution.*

Foods That Heal and Foods That Kill

What to Eat Less Of

After reading all this information, you may ask, *What am I supposed to eat?*

The answer is this: everything in moderation—knowing how the food you eat affects your weight, health, and vitality.

Remember that the human body is composed of approximately 70 percent water, 1–2 percent vitamins and minerals, 0.5–1 percent sugar, 20 percent fat, and 7 percent protein.[3] To function properly the body needs to be fed what it is actually made up of: 70 percent water-rich alkalizing fruits and vegetables, 1–2 percent vitamins and minerals, 0.5–1 percent sugar, 20 percent healthy fat, and 7 percent healthy proteins.

Are these the kinds of foods most of us have on our plate every time we eat?

Obviously not, otherwise we would not be up against the fact that more than 64 percent of us are overweight or obese.[96]

Dr. Haas asserts that the average American gets 75 percent of his or her calories from only 10 types of food and drink.

It is customary for Americans to drink alcohol or soft drinks[97] and eat huge quantities of acid-producing packaged and unhealthy fried and cooked foods. Fast food, caffeine, animal foods[98] such as beef,[99] chicken,100 and fish with a few token vegetables on the side, and lots of desserts,[101] compose much of the American diet. This is one reason why the U.S. has dropped from the healthiest nation in the world a century ago to number 100 today. America, one of the healthiest nations 100 years ago, has become one of the unhealthiest, with heart and coronary disease the number-one killer, cancer number two, and obesity and epidemic afflicting 64 percent of the population.

Overweight as a result of our misguided eating habits, our bodies are actually starving for nutrients (vitamins, minerals, essential fats) and keep asking for them through the sensation of hunger. Thus, we feed them more of the same old stuff that they cannot digest—overly processed and cooked foods with no enzymes, too much salt, too many refined sugars, the wrong fats, too many processed carbohydrates, too much protein, and all kinds of toxins (herbicides, pesticides, antibiotics, hormones, preservatives, irradiation).

What does eating the wrong foods have to do with our ability to lose weight?

The short answer is ***energy and inflammation***. By eating the wrong foods and foods that are not meant for human consumption, we force the body to spend all of its energy on the digestion and elimination of these foods. This is why we feel tired and sluggish after such a meal. The body doesn't have any energy left to eliminate toxins. Therefore, the toxins remain there as extra weight until we have the energy to deal with them later. If we continue to eat too much of the wrong foods, that *later* never comes, and we end up getting heavier and heavier. The cornerstone of weight loss is detoxification that is entirely dependent upon energy.

....

Weight loss secret:
Eat less acidic foods.

In order to lose weight, you need to alkalize your body by eating less acid-forming foods such as:

1. Meat
2. Dairy
3. Alcohol
4. Caffeine
5. Processed fats
6. Sugar-based food
7. Sugar-based drinks such as soft drinks

Note: **"Desserts" spelled backwards is "stressed"**—a body out of balance.

....

What to Eat More Of

The correct diet needs to be a lifestyle diet that is fun and healthy at the same time. It should be a personalized diet that takes into account the overall health situation, the genetic imprint, and the particular needs and likes of each individual.

To lose weight and avoid inflammation you must significantly alkalize your body.

Although I have been a vegetarian since 1992, my intention is not to tell you what to eat or not to eat, but to give you information with which you can make intelligent choices. I want to empower you with knowledge and encourage you to come up with a diet that makes you happy, fits your body type and needs, and complements your lifestyle. I highly recommend beginning today, wherever you are.

Before eating your next meal, remember that you need to match your body structure (70 percent water, 1–2 percent vitamins and minerals, 0.5–1 percent sugar, 20 percent fat, and 7 percent protein) with what is on your plate. In other words, if you are healthy and want to lose weight fast and keep it off forever, follow these basic nutritional recommendations for every meal:

Summary of nutritional weight loss secrets

1. ALKALIZE YOUR BODY BY:
   - **Increasing your consumption of green vegetables** (such as green salads, cucumbers, zucchini, etc.) to as much as 70 percent of each meal, thereby reflecting the makeup of your own body.
   - **Consuming more essential fats found in avocados, olive oils, flaxseed oils,** and other oil blends such as Udo's Choice Perfected Oil Blend.
   - **Eating foods of a variety of colors and tastes to get all possible nutrients, vitamins, and minerals from the food directly.**
   - **Reducing refined carbohydrate intake** such as white rice, cereals such as Cheerios and corn flakes, and white flour–based products such as pasta and white bread. Instead, consume whole and unprocessed carbohydrates such as whole wheat and whole-grain breads and pasta, as well as brown and wild rice.
   - **Increasing your intake of fiber and low-sugar foods** such as asparagus, kiwi, bean sprouts, beet greens, and broccoli.
   - **Consuming one gallon of green drink throughout the day** to encourage the body to release fat.
   - **Combining food properly.** If you are not vegetarian, decide up-front whether you want to have a protein (meat or fish) or carbohydrate (noodles, rice, potatoes) meal, and never mix the two in the same meal. This dish should represent less than 30 percent of your meal.
2. TAKE YOUR SUPPLEMENTS
   - **Supplement your daily nutrition with vitamins, minerals, and enzymes for proper digestion and absorption.**
   - **Take enzymes** with each meal to ensure proper digestion and assimilation of nutrients.
3. ENERGIZE YOUR BODY BY:
   - **Applying the 70/30 rule**, which says that every time you eat you should consume **70 percent alkalizing foods such as fresh and raw leafy green vegetables and salads and only 30 percent acid-forming foods such as meat, dairy, and bread.**
   - **Ensuring that the food you consume is of the best possible quality—organic and free of toxins.**

- **Drinking pure water or green drink at room temperature before your meal** and not during or after your meal.
- Reducing alcohol, smoking, and most of all negative thoughts and emotions.
- **Making your transition to healthier nutrition and lifestyle a smooth evolution** instead of a sudden revolution. I personally do not believe in diets and eating plans because I think that you can be much more successful in the long run by introducing the recommendations in this book, one at a time. For some delicious menu ideas, refer to Appendix 1 for a healthy two-week eating plan that respects the recommendations made in this book.
- **Refraining from beating yourself up when you relapse.** Remember that **every moment is a new beginning.**
- **Having fun and focusing on end results.** Make eating fun and reward your successes in weight loss.
- **Celebrating your life and making it a masterpiece!**

....

DAILY AFFIRMATION AND I-CAN-TATION:

All I need is within me now!

Every day in every way I am increasing my mental and physical capacity. I look and feel my ideal weight. I am healthy and vibrant. I am slowing down my biological age daily

- by changing my perception of my body, its aging, and time
- through my daily meditations, prayer, contemplation, yoga practice, and restful sleep
- by protecting myself night and day through light, love, and positive energy. At all times I have a protective shield around my body and my soul, which can only be penetrated by the good and the divine in all things.
- by maintaining a youthful mind and vibrant body
- by eliminating toxins from my body and life on a regular basis
- by automatically and unconsciously blessing my food every time I eat

In this chapter we have addressed all of the important aspects of healthy nutrition that lead to permanent weight loss and well-being. The following chapter will invite you get to know the joy of being in your body. It will help you connect with your body and appreciate your vessel through life and the temple of your soul.

Step 2: Connecting with the Joy of Life – Breaking a Sweat Is Enough

"No citizen has a right to be an amateur in the matter of physical training…. What a disgrace it is for a man to grow old without ever seeing the beauty and strength of which his body is capable."
—Socrates

Did you know?

In his book *Diabetes Danger*, Stanford professor emeritus Walter Bortz argues that **"for every two hours spent watching TV each day, your obesity risk goes up 23 percent and your risk of Type 2 diabetes increases by 14 percent."**

Dr. Bortz states that according to scientific research there are two major reasons for the obesity epidemic: inactivity and overeating. He writes, **"Every survey indicates that we are moving less and less…. A Cooper Aerobic Center study showed that unfit men were four times as likely to become diabetic as fit men over 14 years. A study of 34,257 women in Minnesota revealed that 'any' amount of physical activity lowered the incidence of new diabetes by 30 percent."**[102]

Why you should care about diabetes?

Because **there is a direct correlation between overweight, obesity, lack of exercise, and diabetes** that currently threatens 200 million Americans.

In addition, due to diabetes, overweight, and obesity, **U.S. life expectancy** is dropping significantly, and for the first time in the history of humankind, many children may not outlive their parents.

As a result, **the healthcare cost related to diabetes will soon reach $200 billion per year, an amount that threatens to drive the healthcare system bankrupt.**

If this is not enough to get you to exercise regularly and do anything you can to avoid this terrible disease in your own life, read how Prof. Bortz describes diabetes in *Diabetes Danger*, a book I highly recommend:

"Go to the dictionary and look up the words *horrible, ugly, painful, expensive, selfish, cruel, ferocious, relentless,* and *fearful.* Each of these words describes diabetes…in the most vitriolic terms; the disease deserves it. It is truly horrible. Every single case is a disaster, but the tragedy is that the number of individual cases is going through the roof.… It is the fifth leading cause of death in the United States [and] very soon it may be the number-one killer."[103]

At age 76, Dr. Bortz, who is one of the world's renowned authorities on aging, is still running marathons and enjoys extraordinary health. During an interview, I asked him about his secrets for health, longevity, and vitality. When I asked him, "What is the best diet?" he looked at me with his youthful smile and instead of answering my question, he asked, "For what kind of exercise?" He doesn't believe in diets. The bottom line is, we should eat everything in moderation, he said. He added that as we grow older, our most important organs are not our hearts, lungs, or brains but our legs.

"We were made to move," Walter Bortz II, M.D.

....

Weight loss secret:
Move purposefully for 30 to 45 minutes every day until you break a sweat.

Do that and I promise you that if you eat in moderation and are healthy physically, emotionally, and mentally, you will not only lose weight for good and get beautifully toned, you will *feel great* and you will begin to *fall in love with yourself,* with *who you really are at your core,* and with the *joy of being alive*!!!!

....

You Were Made to Move

I was born in Romania in the late 1950s. The tendency under communist rule was to encourage equality between genders, but girls were still ridiculed when they participated in sports. However, like any child, I was drawn to moving my body, and my parents were very supportive. To this day I remember the winters in

Moldova, the part of Romania where I grew up, very well. They were cold and windy but quite beautiful. We had lots of snow that piled up as high as the house we lived in. I loved to go sledding from the time I got out of school until it turned dark. I remember one day I came home and my mother couldn't take my sweater off. It must have still been wet when I'd put it on and it froze on me. My father asked me to join my fingers together, but I was so frozen that it was impossible. After a few minutes indoors, my fingers began to defrost. I cried out in such pain that my parents had to bring in some snow to cool me off.

We were poor and I received my first doll at age 7, but through some miracle my father got access to and gave me my first pair of ice skates at age 6. And so, despite my early mixed encounters with winter sports, I became quite successful at both artistic and speed skating. I loved it, but in the society I lived in I was considered boyish—not a normal girl. As I grew older, I began to feel less and less comfortable with being an athlete.

After our immigration to Germany in 1974, I maintained a certain level of activity, such as some swimming in the summer and skiing for one week in the winter, but I gave up my great passion for daily sports. Later on, the demanding schedule of my professional career gave me many good reasons not to work out regularly, and by the time I gave birth to our son at age 38, I had a serious weight problem. I was more than 38 pounds overweight.

The hypnosis of my own social conditioning and the environment I lived in provided me with all kinds of excuses not to look at reality. I kept telling myself and others that I was getting older and that it was normal to gain a little weight over the years. What I did not acknowledge was that with the exception of a short time during pregnancy, I had gained all that weight gradually. As I began having a hard time finding the right clothes to wear, I started criticizing the current fashion and photo models. They were too thin and did not look like real women—real women were supposed to have some flesh on their bones, I thought. In reality, this was simply the story I had unconsciously chosen to hide behind.

In addition to being overweight, I was sick often and suffered from a serious case of bronchitis at least twice a year. Each bout knocked me down for about two weeks. Although I considered myself a physically active woman, I was only working out on the weekends, by biking, swimming, or hiking—hardly a commitment to regular and serious physical exercise. However, this would all change after "Life Mastery," a Tony Robbins seminar I attended in Hawaii during the memorable week of September 11, 2001.

The stress prior to flying and the seemingly endless flight at the beginning of September ran my body down, and by the time we arrived at our destination I had chronic bronchitis. The illness threatened to keep me from participating in the very seminar I'd flown in to attend. The weather was magnificent and the blue-green ocean water was out of a dream, but I felt miserable and all I wanted to do was to sleep.

Two days before the seminar began, my husband, a longtime runner, asked me if I wanted to join him outside for a jog. I knew from a previous seminar with Tony Robbins that bouncing up and down strengthens the body's immune system, which speeds up the healing process. So I got out of bed and joined my husband for a run along the beach. I felt miserable. It was as if someone was hitting me over the head with a hammer every step of the way. But I persisted, and my determination paid off. Only few hours later, I felt better and was able to attend the seminar. I continued to run each morning, and my bronchitis went away and never returned. Since then, I have been running every day with very few exceptions, I've lost all the extra pounds, and, at age 44, I have become a marathon runner.

Although I am not recommending everyone become a marathon runner, medical evidence shows that regular exercise not only helps us lose weight but is absolutely essential in keeping us healthy and vital. Thus, while Step 1 of this program looked at nutrition, Step 2 focuses on the role of regular exercise for successful weight management, reducing signs of aging, and most of all, generating "happy hormones" in the body.

What You Are Up Against

Sedentary Lifestyle

Weight loss experts consider a sedentary lifestyle and lack of regular exercise major factors in weight gain.[104]

Simply put, if we don't move, we cannot burn the calories we eat. Instead, they stay with us and get stored as fat.

In our society, we rarely go shopping without a car or go to work by bike or on foot. We sit in an office for hours at a time and go home only to sit down again in front of the TV. Television has a serious hold on many of us. To lose weight, we might have to rid ourselves of not only a food addiction but also a television addiction. According to scientists Robert Kubey and Mihaly Csikszentmihalyi, "People who watch a lot of television can exhibit symptoms similar to substance dependence, including making repeated unsuccessful efforts to reduce use and even experiencing withdrawal when use stops."[105]

If we want to lose weight and keep it off permanently, we need to adopt a lifestyle that is in line with our innate nature. This includes honoring the fact that the body was made to move.

The U.S. Surgeon General recommends that American adults exercise for 30 minutes a day and children for 60 minutes a day. More exercise should be added to "prevent weight gain, to lose weight, or to maintain weight loss…especially combined with healthy eating."[96]

Lack of Time

I don't know about you, but I never seem to have enough time during the day to do all the things I want to do. We all have to work to make a living, and some of us even have two or three jobs to get by in a society that overvalues material things. In addition, we have to take care of children, families, and partners. With all of that on our plates, it seems we can never find the time to take care of our bodies—our vessels through life. And yet, that comes back and bites us the hardest, for our bodies are the foundation for everything we want to do in life.

> **Where can you get the time to exercise? How can you make time to engage in one of the most important aspects of losing weight and keeping it off?**

Making time for what is important is always a matter of intention. If we really want to do something, we will not only find a way but also *make* a way to do it. By gaining a major source of free time, we can begin to serve not only ourselves but society as a whole.

••

Weight loss secret:
How to make time to exercise.

- **Cut down on TV.** Statistics show that in the industrialized world, the average person watches three hours of TV per day. The average American watches seven hours of TV per day. It seems we would rather watch other people living (or seeming to live) their lives than have lives of our own. By reducing the time you watch TV, you also eliminate the media manipulation that tells us how we are supposed to look, what we should eat, as well as what's wrong with us and the rest of the world. I personally stopped watching TV and reading newspapers almost 20 years ago and have never missed them although I continue to be a successful executive in the high-tech industry and beyond.

- **Alkalize your body.** By alkalizing your body through green drinks, green leafy vegetables, and live foods you will become so much more energized that you will need less sleep, Dr. Robert Young tells us. This is time you can then use to exercise. Try it out—you will be amazed at the results.

••

Age

Many people, including myself in the past, use age as an excuse for being overweight.

Getting older in itself does not cause weight gain.

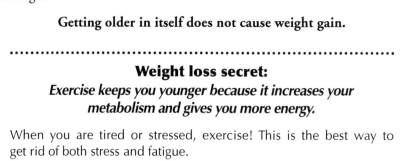

●●

Weight loss secret:
Exercise keeps you younger because it increases your metabolism and gives you more energy.

When you are tired or stressed, exercise! This is the best way to get rid of both stress and fatigue.

●●

The real reason why we gain weight as we grow older is because we tend to move less and as a result our metabolism goes down. As a result of a reduced metabolism, we become less flexible, develop less muscle mass, and become less fit. The truth is that our metabolism slows down with age mostly because we demand less from our bodies due to the sedentary habits we develop over time.

Stress

Another cause of weight gain is living an overly acidic lifestyle (prompted by stress, worry, or wrong nutrition) that forces the body to retain fat in order to compensate for the acids in it. By keeping our metabolism high through regular exercise and eating the right foods, such as alkalizing meals and metabolism-increasing foods, we can prevent weight gain even as we grow older. In addition, regular exercise is the best way to get rid of stress and create a feeling of happiness and well-being.

●●

Weight loss secret:
Find time to exercise through alkalization.

Alkalization can reduce your sleep requirements and stress and increase your energy.

By alkalizing your body through green drinks, green leafy vegetables, and live foods you will become so much more energized that **you will need less sleep**. This is time you can then use to exercise. Try it out—you will be amazed at the results.

●●

For Women Only

When it comes to losing weight, women fight an uphill battle. A woman's body is made to hold on to fat much more so than a man's body. Fat equals fertility, for fat helps produce estrogen, the key to reproduction.

Without women's fat, there would be no humans on earth.

In addition, women have less muscle mass than men. As a result, women's metabolism is 10 to 20 percent slower. Men burn approximately 20 percent more calories at rest than women do. And yet, we live in a society where the woman's ideal body is slim. We should be smart enough not to adopt those beliefs and unrealistic expectations.

••

Weight loss secret for women:
30 minutes of exercise per day is all it takes.

According to research published in 2003 by Harvard Medical School, modest exercise for at least 30 minutes per day can provide significant health benefits for women, decreasing rates of coronary heart disease and premature death.[107]

••

By moving the body regularly we not only lengthen our life span but also increase the quality of the life we live. We let go of unwanted fat and toxins, free our mind and spirit of the load of the past, and begin living a life of meaning, love, and contribution that can take place at every moment.

Did you know?

Studies have shown that healthy people who engage in regular exercise every day for six months can in fact become "addicted" to the feeling of health, vitality, and well-being that exercise provides.

My personal experience of the past three years confirms this fact. If we want to make exercise a regular part of our life forever, all we need to do is commit ourselves to it every day for six months. After those six months, the body and mind cannot stop exercising without giving up the feeling of happiness and well-being.

In 1993 the American Academy of Anti-Aging Medicine published a study in which it confirmed that 14 percent of all deaths in the United States were attributed to and correlated with the level of activity and diet. In addition, the following benefits of regular exercise were highlighted:

1. **Weight loss**
2. **Reduced age markers, mortality, and morbidity**
3. **Increased bone density**
4. **Reduced risk of osteoporosis**
5. **Enhanced flexibility**
6. **Increased strength and endurance**
7. **Reduced chances of injury**

As exercise builds the body's strength, we become leaner and healthier. In addition:

1. **We can build muscle mass so our previously enlarged skin doesn't hang after weight loss.**
2. **Our ability to metabolize sugars improves and reduces our risk of diabetes.**
3. **Exercise helps regulate blood sugar levels** so they don't elevate and increase fat storage.
4. **Exercise increases levels of serotonin—the happy hormone**—as well as dopamine and other hormones responsible for improving the way we feel. Imagine no longer running to the refrigerator when you're feeling depressed or unhappy. Regular exercise keeps our spirits lifted.
5. **Exercise increases the hormones the body releases** including improved HDL (good) cholesterol, growth hormones, and endorphins.
6. **With regular exercise, our mood improves.** We feel happier and less depressed and anxious.
7. Consequently, **our self-image grows**.
8. **Our relationships get better and we feel better overall.**

A Word of Caution

Before starting any exercise routine, you need to make sure the exercise you do is appropriate for your body. If regular exercise has not been part of your life so far, you must get a general checkup with your doctor to make sure you are healthy and to find out what kind of exercise is right for you.

Begin slowly and thoughtfully and listen to your body. It will tell you exactly what to do. In addition, if you want to achieve the best results within the shortest period of time, consider hiring a personal trainer who will set up an exercise routine specially designed for your own needs and goals. A trainer will help prevent injury and keep you on target. For best results you need to make sure to follow an exercise routine at least three times a week, alone or with your trainer.

In addition, always remember to take your pulse before starting to exercise, or to use a heart rate monitor throughout your training. I would encourage you to buy a heart rate monitor. It is a very safe and convenient way to monitor your heart rate during exercise and can be purchased for about $50.

When exercising, never go higher than your target heart rate (THR) unless your trainer, coach, or healthcare professional recommends you go to the next level.

••

Weight loss secret:
Start slowly and have fun.

Keep in mind that you lose the greatest amount of fat at a lower heart rate.

Furthermore, note that sore muscles are caused by lactic acid in the body. That prevents you from losing weight. So go slowly, being sure to superhydrate and alkalize your body.

••

Your maximum heart rate (MHR) is 220 minus your age. For instance, if you are 40 years old, your MHR is 180 (220 – 40). Depending upon your fitness level, your target heart rate should be between 50 and 70 percent of your MHR. Begin with THR of 50 percent of MHR, which is 90 if you are 40 years old (50 percent of 180 = 90). After a couple of weeks, and only if you feel good, increase that by 5 percent every week until you reach 70 percent of your MHR. The best way to tell if you are ready to increase your heart rate is to see if you can hold a conversation during exercise.

While working out you should feel slightly sweaty. If you become short of breath at any time, stop and consult with a physician. You should never feel exhausted or depleted of energy. A little soreness in the muscles will tell you that you have been burning calories and that you are making progress. However, you should never be in pain.

Remember that the body has to retain fat in order to neutralize acid (including lactic acid), to prevent disease and ultimately death. That's why you should work out at a lower heart rate and continue to alkalize your body with lots of green drinks (one gallon per day), alkalizing foods, and a lifestyle that makes you happy and fulfilled. This will ensure that you are both fit and healthy, unlike so many people who may be fit but not healthy.

Breaking a Sweat: Exercise for Weight Loss

Aerobic vs. Anaerobic Exercise

**The most important aspect of exercise is to make it fun
and to be smart about doing it.**

Sometimes when we commit ourselves to an exercise routine, we overdo it. We work our guts out, turn red and sweaty, and produce too much lactic acid. The body then becomes acidic and the next day we wake up with immense pain in our muscles. We worked out anaerobically (without oxygen) instead of aerobically (with oxygen)—and pain is always the body's response to such wrongdoing. Based on what we learned in Step 1 of this program, if we want to lose weight fast, we need to keep the body alkalized at all times. Producing lactic acid during exercise creates exactly the opposite condition. Thus, we have to be very smart about the way we exercise to achieve maximum benefits for both weight loss and fitness. The key to smart aerobic exercise is to watch the heart rate and keep it within a certain range.

. . . .

Weight loss secret:
Aerobic exercise burns fat.

Therefore, this is the type of exercise we want to do for weight loss. Through aerobic exercise, you:

- achieve high endurance
- exercise the heart, lungs, and lymphatic system

Increase your metabolism by building muscles without lactic acid. Remember, the lactic acid prompts the body to retain fat instead of letting it go.

By increasing lean muscle tissue and decreasing fat mass, you burn more calories even when you are not exercising.

. . . .

Muscle is a highly metabolically active tissue that demands more calories for maintenance than fat tissue.

The more muscle we can develop, the more efficient our bodies become at burning fat. Additionally, with more muscle, the body appears more defined and firm. And, of course, we have more strength at our disposal.

Optimal Exercise for Burning Fat

When we engage in low-intensity exercise, approximately 70 percent of the energy used for muscle contraction comes from fats and about 30 percent from carbohydrates. As the intensity of the exercise increases, there is a shift in energy from fats to carbohydrates (ultimately sugars). During high-intensity exercise (with the heart rate at 70 to 80 percent of maximum heart rate), almost 100 percent of the energy comes from carbohydrates, as long as an adequate supply is available.

However, with heart rates of 50 to 70 percent during extended exercise, there is a gradual shift from carbohydrates back to fats and proteins as energy. Within this range is exactly where we want to be when we exercise.

••

Weight loss secret:
Maintain a low heart rate to burn fat.

For optimal fat burning, I recommend exercising at a level hard enough to raise your heart rate to 70 to 85 percent of your maximum heart rate, which is expressed as 220 minus your age. The body burns more total fat calories at higher intensities.

Burning fat provides a much better and longer lasting source of energy than burning carbohydrates. And it helps you lose the fat you don't want.

••

In low-intensity exercise—20 minutes or longer at around 50 percent of maximum heart rate—fat supplies as much as 90 percent of fuel requirements.

Higher intensity aerobic exercise at roughly 75 percent of maximum heart rate burns a smaller percentage of fat (around 60 percent), but results in more total calories burned overall—including more fat calories.

At 50 percent of maximum heart rate, the body burns approximately seven calories a minute, 90 percent of which come from fat.

At 75 percent of maximum heart rate, the body burns 14 calories a minute, 60 percent from fat. So at 50 percent intensity, where 90 percent of the calories are from fat, we are burning only 6.30 fat calories per minute (.90 x 7 calories/minute). At 75 percent intensity, where only 60 percent of the calories are from fat, we are burning as much as 8.4 fat calories per minute (.60 x 14 calories/minute).

If it is difficult to exercise at a high intensity, try increasing the length of exercise time. The body can burn just as many fats at a lower intensity by working out longer as it can by exercising at a higher intensity for a shorter duration.

The above fat-loss theory tells us that we could burn more fat as a fuel source with lower intensity training (50 to 60 percent of maximum heart rate). So if we are embarking on a fitness program for the first time, it is in our best interest to start out exercising in the lower-heart-rate ranges and gradually increase exercise intensity as the body adapts to the physiological stress of exercise. This ensures we keep burning fat instead of sugar, which is what we want to accomplish through an exercise program for weight loss.

Let us take a look at the types of exercise that support this endeavor. We'll discuss cardiovascular training, strength training, and flexibility training, as well as awareness training.

Cardiovascular Training

Aerobic exercise is the best way to improve cardiovascular activity, and for good reason. Aerobics has become and stayed popular over the years because it provides numerous benefits:

- **Permanent weight loss**
- **A healthier heart**, leading to greater exchange of nutrients and waste output
- Higher amounts of oxygen used at the cellular level for the entire body, leading to **better physical conditioning**
- **Slower resting heart rate**, which may help the heart last longer
- **Better sleep**
- **Better blood circulation** for nutrient transport and waste removal
- **Improved ventilation efficiency and reduced breathing frequency**
- **Greater oxygen utilization**
- **Less lactic acid production**
- **Higher levels of fitness**
- Increased levels of happy hormones, leading us to feel healthy and vital

••

Weight loss secret:
Make sure you break a small sweat every time you exercise your body, but don't overdo it.

Note: *No pain, no gain* should be erased from your vocabulary because it is not good advice within this context.

••

Strength Training

I cannot emphasize enough the importance of developing the strength of your body. Clinical studies on strength training in older populations (ages 50 and up) have shown that regular strength training:

- **Has a profound effect on building muscle.**

- **Increases bone density.** During periods of inactivity, bone density returns to pre-exercise levels very quickly. So it is important to maintain a regular strength-training regimen.

- **May reduce the risk of fractures** caused by osteoporosis by improving the dynamic balance of the body, including the skeleton, muscle mass, and overall level of physical activity.

....

Weight loss secret:
Building your muscles builds your bones.

Make sure to get a good trainer who will help you avoid injury.

....

On a personal level, as a newly converted marathon runner, I can say that without strength training twice a week I would not have been able to run a marathon. Although I am not recommending marathon running for everyone, I would encourage you to get all the benefits from strength training, such as increased muscle tone, strength, size, and endurance. In turn, better-developed muscles improve posture, reduce back pain, create greater metabolic capacity, increase resting metabolic rate (RMR), increase bone mineral density, and improve overall physical function including higher overall flexibility.

Flexibility and Mobility Training

We need to stretch, not only before and after exercise, but also in the middle of the day and especially if we have a sedentary occupation.

....

Weight loss secret:
Stay flexible through stretching.

Make sure to stretch before and after each workout.

Stretching reduces muscle injuries and helps maintain and increase flexibility. Opinions vary on how long we should hold each of the stretches. From personal experience, I would recommend a minimum of 15 seconds and an ideal of 60 seconds for each muscle.

....

The exercise menu we developed for this program provides several flexibility exercises. However, I believe that yoga and Pilates are ideal for stretching every muscle group, improving spinal flexibility, increasing blood circulation, and improving muscle tone.

In addition, I would highly recommend visiting a chiropractor once a month to make sure the core of your body, the spine and the skeletal system, is aligned and stays flexible.

Awareness Training

Awareness training means developing the habit of taking every possible opportunity to stay physically active and to keep moving your body. For instance, you can train yourself to always:

- **take stairs to a destination instead of an elevator**
- **walk or use a bike for local errands**
- **walk to a park** to have lunch during a workday instead of remaining in an air-conditioned building
- **think twice about using the car.** Come up with **alternatives like walking, jogging, or biking.**
- **substitute a brisk walk for TV time.** At the very least, get on a Stair-Master® while watching TV.

··

Weight loss secrets for exercise

1. **Start small.** As someone who has gone through this, believe me, the hardest part is getting started. So set yourself up to win by starting small. If you're breaking out of a longtime sedentary lifestyle, begin a new exercise program by walking three times a week. For the first week, walk just 15 minutes at a time, at a slow pace. Gradually add more workout days and extend the workout time from 15 to 30 minutes, then from 30 to 45 minutes. Finally, pick up the pace! After eight weeks, walk 45 minutes five days a week at a fairly brisk pace. This should be easy! (Refer to the exercise menu in Appendix 2 for details.)
2. **Increase intensity slowly**. One easy way to add a bit of intensity to a walk is to add some additional weight, such as carrying a bottle of water in each hand. I prefer using a weighted vest instead of walking with free weights or ankle weights. Free weights and ankle weights can do more harm than good, since they concentrate the weight on the arms and legs and put undue stress on the joints.
3. **Blend cardio and flexibility**. For optimal results, perform the cardio and flexibility training together in one

workout, three to five times a week, whether at home, at the gym, or while traveling.

4. **Remember to stretch.** Always begin and end a workout with stretching. This prevents muscle injuries and ensures against shortening of the muscles. The best way to learn how to stretch properly is by taking a yoga class.

5. **Warm up and cool down.** To warm up, walk around while gently swinging the arms and raising the knees up to waist level (or as high as possible). Gently stretch the muscles of the calves, the backs of the legs, the waist and the back. Hold each stretching position for 30 to 45 seconds. Go to the point of tension but not pain. Breathe deeply and pay special attention to those parts of the body where the stretch is focused. Repeat this process immediately following the workout.

6. **Breathe deeply.** Breathing is the most important thing in life. And yet, most of us do not breath properly and deeply enough. From Tony Robbins I have learned an amazing breathing technique that I practice three times a day. It makes me feel great, full of energy, and totally awake. The instructions: Breathe deeply in your abdomen while counting (let's say to 10), hold the breath for four times that amount (40), and then release it for twice that amount (20). Do that 10 times in one session three times per day. Then listen to your body. You will be amazed at how good it feels.

7. **Have fun.** For optimal benefits, it's important to have fun while exercising. So choose a pleasant setting, add music to your workout, think positive thoughts or affirmations, or listen to empowering tapes.

8. **Gain more.** It would be a lie to pretend that I loved working out when I first began. I did it because intellectually I had accepted the fact that I had to do it if I wanted to stay healthy while growing old. And since my life is driven by growth and contribution, I began working out by listening to fun tapes by Deepak Chopra, Tony Robbins, Wayne Dyer, Ram Dass, Louise Hay, and so many other experts from whom I could learn valuable lessons. Today I listen to tapes I have created that contain my own affirmations and goals in life. These tapes help me grow every day. They remind me every morning of what I am grateful

for, of who I love and who loves me, as well as what I am about and what I want to achieve in life. By doing this I have more fun working out, I get more motivated about my goals, and I maximize the use of my time.

9. **Hydrate.** Moderate exercise in a temperate climate can result in the loss of half a gallon of water per day, so be sure to drink enough water throughout the day while working out. Remember, this is in addition to the eight glasses needed each day for normal, healthy functioning. Since regular, unfiltered tap water, or even bottled water, may be full of contaminants, consider using a home appliance that filters water.

10. **Drink green drinks.** Consume a green drink while training to keep hydrated and alkalized.

11. **Keep at it.** Stick to an exercise routine religiously whether at home or on the road. Remember that your body is the foundation of everything you want to achieve in life. On a plane, flight attendants teach us to put oxygen masks on ourselves first before we help our children. So too, we must take care of ourselves first so that we can take care of others.

12. **Stay committed.** Get a buddy for workouts. A workout buddy helps us stick to our commitment and workout routines, whether we feel like it or not. Do anything it takes to keep your commitment to your regular physical exercise.

13. **Handle relapse well.** You can start again at any moment. Please do not beat yourself up if you slipped from your routine for a while. You know what to do to get back on it, so do it and forget about the past. You always have the now. So put on your shoes and gear and begin moving to the rhythms of your favorite music.

14. **Change your identity** – become an athlete in your mind first. The key factor in changing anything we want in life is not what we do, but how we feel about it. So if you want to make exercise an integral part of your life, you need to attach athleticism to your identity. Seeing yourself as a fat person who hardly moves at all will not get you into your running shoes; visualizing yourself as a beautiful and happy athlete will. So while working out, repeat to yourself, "I am a beautiful, happy, and healthy athlete." You will be amazed at the results.

15. **Celebrate**. After each exercise session, celebrate. Thank your heart, legs, arms, skin, and your entire body for its support. Be happy and grateful and jump up and down to give your brain this message of pleasure so it will want to remind you to exercise again tomorrow.

Appendix 2 offers a one-week exercise menu that contains all of the recommendations made in this chapter.

It is never too late to become physically active. If I can become a marathon runner at age 44 without ever having run before, you can do it too, if that's what you want. Those who have known me for a long time make fun of me by reminding me how much I used to hate running and how I used to emphasize that I was a swimmer, not a runner. Today everything is different.

It doesn't matter what you do as long as you move your body regularly and for 30 minutes per day. If you can do that every day for six months, you will want to keep moving until the last day of your life. That's how good, energized, and happy you will feel after each workout.

I would caution, however, against diving headfirst into a vigorous exercise regimen without giving the body an opportunity to adapt to a new routine. That's a setup for failure. Remember, exercise is a lifestyle change, so it's important to adjust gradually.

I-can-tation/Affirmation/Meditation:

I love and I exercise my healthy and vibrant body regularly with joy. I say "yes" to life and allow for change. I am open and follow my heart. I decide today to totally commit to my health and well-being and to begin to exercise regularly.

The next chapter will show you how you can increase your level of energy and vitality even more. It will support your weight loss plan by showing how you can lose some extra pounds that will never return just by cleansing and detoxifying on a regular basis.

Step 3: Stop the Enemy – Cleaning Up the Mess through Cleansing and Detoxification

"Go confidently in the direction of your dreams. Live the life you have imagined."
—Henry David Thoreau

Did you know?

You are a candidate for detoxification if you:

- suffer from obesity
- have frequent headaches, back pain, or joint pain
- feel bloated, congested, or sluggish; lack energy and vitality; or suffer from insomnia
- do not have at least one bowel movement per day
- have allergies and suffer from food cravings
- have indigestion, arthritis, respiratory problems, or hemorrhoids
- suffer from acne, psoriasis, or dry skin.[5]

As I was working on the current edition of this book, Al Gore's book and movie called *An Inconvenient Truth* were released. "What a coincidence!" I thought. I couldn't help but see the obvious parallel between our physical bodies and our extended body, our Mother Earth.

It is pollution that is a major contributor to bringing our planet out of balance and it is also pollution that is a major contributor to overweight and disease in our own bodies.[108]

This is especially true for us in the Western world, with India and China gradually following suit. Statistically, Westerners are not only the fattest people on this planet, but also the biggest planetary polluters. I remember meeting former Vice President Gore in Puerto Rico in December of 2004. During our dinner together, I asked him when America would ratify the Kyoto Protocol, whereby countries agree to reduce pollution to prevent further planetary destruction. Being the diplomat that he his, Mr. Gore didn't respond directly to my question but instead shared with me how hard he was working with both German Chancellor Gerhard Schroeder and French President Jacques Chirac to get Russia to sign the Kyoto Protocol first. Luckily, he succeeded, and Russia ratified Kyoto in early 2006. We are systematically making progress at the global level and I hope that our children will not inherit a planet in crisis from us.

There is hope, and as Al Gore continues to work to get one country after another to sign the Kyoto Protocol, we too must begin, one by one, to stop the pollution of our own bodies for our own and the collective good.

Why Should You Care?

Let me ask you something: *How often do you brush your teeth? How often do you take a shower? Why do you do these things?*

I don't know your answer, but I believe we wash ourselves a couple of times per day because it is part of our lifestyle; it is a normal practice for good hygiene and it feels good. Brushing teeth and taking showers are part of the normal routine in Western society, but the freedom of good hygiene is a privilege that billions of people on Earth still do not enjoy.

For the first 16 years of my life growing up in Romania, we had no running water and no indoor bathroom. I brushed my teeth only when I remembered and took a bath once a week in a small metal bathtub. The bathtub was brought into the family room, which also served as our kitchen and my bedroom. Using coal or wood, we heated enough water to fill up the bathtub. As the youngest, I had the privilege of being the first one to take a bath. My parents bathed in the same water I did. As you can imagine, I don't have enough words to express my gratitude for today's amenities.

Unfortunately, having good external hygiene is not enough to stay healthy.

So let me ask you another question: *How often do you intentionally clean yourself on the inside? I mean your digestive system, liver, or bloodstream.* Ninety-eight percent of the population would answer "rarely" or "never." Cleansing and detoxifying is not what we normally do in our society.

The development of our industrialized society came with a big price tag. It happened at the expense of pollution of our soil, our water, our air, and ultimately, our bodies. As a result, it is no longer enough to take a shower, cleansing only the outside. Cleansing ourselves inside has become mandatory if we want to stay healthy, look good, and have abundant energy. You would be amazed and alarmed if you could see what clogs the intestines of humans, especially those among us who have suffered from overweight or obesity for years.

Here is an example:

Figure 4: Example of hardened fecal mater eliminated after an intestinal cleanse (printed with the friendly permission of Richard Anderson)

How Do You Know If You Should Detox Your Body?

We were made to be healthy and vital. For instance, if we undergo surgery, the surgeon may perform the surgery, but who is actually performing the healing? It is the wonder of the human body that has the tendency to be healthy unless we impede it.

Did you know?

Every millisecond, the 100 trillion cells in your body work in unison to create your health and vitality. The miracle that is your body can digest food, paint a picture, listen to Mozart, and make a baby—all at the same time. It can do all that and much more if we don't interfere with it.

To find out if you are a candidate for detox and cleansing, let us take a look at what creates imbalance in the human body. If you find any of the factors below apply to you, then you may seriously consider undergoing a cleanse or a detox program.

1. **Environmental factors inside the body.** This category includes:
   a. Overconsumption of acid-producing food and drink such as sugar, processed foods, caffeine, alcohol, dairy, and animal flesh
   b. Overeating
   c. Malnutrition resulting from eating unhealthy, refined, and prepackaged foods
   d. Metabolic disturbances and the resulting inability to properly digest foods due to lack of enzymes, minerals, and vitamins

• •

Weight loss secret:
Health begins at cellular level through detoxification and cleansing.

Remember that a healthy body is at its ideal weight. According to studies performed by the Canadian Task Force on Preventive Health Care, these factors can contribute to defective methylation processes at the cellular level, creating an acidic environment that can in turn lead to inflammation, fatigue, brain malfunction, mood disorders, and overweight.[110]

• •

Defective methylation is a simple biochemical process that affects our genetic imprint and interferes with the detoxification of the body, creating unhealthy cells. These unhealthy cells adapt to the new environment by retaining fat and are prone to disease. This internal environment acts as a breeding ground for parasites, molds, yeasts, fungi, bacteria, and viruses, which create a slew of waste, addictions, and cravings.

2. **Environmental factors outside the body.** The body is exposed to various toxic external factors that are beyond our control. These include:

   a. Chemical toxins in polluted air,[111] both indoors and outdoors
   b. Toxins in our drinking water,[112] including chlorine and fluoride
   c. Dry-cleaning chemicals and household cleaners
   d. Shampoo, toothpaste, soap, deodorant, and shower gel
   e. Office equipment including printers
   f. Electromagnetic pollution through electromagnetic radiation[113] from computer displays, cell phones and cell phone towers, electric razors, electric blankets, waterbed heaters, and more
   g. Chemical emanations from carpets, glue, and building materials
   h. Contaminated foods that contain preservatives, herbicides, pesticides, irradiation, bacteria, and viruses114

Research has shown that all of these influences can lead to genetic damage, health imbalances, and even cancer.[115]

··

Weight loss secret:

Stop the poisoning of your body by becoming aware of and avoiding polluted air, water, electromagnetic radiation, household chemicals, and contaminated foods.

··

3. **Physical pain.** Accidents, physical trauma, and diseases cause pain and often prevent us from pursuing other endeavors and enjoying life to its fullest.

4. **Mental, emotional, and spiritual factors.** This category includes:
    a. Our inner life—the way we think and how we view life
    b. Stress
    c. Financial worries
    d. Job dissatisfaction
    e. Unhappy relationships
    f. Negative thoughts and emotional imbalance

5. **Lifestyle.** Here we have to take into consideration our daily habits, including:
    a. A sedentary and/or stressful lifestyle
    b. Insufficient rest
    c. Lack of exercise
    d. A clogging diet devoid of live foods, nutrients, and enzymes
    e. Failure to detoxify
    f. Addictions to smoking, drugs, and TV

According to the above-mentioned study performed in 2000 by the Canadian Task Force,[116] defective methylation can lead to coronary heart disease, stroke, Alzheimer's disease, and various types of cancer including colon and cervical cancer. Thus, cleansing and detoxification are key to a healthy body, which in turn will tend to rest at its ideal weight.

> **The first and most important step toward losing weight and gaining health and vitality is to stop the vicious cycle of poisoning the body, through cleansing and detoxification.**

....

Weight loss secret:
If you lack energy and vitality you can regain it through cleansing and detoxification.

Many of us have become so accustomed to being out of balance that we have actually forgotten how it feels to be truly healthy, energized, and vital. However, we all remember how energized and joyous we were as children. There is absolutely no reason why this should not be how we live every day. The first step is to cleanse and detoxify; it is a gift we all deserve.

More importantly, when we allow the body to detoxify itself, it no longer needs to hold on to fat tissue to compensate for an acidic environment, and it releases the overload. This weight may never return if you cleanse on a regular basis, and the positive consequence is the creation of health and vitality for the rest of your life.

....

Cleansing and Detoxifying

> *"If liberty means anything at all,*
> *it means the right to tell people what they don't want to hear."*
> —George Orwell

Let's face it: the topic of cleansing and detoxifying is not pretty. It can actually be quite shocking, as it was for me when I first discovered the truth about my own body. Yet I concur with successful dieters and weight loss experts that detoxifying the body regularly is the best present we can give to ourselves. Simply commit to your lasting health, decide, and do it. The results will be far beyond your wildest dreams. Not only will you lose significant weight by eliminating toxins from your intestines and cells, but you will embark on the great journey of achieving and maintaining an ideal weight and feeling more energized, happy, and vital than you may have ever felt before. You deserve that right. Claim it.

If you are not convinced yet, then read what Dr. Bernard Jensen,[117] one of the most widely known authorities on cleansing and detoxifying, wrote in his book *Tissue Cleansing Through Bowel Management*: "One autopsy revealed a colon to be 9 inches (23 cm) in diameter with a passage through it no larger than a pencil. The rest was caked up layer upon layer of encrusted fecal material. This accumulation can have the consistency of truck-tire rubber. It's hard and black. Another autopsy revealed a stagnant colon to weigh in at an incredible 40 pounds." The next figure shows another example of Dr. Jensen's findings.

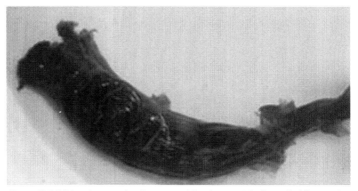

Figure 5: Additional example of encrusted fecal material, also called "mucoid plaque" (printed with the friendly permission of Richard Anderson)

Did you know?

You could permanently lose up to 40 pounds just by cleansing your intestines.[118]

According to Dr. Jensen, more than 90 percent of the overall population in the industrialized world carries such fecal material within their intestines. His findings are in line with my own personal experience and that of my clients. I have not met one person who has not eliminated some form of hardened fecal matter during a cleanse.

My Own Detox Story

Simply out of curiosity, not because I thought I had a problem, I decided in March of 2002 to participate in a cleanse led by world-renowned motivational speaker Tony Robbins. The detoxifying process and the knowledge I acquired through it changed my life forever. In fact, this book would not have been possible without that memorable experience. So I would like to share my experience by showing you the next picture. In it you can see how my blood cells looked before the cleanse. What you see is not a picture of health.

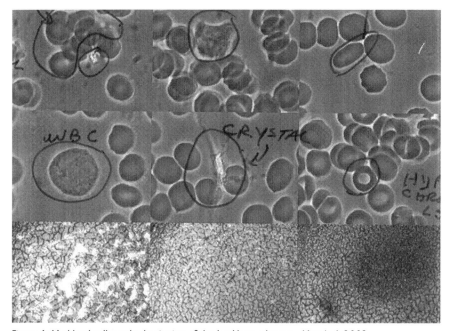

Figure 6: My blood cells at the beginning of the Las Vegas cleanse, March 4, 2002

In a healthy body, the red blood cells are plump, round, and free to carry oxygen throughout the body. As you can see in the picture on the next page, my red blood cells (colored here dark gray) were deformed and lacking in oxygen. As a result, they were clumped together and did not move much, which is a red flag. My white blood cells, indicated with the word WBC, were also deformed and hardly moving. One possible result of such a scenario is that the body's immune system might not respond quickly enough to defend against bacteria, viruses, or other pathogens. This condition could indicate several imbalances, including too much acidity in the system. The black handwriting of my doctor indicates some of the problems I was facing. These were:

- Lack of oxygen (shown in red blood cells clumped together)
- Crystals coming from the bronchitis medicine I was taking
- Lack of iron (indicated by the white holes in red blood cells)
- Lack of folic acid (shown in the oval form of the blood cells)

This was not a pretty—let alone healthy—picture, and I felt it. I suffered from fatigue, irritable bowel syndrome, food reactions, allergies, and low thyroid, and I was constantly sick with bronchitis.

The following picture shows my blood only four days into the cleanse. You can see significant changes.

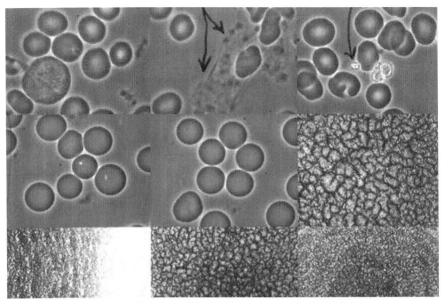

Figure 7: My blood cells after four days of the Las Vegas cleanse, March 8, 2002

The gray areas in the above picture indicate that my red blood cells were now round, free floating, and full of oxygen, which they now could carry to all organs in my body. As you may be able to see from the picture, some filter-organ (i.e., liver and kidney) stress remained. This was the result of the ongoing cleansing process, but the change in the way I looked and felt was significant indeed.

My cleansing experience was not just a wake-up call but a rude awakening. Contrary to my belief, my body had become very unhealthy over the years. The fact that I had lived on a vegetarian diet for more than a decade had not been enough to keep me healthy. I lacked energy and vitality.

What these pictures don't show are the four different types of parasites I was hosting at the time. They were beautifully coexisting and feeding on my body's nutrients while depleting me of my life force. I was constantly tired and irritable, often sick, and miserable. Because this state of affairs had developed gradually, over several years, I had become so accustomed to feeling not quite right that I thought it was normal for my age. In my early forties, I had already bought into the idea that it is normal that the body breaks down as we grow older. Today I know that the body doesn't have to break down if we detoxify regularly, watch our diet, exercise, and live a life of meaning and fulfillment.

···

Weight loss secret:
Don't buy into the social conditioning that we have to gain weight, lose our agility, and become more prone to sickness as we grow older.

Be a revolutionary in your own right and join the many people around the world who live well past 100 and enjoy high levels of health and vitality. Follow the example of the extraordinary people that John Robbins writes about in his latest book, *Healthy at 100*. He writes, "We all have a choice to be either accomplices in the status quo or everyday revolutionaries. We have a choice whether to succumb to the cultural trance, eat fast food, and race by each other in the night, or to build lives of caring, substance, and healing. So much depends on that choice."

···

What Happens During a Cleanse or Detox Program?

First, understand that there are many ways to cleanse and detoxify the body.[119] The most important thing is that you pick one way that works for you and gets you the results you are looking for even if it takes longer. If you have never cleansed before, I would highly recommend making slow but steady changes. Watch your body and how you feel. Make a slow transition to a healthier diet by eliminating some of the foods you know are not good for you. These include dairy, grains, animal flesh, caffeine, sugar, and eggs. First eliminate only one of these reactive foods and watch how you feel. Notice how your weight begins to change, your mood gets better, your allergies begin to diminish, and your skin begins to shine. As you become more comfortable, eliminate another one of these foods and continue to be alert to your body reactions. When you feel strong enough, you may go on a stronger detox process that may contain only fruits and vegetables for a couple of days until you are ready to try a juice fast.

During a cleanse, the body no longer has to deal with digestion. Instead, it uses its energy to eliminate many years of accumulated waste. During the cleanse, toxic accumulations are released from the alimentary canal and poisonous overloads are expelled from the cells, liver, kidneys, blood, and lungs as well as the lymphatic system. This course of action enables the body to rid itself of excess weight, return to its natural balance, and heal itself. It is now empowered to use its own infinite intelligence.

. . . .

Weight loss secret:
Your body cleanses itself all the time and especially during the night.

Cleansing and detoxifying simply means to expand that regular body detox to more hours, days, and even weeks. You will see that your body will honor every single one of your efforts with more energy, vitality and vibrant health.

. . . .

Whether we are aware of it or not, our bodies cleanse themselves all the time, especially during sleep at night. We all notice the odors our skin and mouths emanate in the morning. We even have a word in our society that expresses what we do when we wake up: breakfast. By eating something in the morning, we *break the fast.*

In any event, I would discourage anybody from fasting alone the first time. Join a group; attend a fasting week.[120] Most of all, enjoy reuniting with your higher self, for fasting can often become a journey to your soul.

A Word of Caution

If you have a serious health condition, are pregnant, have a low thyroid, or are underweight, be sure to consult a physician before performing a cleanse or a detoxification. However, please note that most medical doctors have not received a proper education on cleansing, nor do they have much experience with it. As a result, they also do not understand cleansing reactions and may not be able to guide you properly. Therefore, it may be wise to consult a naturopathic physician in addition to a medical doctor before undergoing a detox program.

How to Pick the Cleanse That Works for You

There are many ways to perform a cleanse. However, to keep it simple, there are three basic levels of detox to chose from:

1.   ELIMINATION DIET: During this kind of cleanse you continue to eat what you usually eat but you shift your eating habits to become healthier, which in itself will already cleanse your body. To do that, increase your

consumption of organic produce (70 percent of each meal should contain organic fruit, salads, and vegetables). In addition, over the course of several weeks eliminate one after another reactive foods including eggs, dairy, animal flesh, corn, wheat, and sugars, and you will be totally amazed at the changes happening in your body. For more detailed information on the elimination diet, go to the elimination diet section below.

2. SMOOTHIE CLEANSE: During a smoothie cleanse, you drink for one week, or as long as you want, healthy smoothies, which you can make of fruits, veggies, nuts, seeds, and essential fatty acids such as Udo's Oil. This cleanse is much more intense than the elimination diet and the results are beyond your imagination.

3. JUICE CLEANSE: Apart from a water fast this is the strongest and most intense detox method and will bring you the best results during the shortest amount of time. Read the section on the juice cleanse for more details.

FOR BEGINNERS, a simple way to detoxify could be the 30-day Isagenix Cleansing and Detox System.

If you have never cleansed and would like to choose a simple program, I recommend the 30-day Isagenix Cleansing and Detox System, with which I have achieved remarkable results in my practice. The advantage of this program is that it provides an extraordinary network and support system for dieters. These products are available through an Isagenix representative, by calling Isagenix itself, or online for instance at (http://mbozesan.isagenix.com/cleanse_30day.dhtml?inv=0).

I addition, I highly recommend reading *The New Detox Diet* by Dr. Elson Haas, which I consider to be one of the best books on this topic.

Everything You Need to Know to Perform a Cleanse

The detox process produces acids in the body, and we discussed in previous chapters why it is crucial to alkalize the body in order to stay healthy. Thus, in order to protect your body from overacidity and have a successful cleanse, it is important to prepare before you detoxify.

In Appendix 3, called Pre-Cleanse Menu, you can find a menu recommendation that will help you prepare for a cleanse to achieve the best possible results. As a general rule, prior to going into a cleanse process avoid acid-forming foods such as alcohol, caffeine, soft drinks, eggs, dairy products, and animal flesh. Most of all, look forward to the cleanse results and how your skin will be more soft, your thoughts will be clearer, you will begin to feel lighter both mentally and physically, and your overall health and well-being will improve.

Is my body strong enough for a cleanse?

One of the most significant evaluations to make before cleansing is to ensure that your body is healthy and strong enough to deal with the released waste. Alkalization is key. Here is where your knowledge about body alkalization, discussed previously, comes in handy.

To know whether you must alkalize or not, you need to get a pH test. You can buy the pH test strips online[121] or in most pharmacies. I would highly recommend using both the saliva and the urine test. Follow the instructions, and if the test result is lower than pH 7.0, it means that your body is too acidic and that your liver doesn't have adequate electrolyte/mineral reserves available. This may also indicate a health challenge, in which case you must consult with your physician.

In most cases, however, alkalizing your body for one week will enable you to begin a cleanse soon because, as you know, the human body is very forgiving. You can easily get back into an alkaline balance by superhydrating, especially with the use of super green drinks (see previous chapters for more information) and lots of purified water. Also try an exclusively alkalizing diet based on dark green vegetable salads and vegetable juices for one week (Appendix 3 can help you with this too). Then perform an additional test to measure whether your alkaline pH levels have significantly improved. If the situation hasn't changed, please consult a physician. This may indicate a serious physical condition.

If your test is positive—meaning pH 7.0 or above—then your liver has enough alkaline reserves available to deal with the released toxins and to allow for a safe cleanse, which is one of the greatest gifts you can give yourself.

Superhydration

Since the human body is made up of 70 percent water, it is very important that you drink enough water during the day, and especially during a cleanse. A normal adult must drink eight large glasses of water, or 3 liters (three quarters of a gallon), per day. For every 25 pounds of excess weight, you need to drink an extra glass of water. During the detoxification process, it is crucial to superhydrate your body so that the toxins can be carried out as quickly as possible to reduce fat deposits and to eliminate toxins.

Never get to the point of feeling thirsty. Thirst means you are already heavily dehydrated and your body cannot metabolize stored fat efficiently. In addition, you have to make sure you drink high-quality purified water at room temperature. When we consume ice-cold water, we expend energy to heat up the water—energy that could be used toward detoxification. Please do not drink unpurified tap water; it is not good enough.

How to Prevent Headaches and Other Pains During the Cleanse

During the detox process, the body releases many toxins into your bloodstream, intestines, urine, skin, and lungs so that they can be eliminated. These toxins create an acidic environment that can put the body's pH level out of balance.

••

Weight loss & Detox secret:
You can prevent headaches and other side effects during cleansing in the following ways:

1. Through intense hydration
2. By taking essential fatty acids (oils)
3. By cleansing your bowels (see below)
4. By taking supplements
5. By consuming green drinks made from dried green vegetables and stems. These so-called "superfoods" can be purchased in many health food stores, as well as online.[122] In addition to alkalizing your body, green superfoods have been shown to fight free-radical damage, provide the body with essential nutrients, facilitate detoxification, support immune function, and maintain and boost your energy levels during a cleanse.

••

Should you have no access to super greens, you can use (for a short time) baking soda to alkalize. Add a half teaspoon of baking soda in an 8-oz. glass of water and drink it three times a day. Although sodium bicarbonate may alkalize and provide a short-term solution to indigestion, too much bicarbonate can wreak havoc with the body's acid/base balance and lead to metabolic alkalosis. The high sodium content may also cause problems for people with heart disease or high blood pressure. So limit the use of baking soda to a few days only.

Supplements

In previous chapters, I recommended a list of daily supplemental nutrients the human body requires to be healthy. During the cleansing process, we need additional supplements that are designed to support the detoxification process.

I personally take and recommend several products that you can find online or in health food stores. These are in no particular order products by Dr. Udo Erasmus such as Udo's Oil Blend, Super Greens, Probiotics, and Fast Food, and Richard Anderson's cleansing products. Anderson's products include Arise & Shine Alkalizer™, designed to speed up the alkalizing process of the body, Ultimate Food Complex™, Power up!™, and Electro Life.

> **To those who would like a simple supplementation program,** I recommend the InnerLight supplements by Dr. Robert Young, with which I have personally achieved outstanding results. These are the Starter Pack, Alkalizer Pack, and the InnerLight's Complete Program. Unfortunately, Dr. Young's products cannot be purchased in a regular store and must be ordered through an InnerLight sales representative or online for instance at (http://www.innerlightinc.com/sageera/shop.cfm).

....
Weight loss & detox secret:
Taking supplements during your detox is essential to ease the detox process and replenish your system with good health–building components.
....

Digestive enzymes and friendly bacteria are of paramount importance during the cleanse to support the restoration of the intestinal flora. Thus, I recommend a concentrated green powder or green drink during a cleanse because of the drop in pH levels that occurs during the detox process. In addition, I would also recommend a multimineral, a multivitamin, and chlorophyll—a fruit concentrate with enzymes and antifungal properties. In addition to taking digestive enzymes, take an anti-yeast product as well as an anti-parasite formula containing black walnut hulls.[123]

Deep Breathing

Shallow breathing is characteristic of our society. As a result, we do not provide our bodies with enough oxygen. The effect is often lack of energy, vitality, and even disease. Oxygen is the catalyst in creating ATP (adenosine triphosphate), the energy source of the body. Breathing correctly during your cleanse is very important to support the elimination of waste through the lungs. You can do this by breathing consciously at least three times a day.

....

Weight loss & detox secret:
*You can detox faster by breathing in a   cer-
tain pattern.*

For instance, breathe in while counting to a certain number, for example 10; then hold your breath for four times that amount (40); then
release it for twice that amount (20). Do that 10 times, three times a
day, and listen to your body. You will be amazed at how good and how
energized you feel.

....

Exercise

We especially need to exercise while we're detoxing the body. Regular exercise increases metabolism, which enables detoxification throughout every
organ, including through the skin via sweating. Personally, I have kept my
daily running routine even while fasting. However, I would only recommend
vigorous exercise to people who do that on a regular basis. Otherwise, I recommend moderate exercise such as brisk walking, swimming, yoga, working
with a personal trainer for structural support, Pilates, and especially rebounding. Rebounding is a marvelous way not only to detoxify but to develop and
sustain a healthy immune system.

....

Weight loss & detox secret:
You can detox faster by exercising.

....

Rebounding means simply jumping up and down like a child. You can
do this on your bed—ideal when you travel—or on a professional rebounder.
In fact, I recommend that every home have a rebounder that people use for
10 minutes per day. I believe from experience that using a rebounder daily
can function as an insurance policy against colds, flu, and other minor health
challenges.

Detoxification Through the Skin

The largest organ in the human body is the skin, which, when stimulated
appropriately, is also the greatest generator of growth hormones and immune
cells. In addition, we can use this marvelous organ not only to improve our
overall health and well-being, but also to optimize the detoxification results
during a cleanse.

....

Weight loss & detox secret:
You can detox faster through massage, sauna, and hot mineral baths.

....

You can accomplish skin detox in the following ways:

- **Skin exfoliation.** Use a loofah pad or natural hair brush to brush the skin either dry or wet. If preferred, add a body scrub, available in any health food or cosmetic store.

- **Massage.** Being the body's largest organ, the skin produces more growth hormones than any other organ. These hormones keep us healthy, vital, and youthful. The skin generates these hormones naturally, but we can increase the quantity through stimulating the skin by touch and massage on a regular basis. Massage also aids in detoxification through increasing circulation in the body, specifically by increasing the flow of lymph fluids, thereby helping to release trapped toxins. Just like a regular sauna, the massage habit can be a ticket to health and well-being. This is especially true when the massage is conducted during a cleanse. Receiving a massage from someone else can be the ultimate luxury. If that is not possible, you can self-administer a massage daily using warm sesame oil.[125] Begin with the scalp and move down to the toes while massaging every single part of the skin. Simply enjoy this gift of love to yourself.

- **Mineral baths.** Before and after your massage, take a long mineral bath. Many of us know how great we feel after soaking in a Jacuzzi for a while. Detoxifying feels the same way and is even better because it is free of the toxic chemicals usually used in a Jacuzzi. However, Jacuzzis have various purification chemicals in the water to ensure a safe hygienic environment over long periods of time. That's why I do not recommend using them too often. But during your cleanse I recommend taking a long bath in a regular bathtub and adding Epsom salts. You can purchase these in any health food or drug store. If a nearby spa provides mud baths, please indulge in this luxurious experience.

- **Brushing teeth.** We detoxify even through the mouth. During the cleansing process your tongue and teeth will develop a thick coating, which will create a strange feeling of heaviness in the mouth. Other people will notice it as well, so I recommend brushing your teeth more often than usual.

Why Is Sauna So Important for Your Health?

"Sauna is a poor man's drugstore."
—Finnish proverb

Going to a sauna, a Finnish invention, every week, and really sweating is the best way to stay healthy and prevent disease throughout your life. During a cleanse, a sauna speeds up the detoxification process. In the sauna instructions below, you can find out how to take a sauna correctly to achieve optimal results.

Step 1: Do not drink or eat anything for two hours prior to a sauna. Do not drink anything during the sauna even if you are thirsty, for your intention is to get the toxins out of your cells, and not the water you have just consumed.

Step 2: Take a hot shower and exfoliate your skin with a body exfoliator or with a brush (dry or wet).
   • Make sure your body is warm when you walk into the sauna so that you start to sweat immediately.

Step 3: Go into a dry sauna and sit there 8–12 minutes. You will know soon which of the levels is best for you. If you are a sauna beginner, you may want to sit on the lowest level at first and move up as you become more accustomed to the temperatures. However, you should know that the higher up you sit the hotter it is and the more intense the cleansing. While in the sauna:
   • Close your eyes and enjoy the beautiful experience your body is giving you. Meditate or contemplate something nice and pleasant. Do not talk or read anything because ink becomes very toxic at high temperatures.
   • Brush your skin with a Loofah pad while in the sauna to encourage exfoliation and sweating. It will also help you endure the heat much better until you start sweating.
   • After a few minutes notice how you begin to work up a good sweat.
   • Listen to your body—it will know when it has had enough. However, if you can, push yourself gently and move a step up. If it becomes too hot for you, go back down.
   • Make sure you have been sweating for at least five minutes before you leave the sauna.

Step 4: Go out into the fresh air (preferably outside), into the snow if available, and take a cold bath in a lake as they do in Finland, if at all possible. Breathe deeply while you walk around and enjoy the experience.

Step 5: Take a shower and give your feet—or entire body, if you can take it—alternate hot and cold baths three times. The last bath before the break should be hot.

Step 6: Relax for the same amount of time you spent in the sauna.

Step 7: Repeat steps 1–6 three times. Make sure the last shower you take before leaving is warm.

Step 8: Slowly caress your skin. Notice how soft and supple it has become. Give yourself a self-administered massage with your favorite body lotion.

Step 9: Embrace the gift of love that you have just given yourself and celebrate!

Now that we have addressed detoxification through the lungs, kidneys, skin, and bloodstream, let's find out how you can cleanse your bowels.

Bowel Cleanse

"Keeping your bowel clean is the single most important thing that you can do for your health!"
—Dr. Bernard Jensen

All inner organs including the brain, heart, liver, lungs, kidneys, and hormonal glands—in short, each of the 100 trillion cells in the human body—are totally dependent upon a properly functioning digestive system.

The intestinal tract is the hub of the entire body. The bowel feeds the blood, which carries all nutrients and oxygen to every cell in the body. If the bowel is clogged with waste, the blood becomes badly contaminated and we end up bathing in our own junk on the inside. At the beginning of this chapter you saw two pictures that showed how bowel pollution looks in some people. It is essential to keep your bowels healthy in order to maintain a steady, healthily oxygenated flow of nutrients to your organs.

According to Dr. Bernard Jensen,[118] 90 percent of people in our society have polluted their bowels with unimaginable filth and thus have weakened their digestive functions. In such an environment, even good food can become toxic. As long as this waste remains inside, the body grows weak. We become more prone to deficiencies and more susceptible to disease.

....

Weight loss & detox secret:
Colon hydrotherapy[126] and regular enemas are two of the most important things you can do to maintain healthy bowels.

A healthy body at its ideal weight will be your reward.

....

When I began my fast during that memorable cleanse of 2002, my body started to detoxify. It happily threw off all the waste it could find through my skin and into my bloodstream, intestines, and kidneys. My body odor increased and I had terrible breath. My head throbbed and I felt really nauseated. But there was nothing in my stomach because I hadn't eaten for two days. I felt so bad that I almost fainted. My nose was running like a broken faucet. I was severely constipated and my skin was irritated and itchy.

As anyone would assume, I thought my agony was caused by what I was currently doing—namely, fasting. I began questioning my presence at the cleanse. I could not believe that I was actually paying money—and not a small amount—for this misery! Luckily, I was in the perfect environment and immediate help was at hand. Dr. Herbie Ross[127] came to my rescue. After I underwent a few of his chiropractic techniques, my nausea disappeared and my bowel began moving. An enema, followed by a colon hydrotherapy, brought great relief. I later learned that I had been facing what is generally known as a *healing crisis*—the first step and a great opportunity to heal both body and mind.

To help you avoid the misery I went through, I would like to share with you how you can perform a simple bowel cleanse at home in case you don't have access to a clinic that can perform a more thorough colon hydrotherapy. The bowel cleanse you could perform on your own is called an enema.

How to Self-Administer an Enema
SUPPLIES

- One reusable enema kit (bought online[128] or at any drugstore)
- Two liters (two quarts) of purified water (boiled tap water is fine) at room temperature
- Super greens, if available

PREPARATION

- Apply 1 teaspoon of green drink to one liter (one quart) water at room temperature and mix it well.
- Fill enema container with the water and the greens.

DIRECTIONS

- Follow instructions on enema kit. (Make sure a lubricant is included in the kit; if not, buy one yourself.)
- Perform enema in the bathroom. (Lock the door for uninterrupted privacy.)
- Lie down on your side, your back or get on your knees
- Take three deep breaths and relax—then insert the tube into the rectum and release its contents.
- During the release process, massage the belly from the lower left side up the rib cage to right side, then down.
- If you feel like going to the bathroom, breathe through it—the sensation will disappear soon.
- Keep massaging and go deep into the abdomen to support the release of feces. Keep massaging for 15–20 minutes, if possible.
- Release the contents by moving your bowel.
- Repeat whole process at least one more time until you feel that your colon is empty.
- Perform this procedure every day during the first week of your cleanse. Take a probiotic pill with friendly bacteria after your enema or one hour before your next "meal."

CLEANUP

- Clean and disinfect the equipment thoroughly.

Dramatic Signs of Healing: The Healing Crisis

The healing crisis happens when the body is getting stronger and cleaner during the cleansing process. When we stop eating, the body realizes the amazing opportunity for cleansing and begins dumping all stored toxins into the bloodstream, intestines, kidneys, skin, and lungs.

A healing crisis can be soft or harsh, and it can come regularly in the process of restoring health, which sometimes can last over a period of several years. Some people get headaches or joint pains, some people get diarrhea, back pain, or skin rashes. Whatever it is, welcome it, because it is a clear sign that your body is healing. Taking an enema or a hydrocolon therapy, going for a walk, taking a dry sauna, or soaking in the bathtub will provide instant relief. If uncomfortable conditions persist, consult with your naturopathic physician or your regular doctor if he or she is well versed in the process of cleansing.

•••
Weight loss & detox secret:
In a healthy body, pain during the cleanse can be a healer.

The healing crisis can actually be a sign of progress. It is an unavoidable step on the way to healing. In his *Doctor-Patient Handbook,* Dr. Bernard Jensen writes, "By allowing the healing crisis to run its course and continuing to support the body to cleanse itself, we can purge ourselves of the latent seeds of past disease and disorder…the body becomes determined to remove them! When this healing crisis passes, health returns, more vibrant and invulnerable than ever…. You earn this crisis through hard work. It comes through a sacrifice, giving up bad habits, taking a new path—cleaning up your act by replacing negative patterns with positive ones in your life, working within the laws of nature."
•••

Parasite Cleansing

Like most of us, I had learned in school about intestinal parasites. I believed only people in developing countries suffered from them and not me or others like me who lived in the industrialized world. I had no idea how wrong I was until day four of my 2002 cleanse, which I mentioned earlier. I had just taken an enema and gone to the bathroom. What I witnessed there blew my mind. In the toilet bowl, I saw a wealth of small and large creatures that had just come out of me. They were intestinal parasites eliminated by my body along with the bodily waste and toxins.[129]

•••
Weight loss & detox secret:
Detoxing helps eliminate parasites from your system.
•••

In my total shock I went for help and learned that my misery was caused by outside creatures such as yeast (*Candida Albicans*) and parasites, which were dying during the cleanse. They were being deprived of their nutrition and had to go. While vanishing, they eliminated their own waste, which of course added to my own misery.

After the cleanse I attended a retreat with David Wolfe, one of the foremost authorities on raw food and nutrition. During my stay there I was tested and diagnosed with four different types of parasites. It took me another six months of intense detox processes to rid myself of these parasites and bring my body back into balance. While at Wolfe's retreat, I made an additional amazing discovery.

I was introduced to the work of Richard Anderson[130] and discovered the "mucoid plaque" in my own body.

Encrusted Fecal Material

At the beginning of this chapter, you had the opportunity to see some pictures of disgusting encrusted fecal matter that was eliminated by people during intestinal cleanses. In his book, *Cleanse and Purify Thyself*, Anderson describes how he first learned about this plaque and how the elimination of it helped him journey away from terminal cancer into healing. He defines mucoid plaque as "the unhealthy accumulation of abnormal mucous matter on the walls of the intestines."

In volume one of the *Textbook of Gastroenterology*, we find this matter being described as a layer of mucin or glycoproteins. This mucin is made of 20 percent amino acids and 50 percent carbohydrates. Furthermore, it is "naturally and appropriately secreted by intestines as protection from acids and toxins."[131] Dr. J. Rainer Poley states, "This layer of mucus, when adhering closely to the mucosal surface, probably functions as a barrier to membrane digestion and most likely also to absorption…. Where, with increasing age, the mucus layer becomes more pronounced and widespread…it is hypothesized that the 'mucus barrier' interferes with membrane digestion and absorption."[132]

Through this layer, the body seems to protect itself from toxins, drugs, herbicides, pesticides, parasites, heavy metals, and acid-producing foods such as meat, dairy, and packaged foods. Unfortunately, the intestines cannot remove this layer alone. As a result, it grows bigger, thicker, and harder over time. Just as garbage attracts rats that come to eat, so does this matter become the home of a series of parasites and bacteria, which feed off the collective waste accumulated there.

As you look at it from the weight loss perspective, you need to consider removing this mucus layer, which can ensure that you lose unwanted weight—up to 40 pounds, according to Dr. Jensen—forever. Afterwards, if you change your lifestyle, adopt a less acidic diet, and continue to cleanse regularly, you can support your body to get back into balance without having to create that mucus ever again. If you are interested in removing this matter from your intestines, I recommend Richard Anderson's program.

Emotional Cleansing

During a detox process, we not only eliminate toxins from our physical bodies but we also purge mental and emotional garbage from our system. As a result, we can experience a whole host of emotions, from total happiness and serenity to anger, anxiety, and depression. Research shows that as we detoxify, we also shed the emotions we experienced while eating that particular food in the past. Through a cleanse, the reverse process can occur and we may relieve ourselves of these past emotions.

Dr. Otto Buchinger Sr., one of Germany's most famous fasting therapists, said, "Fasting is, without any doubt, the most effective biological method of treatment…. It is the 'operation without surgery.' While fasting, the patient improves his or her physical health and gains much. But he or she will have neglected the most important thing if the hunger for spiritual nourishment that manifests itself during fasting is not satisfied."

••

Weight loss & detox secret:
Detox is your opportunity to eliminate emotional garbage from your system.

Be very gentle and patient with yourself through this process and allow that gift of releasing negative emotions to unfold. To support yourself in this process I highly recommend going for a walk in nature, daily meditation, prayer or contemplation, and journaling.

••

An alternative to psychotherapy, journaling costs nothing and is an extraordinary tool for self-discovery. Your journal can become your most intimate friend that is always available to you when other people are not. In your journal you can pour out your heart and soul, and share your greatest fears, anger, frustrations, and desires without negative consequences or fear of criticism. If done regularly, your journal can keep you on your life's course. It can become your greatest companion in your spiritual path, bringing you clarity about your own identity, your life goals, and whether you are aligned with them or not.

The Elimination Diet

According to Dr. Elson Haas, author of *The False Fat Diet*[10] and *The New Detox Diet*, an estimated 80 to 90 percent of overweight people have food allergies and food cravings. Correcting these helps return the body to normal weight and health. Food reactions and cravings are triggered by the inability of the body to completely digest the foods we eat. This is due to the poor quality of foods in our society, age, stress, unhealthy eating habits, or lack of proper enzymes. As a result, the body doesn't recognize the ingested food; it decides that the food is an enemy, much like bacteria, viruses, or parasites, and treats it as such. When these partially digested foods enter the bloodstream, the immune system attacks them. The results are often metabolic disorders such as overweight, obesity, fatigue, severe hormone imbalances including immune disorders, bloating and swelling (called "false fat" by Dr. Haas), water retention, and food cravings.

What can you expect from the elimination diet?

Research shows that you can lose significant weight—**up to 5 pounds per week** (both false fat and real—adipose—fat)—during a detox program by:

1. **Identifying and eliminating** reactive foods from your diet for a couple of weeks until your body regenerates itself
2. **Cleansing and detoxifying** your body, which will help heal your food cravings and food addictions
3. **Slowly reintroducing formerly reactive foods** after a couple of weeks of cleansing and detox
4. **Replenishing** your body with health-building foods and supplements, which will help create health at the cellular level.

The Elimination Process

According to Dr. Ellen Cutler, the most highly reactive foods are milk, sugar, peanuts, corn, and eggs. As a (typically allergic) reaction to these foods, your body stores lots of water (false fat) in your body. To lose that false fat you need to desensitize yourself from those foods by:

- Identifying the foods you are reactive to
- Eliminating these foods from your diet one-by-one for the next two weeks while your body heals
- Cleansing and detoxifying your body through (preferably) a juice cleanse
- Replenishing your body with healthy foods and supplements (digestive enzymes, vitamins, and minerals)
- Slowly reintroducing the formerly reactive foods
- Getting back to your regular routine and incorporating healthier habits to support your weight loss process

How to Identify Reactive Foods

To find out which foods you are reactive to, **stop eating wheat, milk and dairy products, sugar (including fruit), peanuts, corn, and eggs for the next two weeks.** Do not worry, you will be able to eat these foods again, this process is temporary. When you stop eating foods you are reactive to, your body will begin to regenerate and heal. In the meantime, pay particular attention to any cravings you have for any of these foods. That is a sign you are reactive to that food.

To make this process faster and more complete, I would highly recommend consulting your physician and asking him or her to refer you to a clinic where you can do an allergy test. The results of that test may give you an entire list of foods you should be avoiding until you have performed a thorough cleanse and fast and you can reintroduce them into your diet.

Motivation Is Everything

I know from personal experience that going through such an intensive restructuring of your life and habits can be disturbing and difficult. Yet being disturbed and unhappy with the current situation is what makes change possible in the first place. As long as you make your current state OK you will not change and you risk becoming more and more unhappy until the day comes when you have had it.

Make today that day and give yourself the gift of freedom from addictions and overweight forever by deciding to stick to this detox and elimination process for the next two weeks.

How to Eliminate Reactive Foods

For the next two weeks, stop eating wheat-based breads and pasta, rice, potatoes, processed and packaged goods including cookies, sugar of any kind including sweet fruits and candy, eggs, and milk and dairy products such as ice cream.

You can eat plenty of organic salads, vegetables (avoid carrots since they are high in sugar), legumes, lean meat and fish of organic provenance as well as tofu if you are vegetarian. However, there are people who may be allergic to soy as well (tofu is made of soy). Find out by elimination if you are reactive to it. And no alcohol for two weeks, please.

To support you through this process and make it easier to go through it, do the following:

- **Alkalize the body.** Drink one gallon (four liters) of green drink per day.[65]
- **Eat three large meals** (salads and steamed vegetables mostly) **and two snacks per day.** As a snack you can eat bell peppers, tomatoes, cucumbers, and soaked nuts and seeds. Appendix 3 of this book contains sample menus for during this time. However, you can get more ideas about what to eat in Shelley Redford Young's books[2] *Back to the House of Health* and *Back to the House of Health 2.*
- **Exercise daily.** Make sure you continue to perform your daily exercise. This will not only help you detoxify but will keep you away from your refrigerator and prevent you from fantasizing about food.
- **Do visualization exercises.** Support yourself through daily visualizations of your beautiful body and dream wardrobe.

- **Get a support system.** Before embarking on the elimination diet, be sure to make a public statement about it to your friends, so you commit yourself openly to your new lifestyle and ideal weight. In addition, enlist the support of your family and friends. Ideally and most importantly get yourself a buddy who will do this with you.

One more thing during the elimination phase: Massive supplementation

As your body begins eliminating fat and stored toxins, it needs to replenish itself. In an ideal world, we would get all of our nutrients from food and would not need any supplements. However, we do not live in such a world.

- Take daily supplements to help give your body what it cannot receive through food. Vitamins and minerals can be taken separately or in one pill. It is very important, however, to know that some vitamins are water-soluble and others need oil to be absorbed. Supplements that need oil for absorption must be taken with a meal that contains some fats. In Step 1 of this book you can find a detailed description of the most important supplements and how they contribute to your health.
- Take probiotics daily to ensure the health of your intestines with friendly bacteria.
- Take digestive enzymes with each meal to support your digestion.
- Take essential fatty acids. They help you heal and replenish your body at the same time that they keep you satiated and stop you from hunting for foods and giving in to your cravings. Make sure you take at least three tablespoons of essential fatty acids such as primrose oil, flaxseed oil or—my preference—Udo's Choice Oil Blend, which you can get at any health food store or online.

The Juice Cleanse

The juice cleanse is a much stronger detoxification process than the elimination diet or the smoothie cleanse. However, it has the fastest and the deepest results. One of the most popular fasts I know and recommend is the Master Cleanse (go online for more information). However, for best results and if you have never done such a cleanse, join a support group or go to a fasting retreat. Making this investment of time and money will be the best thing you have ever done for yourself.

Stop Eating Regular Food

The human body doesn't like sudden changes. Therefore, a juice cleanse should begin with eating less and less until the stomach switches into detoxification mode, where we are not hungry anymore. This is the least known point about fasting. Most people do not cleanse because they are afraid of walking around hungry. And I totally agree with that. Nobody likes to be hungry. It is against nature and our survival instinct. However, during a proper cleanse we don't want to eat.

Weight loss secret:
During a juice cleanse you are not hungry.

To get to the fasting point, we need to be very kind to ourselves and allow for a gradual reduction in the amount of food we take in. The beauty about the process is that when we decrease our food intake, our organs begin eliminating waste immediately. This gives us the benefit of cleansing even while we are still ingesting small amounts of food. The energy previously used for digestion is now being used to detoxify and eliminate waste. On the last day before the cleanse begins, eat only green salads or fresh organic fruits.

During this phase, toxic accumulations are released from the alimentary canal, and poisonous overloads are expelled from the cells, liver, kidneys, blood, and lungs as well as the lymphatic system. This course of action enables the body to rid itself of excess weight (2–5 pounds, or 1–3 kg, per week), return to its natural balance, and heal itself.

Nutritional Intake

During a juice-based cleanse, you will consume freshly squeezed juices three times a day. The juices can be made from wheat grass, which you can buy or grow yourself from sprouted grains, as well as dark green vegetables or legumes. These juices alkalize the body and provide plenty of vitamins, essential amino and fatty acids, minerals, probiotics, antioxidants, and digestive enzymes to ensure optimal functioning. The essential fatty acids (Omega 3 and Omega 6) are crucial. As an outside source of Omega 3 and Omega 6, I would highly recommend taking one of the best blends of essential oils on the market today—Udo's Choice Oil Blend.

This is the most effective way to cleanse, and because you will not be eating any solid foods, the body no longer has to negotiate through a poor digestive process. Instead, it uses its energy to eliminate many years of accumulated waste and rid itself of food reactions and sensitivities.

A short juice fast of one or three days is safe for most healthy people as long as you drink enough fluids to help your body eliminate fat and toxins. Trust me, your ancestors fasted regularly. However, some people shouldn't fast. These include pregnant or breastfeeding women and people with heart problems, diabetes, cancer, or other chronic illnesses, or people who are underweight.

Juice Cleanse Guidelines

- **Choose the right time.** If you have never done a juice fast, choose a weekend so you have enough opportunities to relax, stay away from people who are eating, and enjoy the process.
- **Decide how many days to cleanse.** Remember that your body is actually fasting every time you sleep. That's why we call the first meal of the day *break-fast*. You can take advantage of that by continuing the fast during the day. You can do the cleanse for one to three days. If you want to fast longer than three days, I would highly recommend doing it on a specialized retreat such as the ones offered by David Wolfe or Gabriel Cousens.
- **The juice cleanse process:**
  a. Throughout the day consume juice, preferably self-made, instead of regular food.
  b. The juice, which I recommend you make yourself using a juicer or a blender, can be made of fresh organic vegetables or fruits.
  c. Dilute the juice with water to avoid the feeling of hunger. I would highly recommend drinking more vegetable juice than fruit juice, because fruit juice has too much sugar. Avoid high-sugar fruits such as bananas.
  d. Consume one gallon (four liters) of green drink daily during the juice cleanse.
  e. Drink plenty of water to flush out released toxins.
  f. To each of your juice meals add one tablespoon of essential fats, such as Udo's Oil.
- **Healing crisis.** During the cleanse you can expect to feel strange. As your body heals by expelling toxins you may experience headaches, lightheadedness, dizziness, fatigue, irritability, or severe cravings. Drinking more water at room temperature, taking an enema, going to a sauna, working out, or taking a hot bath are all ways to mitigate these discomforts, which disappear as the body becomes healthier. If the discomfort doesn't stop, consult with your physician, who has hopefully been trained on fasting and cleansing.
- **Supplements and medications.** Continue to take your enzymes, probiotics, vitamins, and minerals. In Step 1 of this book you can find a detailed description of supplements. Make sure you continue to take any medications you have been prescribed by your physician.
- **Food cravings.** As you eliminate the reactive foods from your system through cleansing and detoxifying, the body resists at first and you

may experience discomfort similar to that of a smoker in withdrawal. Within less than 48 hours, the reactive foods will leave the body and you will begin to heal. The food cravings will subside and a natural weight loss process continues. Taking supplements will help you through this process.

- **Walking and breathing.** During your juice cleanse make sure you continue to walk daily and breathe consciously on a regular basis. Both help release food cravings, detoxify, and make you feel better and more energized.

- **Emotional cleansing.** During this time, you will probably experience a whole host of emotions, from total happiness and serenity to anger, anxiety, and possibly even depression. Scientists tell us that emotions we experienced while eating foods in the past are stored in the body and that as we detoxify, we shed the emotions that are associated with those particular foods. Thus, be very gentle and patient with yourself through this process. Give yourself the gift of releasing negative emotions forever. To support you in this process I highly recommend journaling and meditation.

Breaking the Cleanse

This section should actually come at the very beginning of this chapter, for it is more important than anything else I've written here.

••

Weight loss & detox secret:
Breaking the detox is more important than the detox itself.

How you break your detox determines whether you will gain more weight or continue on your path to your ideal body. Breaking a cleanse in the proper way ensures long-lasting success and establishes sustainable eating and lifestyle habits, as well as permanent weight loss and healing.

••

During the cleanse, your body has become accustomed to eating in a healthy way or not eating at all if you did a juice cleanse. So be gentle and loving with yourself.

To properly break the detox, follow a few simple rules:

1. **If you did a juice cleanse, begin by eating a soaked dried prune or a little bit of apple the first morning after your cleanse.** Eat

very slowly and eat very little. During the juice cleanse your body became accustomed to not eating. Remember that the body doesn't like sudden changes. So be gentle and loving to yourself. Listen to your body very carefully, not only through your eyes but through your stomach. It will tell you when it has had enough food. You will notice that satiation comes very quickly. This is your chance to set habits for losing weight and keeping it off permanently. Take advantage of this opportunity. It is true personal power.

2. **Eat organically grown raw, fresh foods for the same amount of days as you fasted.**[135] If you did the juice or smoothie cleanse for eight days, eat raw foods for the following eight days. If possible, blend all food for the first three days to make it easy for your system to begin digesting again. Follow the Post-Cleanse menu in Appendix 3.

3. **Chew your food very thoroughly** (30 times) before swallowing it. Add new food to the mouth only after the previous bite has reached the stomach. That will ensure proper digestion.

4. **Sit down while eating.** Do not watch TV, do not read anything, and do not talk while eating. This allows you to enjoy every bite, and food will taste better than ever before.

5. **Exercise every day.** You can walk, run, swim, bike—anything that gives you pleasure. If you do this for six months you will never stop for the rest of your life, because regular exercise will have become part of your daily routine just like brushing your teeth or taking a shower.

6. **Continue to expand your knowledge about nutrition, as well as your knowledge of emotional and spiritual mastery.**

7. **Commit to a higher standard in life by adding new habits to your daily agenda.** You probably never leave home without performing your daily hygiene. You need to make the same commitment to your newly gained body and sense of self. Begin taking an enema at least once a week and cleansing twice a year, in addition to going to a sauna each week and eating mostly raw fresh salads and vegetables.

8. **Share this knowledge and experience only with people who are supportive.** Be selective about the people with whom you share this information until you are strong enough to encounter those who might, in the beginning, question your new lifestyle. Like a newly planted tree that needs to be watered and cared for until it is big enough to give shade to others, your new sense of self and lifestyle habits must be protected. Once you are strong enough, you can help other people in your environment who badly need your support.

9. **Most of all, reward yourself** (but not with food) **and celebrate** with something you will remember forever. Congratulate yourself on your success and have fun with your new life!

How to Reintroduce Formerly Reactive Foods

During the process of slowly introducing formerly reactive foods back into your diet, you need to know that the more cravings you had for a certain food (withdrawal symptoms), the more allergic your body was to that food and therefore the more careful you have to be before you can reintroduce it into your diet. If you are still craving a certain food do not eat it yet; continue to keep it out of your diet. For instance, if you crave ice cream you are most likely allergic to milk or eggs or both. Therefore, eat a little bit of ice cream made of soy and continue the alkalization of your body and the elimination process. Your cravings should go away in less than a week. Then you can begin reintroducing those particular foods one by one and seeing how you feel.

Begin reintroducing foods very slowly and one at a time. You have all the time in the world! Choose one food you would like to reintroduce and add it to one meal per day. Watch what happens. If you begin to feel bloated, pass gas, have cravings, or in the worst case gain weight again, you are most likely still allergic to that food and your body has begun storing false fat to protect itself from it. Since you are reintroducing the reactive foods one at a time, you will be able to identify which food is causing the discomfort. Eliminate that food for an additional 10 days before you attempt to reintroduce it again so your body will be able to continue healing the reactivity.

Celebrate

Recognize the fact that this juice cleanse has renewed your motivation to take care of yourself and to live well and has given you a new appreciation for your body, food, and hunger. Celebrate your achievement with something you will remember forever. Congratulate yourself on your detoxification success and have fun with your new insights and improved quality of life!

Physical Pain and Other Challenges

Physical pain can be an obstacle to losing weight. If our body is uncomfortable, we tend to forget everything else and focus entirely on our aches and pains. We may move less and eat unconsciously, including larger quantities and unhealthy things, just to compensate for the pain we feel. Under all circumstances, I recommend consulting a physician to address and heal chronic and acute pain before embarking on any lifestyle change including a detox program.

As you detoxify you have the opportunity to reduce your physical pain, if you have any. If your pain gets worse make sure to consult your physician.

Chiropractic, Acupuncture, and Energy Psychology

Under normal conditions and more often than not, we may be in pain because our body's structure is out of line. Nerves get compressed and create pain. Visiting a chiropractor on a regular basis will ensure that your skeleton and muscles are in line and supporting you optimally. Acupuncture and kinesiology are two other powerful techniques that can get you out of pain and bring about healing through noninvasive, nonchemical means. Fred Gallo is one expert I admire and highly recommend for his ability to heal emotional and physical pain through a technique he developed called "energy psychology."[136] We can easily learn these simple techniques to alleviate several kinds of body pain including migraines and simple headaches, fatigue, heartburn, and back pain, especially during a cleanse process.

Another important component in the relief of physical pain is regular exercise such as yoga, biking, swimming, walking, or hiking. Of course, all such activities should be done intelligently and under regular expert supervision when needed.

In addition, note that eating and metabolic disorders, as well as immune deficiencies, can all lead to physical pain of various kinds.

Addressing Immune Deficiencies, Eating, and Metabolic Disorders through Cleansing

The old-fashioned and very unfair view is that people with eating disorders such as compulsive eating, anorexia, and bulimia (mostly women and girls, who count for 95 percent of all cases) have troubled psyches and need to be treated with Prozac-type drugs. While I believe that a certain percentage of people do need drugs to treat their chemical imbalances, researchers and experienced doctors maintain that a large percentage of patients can be healed through cleansing and by addressing food reactions[14] along with emotional and spiritual issues.[137]

Food reactions and the inability to properly digest our food lead to significant metabolic disorders in the body. As ingested and unidentified food macromolecules leak into the blood vessels, the immune system becomes stimulated and begins fighting. At this point, the entire endocrine (hormonal) system is activated and eventually becomes exhausted. This imbalance may manifest in the form of disturbed function of the thyroid and adrenal glands. This, in turn, can lead to the inability of the body to properly burn fat, which leads to weight gain. Insulin levels also may get out of balance, in which case food energy gets converted into fat and may contribute to low blood sugar levels or hypoglycemia.

Other metabolic disorders caused by food reactions can lead to low serotonin levels and then manifest as bad moods, depression, lack of energy, migraines, insomnia, and other physical and mental disturbances. These imbalances may lead to pain in various areas of the body but can still be healed by cleansing and adhering to an alkaline lifestyle through green drinks and alkalizing foods, as well as taking proper enzymes under the guidance of an expert. In her book The Food Allergy Cure: A New Solution to Food Cravings, Obesity, Depression, Headaches, Arthritis, and Fatigue, Dr. Ellen Cutler shows how enzymes and proper nutrition can bring about quick healing and permanent weight loss.

Environmental Factors Outside the Body

Unfortunately it is not enough to cleanse the body, eat healthily, exercise daily, and take control of our emotional life. We also have to take into consideration and stop the host of chemical toxins found in polluted air, drinking water, dry cleaning, shampoo, toothpaste, deodorants, creams, and lotions. We also need to be alert to contaminated foods that include chemical toxins, preservatives, herbicides, pesticides, irradiation, bacteria, and viruses. All of these elements undermine our well-being and keep us overweight.

We need to become more critical, ask more questions, and develop the habit of reading the labels not only on food but also on shampoo, deodorant, and toothpaste. We need to reduce the risk of taking in chemicals from dry cleaning and make sure we live and work in an environment that provides clean air and proper water. By purchasing organic foods, we not only support our own health but also the environment and those farmers who are aligned with natural cycles and are currently struggling to survive.

Healing Lifestyle Addictions through Cleansing

Food Addictions

As stated before, most food addictions can be addressed through cleansing and detoxification. Developing awareness, cleansing, fasting, and supplementing with enzymes can create a healthy environment free of cravings. Through a detox process, the body can come back into balance and help us receive the necessary nutrients to rid us of unhealthy food addictions.

Smoking, Alcohol, and Drugs

It is widely accepted that an addiction to smoking, alcohol, or recreational drugs is likely to kill us. A detox process is the best step in avoiding this fate. In addition, I would like to emphasize that healing these addictions happens the same way we heal food addictions—not by sheer force but by creating awareness and asking ourselves who is actually the master of our lives. Are we in control, or are our addictions controlling us? We can get professional help and train ourselves to observe the cues that lead us to those addictions. Next time you want to give in to your addiction, take a moment and ask yourself if this is really who you are and how you want to live. At the cue, replace the disempowering activity with something that gives you pleasure without harming you. Celebrate every time you manage to succeed, and stop beating yourself up when you relapse. Instead, start anew knowing that every moment is a new beginning.

TV Addiction

As mentioned before, statistics show that in the industrialized world we lack sleep but watch too much TV. It is fascinating how often we seem to prefer watching other people living their lives rather than having meaningful lives of our own. We seem to believe what the media and advertising tell us even though we are constantly being told that we are not cool enough until we eat or drink this, or that we don't smell good enough until we buy that deodorant, or that our hair or skin don't look good until we put this or that on and so on.

As you detoxify your body, think about the negative messages that tell us what we should be thinking or doing. Ask yourself if this is how you want to live. If not, change it. Do what you want and begin advertising in your own head the thoughts that are most important to you. Remember that you are the only person thinking in your head. Do not allow other people to change that. You will be amazed at the results.

During your cleanse, reduce the amount of time you watch TV, and you will see how that will free up a major source of time, which you can use to pamper yourself, connect with your loved ones, or serve your community.

Mental, Emotional, and Spiritual Environment

If we live a life of emotional disturbances, we become victims of outside forces such as social conditioning, job dissatisfaction, unhealthy relationships, bad habits, financial worries, and other stress factors that can color how we feel and think about our lives. It is extremely important to learn the skills that allow us to fulfill our life's mission and goals without sacrificing our boundaries.

During your cleanse you have an extraordinary opportunity to address all of your mental and emotional issues that come up. You can do this by getting professional help, practicing meditation, attending self-growth seminars, joining a self-help group, reading books, and listening to tapes that help you grow spiritually and emotionally. It is a beautiful journey to the core of who you are, to the beautiful person that you are. Begin that journey today. It is the first step of the rest of your life.

ON CLEANSING AND DETOXIFICATION:
SECRETS TO REMEMBER

1. **Cleansing and detox is your ticket to permanent weight loss, health, and vitality.** Do it twice a year, and your allergies, fatigue, headaches, insomnia, constipation, and other diet-related ailments will go away.
2. **Make sure your body is alkaline** going into the cleanse.
3. **Pick a cleanse that fits your lifestyle and will be easy for you to do.** You can choose between a juice cleanse, a smoothie cleanse, and an elimination diet. Your body will thank you a thousandfold. If you can afford it, make cleansing a cause for celebration and fun by going to a retreat to do it so you get all the support you need from people who are committed to your health and vitality.
4. **During the cleanse,** superhydrate, alkalize, replenish with supplements, exercise, take enemas, get massages, go to a sauna, write in a journal, and meditate.
5. **Beware of healing crisis.** If you have a headache or feel bad during cleansing, see it as a good sign. Drink plenty of water, take an enema, draw a bath, and go for a walk. If pain persists more than two days, consult with your physician.
6. **Breaking the cleanse is more important than cleansing itself.** How you break the cleanse determines whether you lose weight for good or gain more weight than you had before. So carefully follow the guidelines for reentry.
7. **After the cleanse:**
   a. **Stop the pollution.** Begin reading labels, and do not put anything into the body that contains ingredients that are incomprehensible. This includes the chemical additives found in food and personal hygiene products such as creams, deodorants, and shampoos. Avoid foods that are chemically preserved, contaminated with growth hormones, irradiated, or likely to contain toxic chemicals, fungus, mold, or bacteria. Whenever possible, avoid meat, dairy, alcohol, caffeine, soft drinks, and processed foods, which create an acidic state in the body.
   b. **Superhydrate your body.** It is very important to drink enough water during the day in addition to eating water-rich foods. The normal adult should consume eight large glasses of water or three liters (three-quarters of a gallon) per day. However, for every 25 pounds (12 kg) of excess weight, we need to drink an extra glass of water.

c. **Consume alkalizing food and drink.** Eat live foods like leafy green vegetables, such as broccoli, kale, and spinach, and low-sugar fruits. These highly biologically active foods ensure alkalinity and combat fungus, molds, parasites, and bacteria. They create the foundation for the body to lose weight fast and keep it off easily. Green foods are powerful because they're loaded with healthy phytonutrients (which combat fungus), essential amino acids (building blocks of cells), enzymes (essential in breaking down, digesting, and absorbing nutrients from foods), antioxidants (a buffer from free radicals, which create acidity), vitamins (which facilitate and process chemical reactions), and minerals (which repair, regenerate, and maintain the proper electrical balance).

d. **Consume green drinks.** I recommend drinking one gallon (four liters) of green drink per day.

e. **Take essential fatty acids.** Essential fatty acids help build cell membranes, aid in the production of hormones, support the body in buffering and neutralizing acids, and raise metabolism. Take three tablespoons of essential fatty acids (flaxseed oil, avocado oil, primrose oil, or extra-virgin olive oil) per day.

f. **Get protein from organic sources.** The human body needs protein, also called essential amino acids, as the basic building blocks of cells. However, we don't have to consume heavily contaminated meats in large qualities to get the protein we need. Other sources of protein are broccoli, which contains 45 percent protein, or wheat grass, which contains all of the essential amino acids our bodies need. If you must consume protein of animal origin, make sure it is organic.

8. **Continue to conserve energy in these ways to lose weight and to heal:**

   a. **Eat moderately.** There is no better way to lose weight than by eating less food. Practicing portion control, eating less, and not eating between meals helps cleanse the body.

   b. **Combine foods properly.** By eating simple live foods and combining them properly, we make it easy for the body to digest and to use the leftover energy for elimination and detoxification purposes. Decide before each meal if you're going to have a protein-based or a carbohydrate-based meal. Then, leave out the one food you decided against and add salad and vegetables to your meal in a ratio of 70 percent veggies to 30 percent for the rest.

   c. **Chew properly,** taking the next bite only after swallowing what you currently have in your mouth.

    d. **Keep warm.** During colder months in colder climates, dress warmly, stay out of drafts, and keep the head and feet warm and comfortable at all times to save energy.

    e. **Don't drink water during meals.** Drinking anything during a meal dilutes the gastric secretion and leads to a longer digestion process, which requires the body to dispense even more energy to digest the food. This is energy that you could and should be using to lose weight.

9. **Celebrate eating.** To lose weight we need to make eating a true celebration. We can do this through eating consciously, enjoying every single bite, and maximizing the experience of taste in the mouth.

10. **Take supplements.** Complement—I prefer the word *complement* to *supplement*—healthy foods with additional antioxidants, enzymes, vitamins, minerals, and fiber.

11. **Get enough rest.** If possible, go to bed before 10:00 at night and get up before 6:00 in the morning. Do not eat anything two hours before bedtime to allow the body to use up the energy of the ingested food.

12. **Exercise.** Brisk walking for 30 minutes a day, rebounding, swimming, biking, and hiking are all effective ways to work out. Try to do your exercise outdoors to take advantage of the natural light that stimulates the production of happy hormones and strengthens the immune system.

13. **Cultivate happy thoughts and healthy friendships**. We can eat the best foods but if we are unhappy we create the same toxic and acidic environment that makes the body hold on to fat. Becoming the master of our thoughts is just as important as eating the right foods and exercising. Become very selective about what you put into your brain, and make sure you surround yourself with people who support you and your new healthy lifestyle.

14. **Apply the power of intention**. Your intention to be slim and healthy will ensure that the universe helps you stay on your path.

15. **Most of all: Celebrate your life and make it a masterpiece!**

PART 2

Why We Act As We Do

Step 4: Living a Life of Meaning

*"Most people live, whether physically, intellectually or morally,
in a very restricted circle of their potential being.
They make use of a very small portion of their possible consciousness. . . .
We all have reservoirs of life to draw upon, of which we don't dream."*
—William James

Did you know?

According to scientific research,[138] **most people in our society die at 9 o'clock on Monday morning.**

Being able to die en masse at the same time is quite an "accomplishment" given the fact that no other being on this planet has a notion of time other than humans.

What does this sad statistic tell us? It tells us that we have become victims of mindless thinking and that we seem to accept our social conditioning without reflection. As a society, we have become accustomed to media manipulation with respect to food, drink, fashion, appearance, and lifestyle. We seem to no longer think for ourselves but rather comply with the requests posed to us from the outside world. It seems that many of us no longer control our own aspirations in life. We have stopped asking critical questions about the messages put out by TV, radio, magazines, and newspapers. We have ceased to find out whether the messages are true or not, and we don't seem to question the role they play in our lives. Do they help us achieve *our* goals in life—or do *we* help *them* achieve their goals with our mindless support? Before we know it, we have become like Pavlov's dog, a collection of conditioned responses. We have become victims of what Deepak Chopra calls the "psychopathology of the average." It seems that as a society we have given up our dreams.

Yet you would not be reading this book if that were completely true for you.

You know that life wants you to live it to the fullest. Life wants you to be *alive* by being who you really are—a magnificent and unique part of nature. Nature doesn't want you to be manipulated by the media and driven by the financial gains of a few to the detriment of many. The ominous *They* do not care if we suppress our emotions and desire for happiness by numbing our senses with junk food, alcohol, cigarettes, drugs, or material things that don't bring us the happiness we seek. These external factors only thwart our true desire for happiness. Without practicing critical thinking, we become accustomed to the belief that external things bring us meaning and fulfillment.

If you are reading this book, you are looking to get more out of life because you know you deserve it. If you are unhappy about your weight, health, job, relationships, or financial situation then you may recognize that each crisis in your life is a wake-up call—an amazing opportunity to grow beyond yourself. The only question is how.

As an inspiration, I would like to share with you what the greatest physicist of all times, Albert Einstein, had to say about who we are, where we come from, and how we can break free from the prison of the mind so we can live a life of meaning:

> *"A human being is part of a whole, called by us the "Universe", a part limited in time and space. He experiences himself, his thoughts and feelings as something separated from the rest – a kind of optical delusion of his consciousness. This delusion is a kind of prison for us, restricting us to our personal desires and to affection for a few persons nearest to us. Our task must be to free ourselves from this prison by widening our circles of compassion to embrace all living creatures and the whole of nature in its beauty."*[139]

Breaking free from the prison of the mind begins with the realization that we are in prison indeed. The next step is to begin to love yourself.

What is in your life today that used to be only a dream? Think about it—what have you already manifested in your life? Is it a relationship, a car, a piece of clothing, a house, a job, a child, a garden, a vacation, a book? What is it and what did you do to invite these things or people into your life? Whether or not you know consciously what you did to succeed, it was your recipe for success. This is what William James calls accessing the "reservoirs of life" in the above quote. It was your dream that inspired you to do whatever it took to make it happen. When we are inspired we are "in spirit"—in line with the power of the universe. We are then living a life of meaning. This is the antidote to failure.

• •

Weight loss secret:
Love your life as if it were the most precious gift you have ever received.

If you love your life then you give it meaning. Living a life of meaning is the most important driving force in your life. It gives you joy and a sense of fulfillment. It makes you happy no matter how fat or thin you are, how shallow or deep your bank account is, and how many material things you have acquired.

More importantly, if you truly love your life you will live a life of meaning and you will be able to enjoy everything you ever wanted. It is the law of the universe.

• •

Furthermore, when we live a life of meaning, we recognize that there is no true failure but rather a chance to learn and evolve to the next level. Each crisis is an opportunity for awakening. At each demarcation point, we can see if we are *fooling* ourselves or not. We develop the ability to see through the web of illusions. We have the opportunity to realize that in our quest for happiness and fulfillment we keep acquiring the *symbols* of love and happiness and not the real thing. We can see that we often mistake the map for the territory—and we can stop doing this.

True happiness comes from within, not from without.

Stephen Hawking, one of the most brilliant theoretical physicists and black hole experts, became world-famous with the international bestseller *A Brief History of Time*, but this is not the only thing that attracted the world's attention. What makes Hawking so appealing to millions of people is his zest for life. He has an extraordinary sense of humor despite his terrible disease (ALS, or motor neurone disease), which has taken away his ability to speak and rendered him practically immobile. People with this illness usually die within a couple of years after the diagnosis, but Hawking's love for life and positive attitude kept him alive and helped him be a role model for all of us. Professor Hawking, who was born 300 years to the day after the death of Galileo, holds the same research position as the famous physicist Isaac Newton. On his website, Hawking writes, "If I were going to die anyway, [my disease] might as well do some good. But I didn't die. In fact, although there was a cloud hanging over my future, I found, to my surprise, that I was enjoying life in the present more than before."[140] Hawking lives a life of meaning.

Do you live a life of meaning? Are you living in alignment with your dreams? If you are, then I'm sure you want more, otherwise you would be a rare human being. If you are not, then begin to make your goals a reality soon, because this is why you're here. Life is about creation and manifestation of your innermost talents and desires, your divine uniqueness. Deep down, we all want to live a life of meaning. This is where true fulfillment comes from. We all want to have the *feeling* that our lives are worthwhile, that we are making a difference in the world. If we don't, we end up in one crisis after another. The most familiar one is the midlife crisis. At midlife, most of us have acquired, or not, what we thought we wanted as adolescents—a career, spouse, family—and we begin to wonder what's next. But how do we know when a midlife crisis has begun? Good question. Sometimes a collection of things occur. Sometimes the turning point is marked by specific events that we remember and find remarkable. Such was one of my first wake-up calls.

My Own Wake-Up Call

My own midlife crisis began several years ago, and I spent the first years of it in confusion, spending about a third of my time reading books, listening to tapes, studying, and going to seminars simply because I didn't know how else to cope. One day, a well-meaning friend—who is known to be clairvoyant and works as a top-level life and image consultant to presidents and heads of state—managed to "take my heart apart" through her predictions about my future. My husband and I had met her through her company that had gone belly-up in the dot-com bust. As a result, her second marriage had also fallen apart. With the best of intentions, she wanted to prevent my going the same route. She predicted that my husband, just like her ex, would soon enter his Uranus period (in the astrological sense), find a younger woman, and leave the family. She advised me to change my personal fashion style, which consisted of beautiful Bavarian/Austrian clothing, buy some modern, more youthful clothes, and cut my hair short to look younger. She basically recommended I change my entire image so my husband wouldn't leave the family.

Can you imagine hearing this from someone out of the blue? A computer scientist, I don't necessarily believe in astrology. So at the beginning, I was in total denial, and I was furious. How dare she tell me something like this? It took me two weeks to admit how much I was hurting and how afraid I was that something like that could truly happen to me. While telling the story on the phone to a friend, I could not help but break down in tears. I was not yet ready to admit to myself that I was actually quite unhappy with my life. Yes, on the surface I was a successful person. I was living a life of abundance and was very grateful for it. But I was 38 pounds (19 kg) overweight, I had many health challenges, I was a workaholic, and I had lost the ability to acknowledge the many little things in my life that could have given me joy and happiness. I had become a pretty unhappy business-oriented person. My femininity, my laughter, and my joy had long since disappeared. I had stopped "singing and dancing," as the Native Americans say.

At a very deep level, my well-meaning friend had given me a different way of looking at my life. She introduced doubt that my life was perfect. While I was not yet ready to face my challenges, I went out and purchased a new wardrobe. I took a picture of Lady Di along to my hairdresser, who cut my hair from shoulder length to short. In my new outfit, with my new haircut, I already felt I was moving in the right direction. But my fat was still hanging onto me, and true fulfillment and happiness had not come along with the shopping spree or the new hairdo. Subconsciously I felt that something was missing in my life, but I didn't know what. In fact, at that point, I was not able to see, let alone admit, that anything could have been wrong. I was caught up in my own social conditioning: at the superficial level, I was doing fine, there was nothing to complain about. I believed that gaining weight was a normal part of aging. The same was true for the various health challenges I faced.

However, as always, when the student is ready, the teacher appears. In my case it was a Tony Robbins seminar called "Unleash the Power Within," which was held in Frankfurt am Main, Germany. The seminar was not simply a wake-up call—it was a major if not *the most important* tipping point in my life.

The seminar began on a Friday afternoon, and by 11:00 that night everybody was ready to perform Tony's signature "fire walk," where seminar participants walk across hot coals as a symbol of their newfound courage and commitment to unleash the power within themselves. It seemed every one of the more than 7,000 people present was ready to walk on hot coals—except me. They couldn't wait to walk toward the virtual realization of their dreams that "waited" for them at the end of the path of coals. But I could not do it.

Following Tony's advice, I simply watched my mind as I stood in front of the hot coals. I was amazed at what was going on in there. In the darkness of the night my husband, who was also attending, and I had lost each other. Regardless, in my head I was bitching about him "deserting" me when I needed him most. In addition, I was afraid that my expensive suit was going to be damaged by the fire and that my purse was going to be stolen while I walked. The truth was that I was scared to death.

What frightened me most was the fact that the person who was scared was *not* I. I did not know that woman. She was certainly not me, Mariana, who would jump at any opportunity to extend herself and learn something new. The Mariana I knew would sing and dance and gladly try out the wildest things. But now I felt confused and torn apart. I didn't know what else to do so I waited for a while and watched hundreds and hundreds of people walk on hot coals. Most of all, I witnessed their souls exalt at the beauty of being alive and free of fear. Everybody celebrated and was in an altered state of consciousness—except me.

I was feeling devastated, sad, and completely lost. I did not know what else to do, so I went to the hotel room and began to cry, and then cried some more. I felt sorry for myself and felt like a failure. I could not believe what had just happened, and I didn't know how to get out of it. I had come to a major turning point in my life. The person who pretended to be me was not in fact who I really was. Not anymore. Something very significant had happened to me.

As I lay in bed feeling sorry for myself, a part of the real me was still alive and began showing itself. I realized that for many years I had been living a lie that had taken me away from my core, my true identity. Instead of getting bigger, my world had become smaller, more restricted, and more fearful. I had given up my dreams and I had stopped growing internally. As soon as I was able to see the truth, I stopped crying and realized I was embroiled in an identity crisis. I knew I had come to a crossroads in my life. If I didn't change in a significant way, my friend's prediction might indeed come true. I could lose everything I had built over many years of hard work, including my marriage and my family, but most of all I realized I was about to lose myself.

As I thought about all of this, I realized that I had been living like this for many years. I had become part of the social hypnosis surrounding me. I had bought into the social conditioning that wanted me to believe that it was OK to be more than 30 pounds overweight as I aged; that it was OK to stop pursuing my dreams; that it was OK not to be living a life full of excitement, love, and passion; that it was OK to be safe and not take too many risks; and that it was OK to stop being childlike. I had become so "normal." I had become a good member of society, someone who doesn't make any waves. I had achieved a certain social status and was spending most of my time and effort defending it. The playful, feminine woman in me had turned into a tough businessman—indeed I had become like a stereotypical male. My short hair now seemed symbolic of that fact. I was materially successful, but emotionally I had flat-lined and lacked true fulfillment.

"Success without fulfillment is failure." —Anthony Robbins

Luckily, my ego was at the end of its rope and did not know how to get out of pain. My little self was ready to grow and willing to receive guidance from my Higher Self. The inner light of my soul could now shine and come through to lead me to my true purpose in life. I was ready to take the next step into the unknown because somehow I knew that I was safe to do it. I was in the perfect environment to go through the process of reconnecting with my true nature and becoming who I really was. It was time for me to grow to the next level.

This experience unleashed a series of massive inner and outer changes. I was back in touch with my true nature and encouraged to live up to my highest potential. I reconnected with my courage, the courage of being alive and living my life to its fullest. I realized that not living up to my true potential was like cheating my life's purpose. I recognized that I might as well be dead if I was not able to appreciate the extraordinary gift of life that I had been given. I was now ready to close the gap between who I really was and what I had become.

Since that remarkable evening, I have done numerous fire walks, jumped several times from telephone poles, leaped twice in the middle of the night from a bridge into a salty river, and traveled several times around the world doing "crazy" things that nourished my soul. My life has never been the same since.

∙∙∙

Weight loss secret:
Your outer appearance is the manifestation of your inner identity.

If you want to lose weight permanently, make sure your identity is that of a slim person. Otherwise you will regain your weight after each weight loss program. You have the courage and the power to create any new identity you truly want for yourself. Simply decide and do anything it takes to get there and you will succeed.

∙∙∙

Through my first (non-)firewalking experience, I found that the beliefs I had that controlled my life were not in line with my identity. I had been unaware of the disconnect up until my life-changing realization that night of the firewalk.

At every moment you must keep guard at the door of your mind.

How was it possible for me to become a different human being than I thought I was? I believe it was my occupation, the environment I lived in, and the stories I had kept telling myself day in and day out. It took that firewalk experience to make me realize how much I had been deceiving myself through stories that were not true. It was not true that it was OK for me to be 38 pounds overweight. It was not true that I liked my job. It was not true that I liked where I lived. It was not true that I lived my passion in life. Right then and there I knew that I had to change my beliefs about myself so that my identity would coincide with my behavior in everything I did. Today I am a totally different person, and my appearance, my profession, my daily activities, my relationships, and my environment are a direct reflection of that. However, I am only at the beginning of my wonderful journey of living a life of meaning. I am more awake.

You don't have to wait for an identity crisis like mine to take charge of your life. You can prepare by being very clear with yourself about your psychological makeup and your own identity, the driving force in your life. The way you live your life is determined by the identity you have and the collection of beliefs you hold true about yourself.

The Power of Identity

Who am I? Who am I really? This is a question that human beings have been asking themselves for thousands of years. In the words of Deepak Chopra, we are "a holographic expression of the entire Universe manifested as a continuum of a probability amplitude of space-time events in the field of infinite possibilities."[141] If this definition sounds too complicated and difficult to understand, you are not alone in your response. However, from the quantum theory perspective this is a quite accurate description of who we really are.

We all have the most extraordinary potential lying dormant within ourselves, but we don't live up to it because we have not learned how to activate this potential. Most of us would define ourselves by giving our name, gender, academic title, or profession. We attach our identity to how we look, what we do, what kind of car we drive, where we live, our social status, and so on. Furthermore, our identity determines how we feel and how we move through life.

However, we are not our identity. We are not what we do. This is why we are called human *beings*, not human *doings*. We are not our *behavior*. Behavior is something we *do* and it can be changed if it doesn't serve us in reaching our goals in life. We can change it because inside us there is something that is everlasting and never changing. *That* is who we really are. This is what Dr. Chopra refers to in his definition.

> **"We are not human beings having a spiritual experience but spiritual beings having a human experience."**
> **—Pierre Teilhard de Chardin**

The quote by Teilhard de Chardin questions where our identity comes from. Regardless of our spiritual beliefs, deep down we all know who we are, which is our true nature. If we ever want to achieve any goal in life that brings happiness and fulfillment, including the perfect weight, we need to tap into that everlasting power of our spirit, our soul. To do that, we have to be able to look through the veil of our social conditioning, our ego identity, and create an identity that is more in line with our true spirit.

What is your identity?

To find out what you identify with at this point in life and see if your identity supports your current goals, take your journal, or use the worksheet provided in Appendix 4 of this book titled "Creating a Life of Meaning," and write down *every* thought (good or bad) you have about your own identity. For example, answer the following key questions:

- How do I see myself as a human being? Am I a parent, a partner, a businessperson, a friend, a contributor to the world?

- What are my beliefs about life in general—about love, relationships, food, dieting, etc.?
- How do I see myself with respect to my weight? Do I perceive myself as fat or thin?

No matter what your current identity or set of beliefs is, the beauty about being human is that you have the *power of choice* and a *free will*. This power enables you to change anything you want. The only thing you need to do then is to become aware of *what you want* and *what you don't want*. You can always train yourself to change what you don't want through the power of intention and attention, because you tend to get what you focus on.

Do Your Beliefs Serve You?

"If error is corrected whenever it is recognized as such, the path of error is the path of truth."
—Hans Reichenbach

Did you know?
We think approximately 16,000 thoughts a day.

The interesting thing is that more than 95 percent of the thoughts we have today are the same thoughts we had yesterday and the day before and the day before that. Where did these thoughts come from? They came from our social environment, parents, relatives, teachers, friends, media, schooling, and so on. The question is, how many of these thoughts are the thoughts we want to think versus thoughts others want us to think? If we want to truly achieve anything we desire in life, we need better control of our thoughts. This is so because thoughts determine our beliefs, and beliefs determine our behavior, including our attitude toward food and diet.

Let us examine and challenge some of the beliefs we hold with respect to food and dieting. Ask yourself if the following beliefs are true for you and how they serve you in achieving your goal of losing weight permanently. Here are some **common misleading notions** many of us have:

- **Food is love.** As children many of us received the best foods when we were sick although we were not at all hungry. As a result, we might still be rewarding ourselves with food. We learned to mistake food for love, but the truth is, **food is food and love is love. Food is not love!**

- **We all gain weight as we age**. I had adopted this common belief because it was very convenient. I felt comfortable hiding behind it. The fact is, if we eat healthily, exercise regularly, and live a life of meaning, we do not necessarily get fatter as we get older.

- **Empty your plate—children are starving in Africa.** Growing up in Romania with very little food and often going to school hungry, I learned early on to appreciate that food is scarce in many parts of the world. But the truth is that if we leave food on our plate, children will *still* be starving in Africa. In fact, if we eat less, we may be healthy and live longer so we can do something to prevent children from starving around the world.

- **Peer Pressure.** We all want to be able to eat what our hearts desire, especially when we go out with friends. We want to be like them and not stand out. We all love to eat pizza, hamburgers, milkshakes, and other foods that are part of our culture regardless of their impact on health. It's fun to eat that way sometimes. But do we want to do that every day? As we become aware of the results of a fast food diet, we need to ask ourselves if we want to be one of two who dies of a heart attack or one of four who dies of cancer. Being smart seems to be more important than being sick and unhappy.

- **Fattening food tastes better than healthy food.** This feels true for a body out of balance because it is out of control. Instead, our addictions and cravings are in charge. Our obsessions and the little creatures that inhabit our bodies (parasites, bacteria, mold, and fungus) now dictate what we should be eating. Once such a body has been cleansed, it will stop craving fattening dishes and delight instead in wholesome foods.

- **Healthy food is boring.** I am amazed how many people ask me how I can have eaten strictly vegetarian food for more than 14 years. They say that vegetarian food all tastes the same. It's boring, with no variety. This is one of the greatest fallacies in our society. I am a great supporter of the new raw food movement in the United States, where supermarkets like Whole Foods and people like Roxanne Klein and David Wolfe are bringing the beauty of wholesome foods to people in the most beautiful and creative ways. Once you have tasted delicious healthy food you will never want to go back to junk food. Your body will cringe if you do.

- **Overweight is inherited.** While I do believe that a certain percentage of people with weight problems inherit a condition that may lead to overweight, clinical studies show that a majority of overweight conditions can be reversed if people decide to take responsibility for their weight and do what is needed to offset genetic tendencies.

- **Diets don't work.** After trying every possible diet and after working with a regular physician—who most of the time has not been trained in nutrition and dieting—many of us give up, believing that nothing can be done to help us lose weight. I would challenge that belief with the fact that scientific research continues to improve, that people do manage to lose weight, and that, while we live, we should never give up, because the moment we do, we die—spiritually first and physically soon after.

- **Death is certain so I might as well enjoy food while I am alive.** Death is indeed a sure thing. Yet what kind of life is one in which the only enjoyment you get is from food, so much so that it ends up killing you? Is there another way to get satisfaction from life other than eating? Can it be that food has taken control of us, rather than us of it? Is it possible that we choose overweight and obesity with all of their horrific diseases over vibrant health, vitality and living a life of meaning?
- **Thinking positive is enough.** While I am a great believer in infinite intelligence and know that positive thinking is an amazing tool to bring about lasting change, I also know that we must take the proper actions to support a positive attitude and absolute trust in divine inspiration.
- **I am stupid.** I used to be guilty of such a belief. Having lived for 16 years in a suppressed dictatorial and communist regime in Romania, I grew up in an environment ruled by fear—fear of going to prison for no reason, fear of not having enough to eat or wear, fear of not being good enough. My fear of not being good enough was further cultivated when I immigrated to Germany. A beautiful and wealthy country, Germany is home to extraordinarily smart and hardworking people who were able to rebuild their devastated country from the ground up after World War II. One of the qualities of Germans is their aim for perfection. In this environment, my belief that I was not smart enough could further thrive and bloom. It wasn't until I became an exchange student with the Bechtel International Center of Stanford University in California that my beliefs that *I was stupid* and *I was not good enough* was challenged for the first time. The people I met there seemed astonished that I was one of only four people and the only woman sent by the German government to Stanford for that program. They seemed impressed that I was a master's student in computer science and that I spoke five languages. These things to which I had paid no attention before suddenly merited respect from other people. For the first time, I started to think that maybe I was not stupid after all. Do you have a similar belief? Then it may be time to question it.
- **I am weak, fat, and ugly and can never follow through.** Most of us who want to master change of any kind encounter times of relapse. Too often, we give up after a few setbacks, thinking we are too weak to change anything. What we need to remember in such situations is how long it took us to learn the old disempowering behavior in the first

place. We need to give ourselves at least the same amount of time to substitute old behaviors with supportive ones. We have to admit that we need help and support and that we are not alone in the process.

....

Weight loss secret:
Throw out your old beliefs and adopt new ones that will help you build a new identity.

....

Take a moment to write down your own disempowering beliefs. You now have an amazing chance to identify negative beliefs and let go of them forever so you can truly be in the driver's seat of your life.

In the worksheet provided in Appendix 4, or in your journal, identify the limiting beliefs you have about yourself. For instance, I believed I was fat, stupid, and ugly and that no matter what I did I wouldn't be able to lose weight. In addition, I thought fashion was going in the wrong direction and my inability to lose weight and keep it off had to do with the fact that I was getting older. What do you believe? Create your own list and be painfully honest, for this is your chance to identify and let go of garbage once and for all.

- What are your disempowering beliefs about life?
- What are your beliefs about yourself?
- What do you believe about your ability to achieve your goals in life?
- What are your beliefs with respect to weight loss?
- What are your beliefs with respect to exercise, food, drugs, and alcohol?
- Do you see yourself as a beautiful, smart, athletic person who is a go-getter and achieves anything and everything you want in life—or do you feel sorry for yourself?
- Are you a victim of self-pity and depression?
- Do you define yourself as an athlete who works out every day and takes care of her/his body or as somebody who doesn't care too much about the way he/she looks?

After finishing the list of your limiting beliefs, simply decide to change them by creating a new set of beliefs that contains desired character traits and values that will support you in all life endeavors from now on. For instance, when I did this I wrote down that I wanted to be a "*beautiful athlete weighing 137 pounds (62 kg) and a marathon runner.*" Today, I perceive myself as more beautiful than ever on the inside, I am at my ideal weight, and I am an athlete and a marathon runner.

What do you value most in life and why?

Develop a list of the values that you treasure and that have guided your life so far. Make sure you list them in order of importance for you. For instance, being a good parent might be more important for you than being a successful businessperson. Are health and vitality on that list? At what rank?

To support you with this process, I am sharing with you my own Life of Meaning poster, which includes my mission in life, my identity, my values and beliefs, my goals and my affirmations, as well as what I am grateful for. Create your own poster and hang it in your office, kitchen, bathroom, or bedroom. It will inspire you daily and keep you focused on your goals when you go off-track.

MY VALUES ARE:

1. FAITH & GREATFULNESS
2. HEALTH & VITALITY
3. LOVE, COMPASSION & LOVINGKINDNESS
4. JOY, CELEBRATION & SELF-RECOGNITION
5. INTELLIGENCE & WISDOM
6. GROWTH & LEARNING
7. PASSION
8. FLEXIBILTY & TOLERANCE
9. ACHIEVEMENT & DETERMINATION
10. MAKE A DIFFERENCE
11. CONTRIBUTION

The mission of my life is to be joy and contribution. My awakening is the awakening and welfare of others.

DAILY AFFIRMATIONS

I have an open and compassionate heart

I have within the light of God as my universal source of faith, intelligence and love

I am divinely guided. I am one with God and a force for good.

I am humble, grateful and aware at every moment of my life.

I have an outstandingly healthy and vital body that I exercise daily with joy

I eat only healthy foods that give me life force, heal my body, reinforce my vibrant health and give me energy and strength.

I let go of old hurts with pleasure.

I have a healthy and loving family life that is enhanced by influential, smart and successful friends and business associates.

I empower people to create a life of true fulfillment for themselves and others

All I need is within me NOW!

My identity is:

- I am one with God, calm and centered
- I live in the field of all possibilities
- I am a daily meditator
- I am a wise & guided leader for Good
- I am joyful, feminine & passionate
- I am a beautiful 62 Kg athlete
- I am playful, warm and caring
- I am humble, grateful and aware
- I am perseverance & determination
- I am intelligent, wise & courageous
- I am an outstanding wife, mother, daughter, friend and leader for Good
- I embrace all challenges of life with great excitement & optimism
- I am manifesting abundance in every area of my life for I am one with God and God is everything!
- I am totally committed to love, contribution, growing and learning.

GRATITUDE

I am grateful to those I love and those who love me.

I am grateful for my open heart, the deep love, compassion and my absolute faith as the guiding forces in my life.

I am grateful for my vibrant health, intelligence and beauty.

I am grateful for absolutely everything in my life right now, the abundance in my life as well as the things that were challenging but that changed my life to the better.

I am grateful to God and all of my spiritual teachers, helpers, healers and supporters

I am grateful for all things that are happening from now on.

I am grateful for my life. I love life!

My top year 2004 goals are:

- Extraordinary love and passion in my marriage
- I continue to grow my outstanding master mind peer group: Wisdom Magnet
- World travels to India, Fiji and Thailand
- I successfully bring wisdom to wisdom seekers and make a difference in the world

Make Your Life a Masterpiece

Imagine being at the end of your life, looking back, and asking yourself:

- What did I accomplish?
- Have I lived the life that I envisioned as a teenager?
- Have I lived out my dreams?
- Have I achieved my highest potential?
- Have I given all I had to give?
- What could I have done differently?
- What would have given me more satisfaction?
- Do I have any regrets?

Take your journal and write down your answers to the above questions. In addition, ask yourself, *Am I currently living to my highest potential? And if not, why not? What could I do differently today to prevent regrets later?* Take the opportunity to do this now; don't put it off. If you do, you'll see that the only person cheated is you.

The beauty about this exercise is the realization that as long as we are not at the end of our existence, we have not only the power but especially the responsibility to redirect our lives toward our true purpose. This process begins with appreciating first what we already have by cultivating gratitude.

Cultivate Gratitude

> *"By giving, you grow"*
> —Sir John Templeton

Having been brought up in communist Romania, I have grown to appreciate the smallest things life has offered me along the way. More than 30 years ago, my parents and I managed to leave Romania and immigrate to Germany, and all we were allowed to take with us were two small suitcases. Although our material life began for us at ground zero, we were able to build a new existence in a foreign country. My parents found jobs and I was able to get an excellent free education. We are full of gratitude to Germany, a country with wonderful people who welcomed us and helped us build a new existence so that we can now help others.

···

Weight loss secret:
Gratitude gives you the sense of sufficiency that helps you let go of weight you don't really need.

···

Based on this and other past experiences, I have learned that I can always start all over again if I really want to. I learned early on to let go of attachments, for there is always something new that life holds for me. As a result, I have come to believe that life is very abundant and rich if I am willing to look for the good in everything. I have learned to cultivate a feeling of gratitude by always living in the *now* because the now is all there is. The past is long gone and the future is not here yet. Therefore, life is nothing else but a collection of *nows*. I make it a priority to live in the present moment and most of all to honor it consciously. To that end, several years ago I began to communicate my gratitude to those around me:

- I always begin my day with a prayer of thanks for all the gifts that life has given me including the love I receive from loved ones but also from those I barely know, such as the cashier in the supermarket.
- I send weekly expressive, fun, or profound notes to my friends to stay connected and to show them my love and appreciation for their presence in my life.
- Everywhere I go I take the opportunity to pay people a compliment and to thank them—verbally and nonverbally—for being in my life.
- I never leave home without a kiss and a hug for all my loved ones.
- I also say a prayer of thanks for my enemies, without whom I would not have grown so much.
- Inspired by my friend and teacher Tony Robbins, I began a couple of years ago to collect magic moments, and once a year I share the most remarkable ones with my friends and loved ones.

These simple techniques help me focus on what's good and beautiful in life. This sense of gratitude makes my heart full of love and compassion and kindness. It nourishes my soul, keeps me growing, and has a beautiful "side effect": the world mirrors my own attitude by reflecting my love back a thousandfold. If I were to die tomorrow, I would be ready because at every moment I have lived a life dominated by love and gratitude.

Now it is your turn. Pick up your journal or worksheet and begin cultivating your own sense of gratitude. Think about everyone and everything in life that deserves your gratitude. To help you with this process I would like to share with you a few very powerful morning and evening questions that I have learned from Tony Robbins and that you may want to use:

- Who do I love? Who loves me?
- What am I grateful about in my life right now?
- What am I proud about in my life right now? What about that makes me proud? How does that make me feel?

- What am I happy about in my life right now?
- What am I enjoying most in my life right now?
- What am I excited about in my life right now? What about that makes me excited? How does that make me feel?

Thank your eyes, nose, ears, heart, and all of your organs for serving you so well. Thank yourself for the opportunity of being able to use a computer and for having access to information and knowledge. Realize that you belong to the few privileged people on this planet who are able to do that. Think of several other ways to express your gratitude and say thank you to Existence on a regular basis. Nurture this sense of gratitude and fill your heart with love for yourself and others.

Cultivate Forgiveness

> *"Judging lets you to be judged."*
> —Jesus of Nazareth

Remember the last time you forgave somebody. How did that make you feel? I don't know about you but every time I forgive somebody, including myself, I feel as if a huge load has been taken off my shoulders. I stop thinking about that person or thing and I feel free. In his book *10 Secrets for Success and Inner Peace*, Dr. Wayne Dyer[142] encourages us to

"Become a person who refuses to be offended by anyone, anything, or any set of circumstances."

By giving up judgment and cultivating forgiveness we free ourselves from the burden of pain, fear, anxiousness, and resentment. By freeing ourselves from such destructive feelings of self-righteousness, we have the energy to focus on our intentions and goals in life. We no longer allow our or someone else's *past* behavior to control our present.

••

Weight loss secret:
Cultivate forgiveness.

Letting go of self-righteousness by forgiving yourself and others helps you let go of the physical and emotional weight attached to it.

"Resentment is like venom that continues to pour through your system, doing its poisonous damage long after you're bitten by the snake. It's not the bite that kills you; it's the venom," Dr. Dyer reminds us.

••

"**Every decision I make is a choice between a grievance and a miracle. I release all regrets, grievances, and resentments and choose the miracle.**"[143] —**Deepak Chopra**

In this statement, Dr. Chopra reminds us how easy it is to forgive ourselves and others. It is only one decision away. When we realize that we are actually one resolution away from happiness, we can practice forgiveness every time we feel the need to be free. This is a very powerful tool that helps us live a life of fulfillment and meaning.

When I have a hard time forgiving somebody and want to stick to my righteousness, I remind myself that by doing so, I am actually allowing that person or past event to control my present moment and possibly my future. I realize that my inability to forgive others, or myself, for that matter, interferes with my inner freedom, my intentions, and my highest goals in life. It puts me in a *re-active* rather than a *pro-active* role, and I give up control to that outer event. Reminding myself that I am actually giving up my power rather than keeping it gets me out of a negative state very quickly.

· ·

Weight loss secret:
Forgiving yourself and others puts the power back into your own hands.

Do not expect yourself to be superhuman. Allow yourself and others to make mistakes and know that if you forgive, you will be forgiven.

Choose the miracle of freedom!

· ·

How Can You Learn to Forgive?

Forgiving someone, including yourself, can be difficult at times, so you have to make a conscious decision to be free. Following is a method for formally letting go of your expectations, disappointments, regrets, and everything else that may bother you.

FORGIVENESS EXERCISE

Assume a prayer, contemplation, or meditation pose. Sit with your eyes closed, your hands resting on your lap with the palms facing upward. Collect yourself and put your attention in your heart. Take 10 deep breaths. When you breathe in, feel how your breath fills every cell in your body with love and light. When you breathe out, feel how all disease, negative thoughts, and dark feelings leave every cell of your body. Breathe in light and love and breath out all darkness that prevents you from being happy and fulfilled. After 10 breaths, go into your heart and imagine a beam of light pulsating there. Join this light and see a picture of yourself or the person you want to forgive and simply say, *"I forgive you wholeheartedly because I realize that you have done the best you could from your state of consciousness."* Repeat that statement from your heart space several times until you really feel the burden of pain leave your body and you can let go. If your attention keeps coming back to that negative feeling of resentment, thank the thought and allow it to move on. Feel the freedom in your heart and feel the feeling of joy that begins to rise. Sit in this position for about 10 minutes or until you know that you have totally forgiven. Feel how the heavy weight has left your body, and rejoice. Enjoy your newly gained sense of love and purpose.

This exercise is a very powerful tool. While it facilitates forgiveness, it also helps us realize we can indeed control our thinking rather than have it control us. This is the *gift of free will* that we all have as human beings. Forgiving others frees us of negative energy and allows us to focus on what we really want in life so we can be happy and fulfilled. By practicing forgiveness, we also allow others to forgive us for our own wrongdoing. By letting go of our own judgments and disapproval of others, we become invulnerable to criticism because we begin to understand the pain of people who have not developed the ability to forgive.

JOURNALING AS A MEANS TO FORGIVE

Apart from prayer or meditation, you can use journaling as a means to find peace and free yourself from the burden of judgment and resentment. Realize in your heart that the presence of this suffering in your life is only a thought that you have chosen to hold on to. As soon as you decide to let that thought go, you will be free no matter what the other person does. It will no longer affect you. Take your journal or the worksheet provided in Appendix 4 and write down the names of the people (including yourself, if necessary) who may have harmed you, cheated you, or criticized you in the past and whom you have not yet forgiven. Ask yourself, *Who else do I have to forgive so I can be free to achieve all my life goals, including that of losing weight?* Write down all the reasons you want to let go and forgive that person. Express all the feelings you currently have toward them so you can be free. Cry if you have to. Tell them everything you ever wanted them to know about how their behavior hurt you. Include your own disempowering behavior that you want to abandon. Write as if you were writing for the garbage can. Do anything that will help you release those negative feelings that hold you back from being who you really are, free of burden. Realize that it is your choice to hold on to this hurt or to let go and be free. Remember that you are the only person thinking in your mind and decide to forgive so you can finally be free. Notice that you are actually playing the same old record over and over again and ask yourself how much longer you intend to play that record. Ask yourself if today is the right day to let go and do it. Take your power back. Realize that this is medicine for your soul. Finish the exercise by sending yourself and others unconditional love and understanding, and enjoying your newly acquired freedom. Having let go of old judgments and criticism, and having embraced forgiveness, you are now ready to fill your heart with gratitude for all the good things that are part of your life right now.

••

Weight loss secret:
Journaling is a powerful medicine for your soul and serves your body.

••

You are now ready to create the future the way you want it, free of the burden of a self-righteous existence. You now have the opportunity to define exactly what you want in life so you become not only successful at having your ideal figure but also at being fulfilled and deeply happy.

Know the Meaning of Your Life

Earlier we discussed the importance of living a life of meaning not only as a means to attaining the perfect weight but also for achieving our life's purpose. If we don't live a life of meaning and fulfillment, a life that aligns us with our true identity and beliefs, we will constantly sabotage our efforts to lose weight or any other goal we want to achieve. In his book *Food Combining and Digestion*, Steve Meyerowitz writes:

> **"If you question successful dieters, you will learn that the only possible way to lose weight is to gain life."**

I would even say that it is crucial to create a life of meaning and total fulfillment where food and the preoccupation with weight become the periphery of life rather than the center. Fulfillment is significant because we can have all the money in the world and all our goals accomplished, including the ideal weight, but if we are not happy on the inside we have failed. We need to understand that all the things we desire have one purpose: to make us happy and fulfilled. If we're not, we need to change either our goals or the way we look at and perceive the world.

Define Your Goals

The first rule in nature is that we either grow or die. Like most people, I was able to experience that natural law firsthand, as I shared with you in the story of my first firewalk. However, my next challenge was to find out exactly what I actually wanted. Why? Because all I could think of was what I *didn't* want. I find this to be true with most people I know.

The first teacher who helped me determine my goals and most importantly how I could achieve them was Dr. Joseph Murphy, in his book *The Power of Your Subconscious Mind*. Like most successful people, Dr. Murphy espouses the philosophy that life gives us what we want only if we ask for it and deeply believe in its manifestation. Born and raised in a communist country with an atheist doctrine, I did not believe in God or any higher power. So I had a hard time following Dr. Murphy's advice in the beginning. But something attracted me to his point of view and I followed his advice.

It was right before I finished my master's degree in computer science that I decided to "try God," as Dr. Murphy put it. I was looking for my first job, asked for the moon, and got it. I asked for a starting salary that was twice as high as the average university graduate's at that time. Yes, it could be argued that it was a coincidence. But then my entire life since must have been a series of coincidences, too. That first experience challenged my entire view of life and its meaning.

Since then I have studied with many accomplished masters who confirm this universal rule. Today I know that the best way to achieve what I want is to *know* what I want. It all begins with writing it down. More than 80 percent of everything I ever wrote down has become reality in my life. Knowing what you want is what differentiates successful people from less successful ones. We all get what we focus on. If we don't tell Existence what we want, we will receive what we don't want because this is all we *know and focus on*. Furthermore, setting goals must be a conscious process and not something left to chance. This is what any successful and accomplished person will tell you.

•••

Weight loss secret:
Only if you make losing weight a measurable goal will you be able to accomplish it.

•••

Now take out your journal or worksheet and write down how you perceive the meaning of your life right now. For instance, as my own poster states, *"The mission of my life is to be joy and contribution. My awakening is the awakening and welfare of others."* Write down how you perceive the mission and vision of your life. Remember that this is a creative process and it doesn't have to be perfect. Write down *everything* that comes to mind without censoring it. Answering the following questions can help you in this process:

- What is the meaning of my life?
- What is the purpose of my life?
- What is the vision and mission of my life?
- Why am I here?
- What do I want to be, do, and create?
- Whom do I want to serve?
- What would the attainment of my life's mission and purpose give me?
- How would I feel if I achieved my vision?

Why Do You Want What You Want?

I am sure you can remember a time in your life when you accomplished something that made you extremely proud. You had an idea you wanted to implement, or you wanted something so badly (a job, a car, a degree) that you became extremely creative in going after it. You did whatever it took to make it happen. You did not mind working day and night or sleeping less. You were driven, so determined to achieve that particular result that no effort was too much for you. Your end vision carried you through all the possible obstacles that came your way until finally you achieved your goal.

Why did you do all that? What was the driving force? You were inspired and totally motivated to follow through. Motivation is the single most important factor in our ability to follow through in life both short-term and long-term. It is the juice that oils our motors.

Motivation is what turns a visionary into a leader.

We are all natural leaders if we know what we want and why we want it. We have proven it in our lives so many times already, whether our goals have been small or large. This is what differentiates those who talk from those who go out and make things happen. We can all become driven by our vision and refuse to succumb to excuses and challenges that occur along the way. By staying motivated, we keep our vision in front of us and turn problems into opportunities for growth. If our motivation is high enough, we find ways to overcome all challenges and unexpected difficulties. We just change our strategies and maintain our enthusiasm and passion.

These are exactly the same qualities you need to apply right now to lose weight and become healthy and vibrant. Just imagine yourself losing all the weight you want to lose and keeping it off forever. You never have to worry again about food, counting calories, or your health. Imagine yourself fitting into your favorite dress and bursting with energy. Imagine yourself receiving compliments from total strangers, sharing the story of your weight success with all of your friends and relatives, and helping others achieve the same goals. Hundreds of thousands of people around the world have achieved their weight loss goals and so can you.

Pick up your journal or the worksheet provided in Appendix 4 and continue the previous process by writing down the goals you have in life. Imagine it is your birthday and you can make any wish you want. Let your imagination flow. Write everything that comes to mind as if you were a child making a wish list. Ask yourself the following questions:

- What are my goals in life?
- What do I want to accomplish at the personal, professional, financial, and relationship level?
- What do I really want?

Prioritize the goals you have for the next 12 months and single out the top three. Then attach compelling reasons to them by answering the following questions:

- Why do I want to achieve these three goals?
- What would that give me?
- How would achieving these goals make me feel?

Now let's focus on and continue with your weight loss goals for a moment. Journal the answers to the following questions:

- **What are my goals for losing weight?**
- **How much weight do I want to lose and in what specific time frame?** Give exact (daily, weekly, monthly, and quarterly) milestones for action items and goals you want to achieve. Make everything very specific in terms of time and exact weight.
- **Why do I want to lose all that weight?** What will that give me? How would that make me feel?
- **Why have I failed to follow through in the past?** What was so difficult? What got me off-track? What will be different this time? What am I willing to do to follow through and make this work?
- **Which concrete actions am I going to take this time to show my total commitment to losing weight?** Whose help will I enlist? Who will I look to for support? What gym will I join? Which books will I read? Which seminar will I attend to learn more and get more support? What will achieving that weight loss goal give me? How would that make me feel?
- **How do I want to measure my success along the way? What am I willing to do to stay on track?**

By completing the hands-on exercises in this chapter, you have shown true commitment to your own personal growth and toward living a life of more meaning and fulfillment. You have made a significant step on your way to reaching your weight loss goal by knowing yourself better and what drives you in life. In the words of the great Roman Marcus Aurelius, you have realized that

"It is not death that man should fear, but he should fear never beginning to live."

You have recognized those fears, and by knowing what you want, you are on your way to more personal happiness and fulfillment.

Three weight loss secrets to remember:

1. Love your life as the most precious gift you have been given. Practice an attitude of gratitude and forgiveness.
2. Your identity must be that of a thin person if you want permanent weight success. Let go of old beliefs and grudges that do not serve you.
3. Know what you want, go after it, and be open to receive the gifts that the universe has for you.

Daily I-Can-Tation:

My body is an expression of health, self-confidence, and happiness. I know exactly what I want, desire, and need, and go after it with total joy and conviction. Every day, in every way, I am deeply grateful and appreciative of the abundance in my life. I love my life and make it a masterpiece.

Step 5: Winning the Game of Life

"If you bring forth what is inside of you,
what you bring forth will save you.
If you don't bring forth what is inside of you,
what you don't bring forth will destroy you."
—Jesus of Nazareth

Not too long ago during a routine cleaning, my dentist revealed to me that one of my teeth was suffering from a disorder called resorption. The medical community does not know for sure why resorption happens but the fact was that my own immune system was attacking my body. I was told that my tooth would eventually have to be extracted because at that point there was no other remedy. At first I went into denial, and for many months I thought I could heal the condition, which I attributed to parasites, through cleansing and proper nutrition. However, when my gums began bleeding heavily despite my taking various measures, I became frightened. Nevertheless, I could not get myself to follow the advice of my dentist and contact the experts in order to begin the therapeutic process.

Instead my fear and inability to get help worsened, and for months, I had terrible nightmares in which I saw myself looking like a monster with a disfigured face. Every night I woke up drenched in sweat and was not able go back to sleep. I am usually an upbeat person, but because I was working hard during the day and was not sleeping well at night, I became a bundle of sadness and depression. I felt sorry for myself, didn't know how to get rid of fear, and hoped that my body would eventually heal itself.

One morning, after another horrible night, I was not in the best mood when I entered the local grocery store to do my daily shopping. In my head, I began complaining about the bread that was not fresh, the salad that was not organic, and the mayonnaise that was added to my sandwich though I didn't want any. By the time I arrived at the cashier's I was pretty upset. As I waited in line, I listened to the conversation the cashier was having with the customers in front of me. The clerk, a man in his fifties, greeted each customer with a welcoming smile, asked if he or she had found everything OK, pointed out that various items were on sale, cracked a joke or two, and wished everybody a wonderful day. When my turn came, I could not help but ask, "Your joy is contagious and you seem to be such a happy person. I'm curious, what is the secret to your joy?" He looked me right in the eye and pulled from behind the cash register a piece of paper, which he handed to me. On it, I read the following poem, titled "Beauty Secrets":

> *For attractive lips, speak words of kindness.*
> *For lovely eyes, seek out the good in people.*
> *For a slim figure, share your food with the hungry.*
> *For beautiful hair, let a child run his fingers through it once a day.*
> *For poise, walk with the knowledge you never walk alone.*
> *We leave you a tradition of the future. The tender loving care of human beings will never become obsolete.*
> *People, even more than things, have to be restored, renewed, revived, reclaimed, redeemed and redeemed and redeemed.*
> *Never throw anyone away.*
> *Remember, if you ever need a helping hand, you'll find one at the end of your arm.*
> *As you grow older, you'll discover that you have two hands: One for helping yourself, the second for helping others.*
> *You have great days still ahead of you.*
> *May there be many more of them.*

The poem, whose sentiments in fact weren't new to me, changed my life that day. The first verse *"For attractive lips, speak words of kindness"* reminded me that what I was most afraid of at that time was ugliness. Yet this was what I was cultivating through my behavior. I had become ugly on the inside. The only thing I was focused on was me, and as a result I had blown my problem out of proportion. I had lost touch with reality and had forgotten that *"if you ever need a helping hand, you'll find one at the end of your arm."* I had lost my power by giving in to the fear that was now dominating me.

Through his poem, that extraordinary man helped me see that beauty is something we do regularly, not something we have permanently. He reminded me that I had to *give* that which I wanted to *receive*. He reminded me of what I had learned many years before from Tony Robbins: that I should be spending 80 percent of my time focusing on the solution and not on the problem. As soon as I got home I called my dentist and my problem was solved.

....

Weight loss secret:
Learn how to handle your emotions and you will win the game of life.

We can and we must learn to handle and bring intelligence to our emotions. This capability is even built in the basis of the word emotions, which comes from the Latin word *motere* – that means the ability to act. As human beings, we are driven by an intelligent brain, which can help us control our emotions. This is what differentiates us from primates such as monkeys who act before thinking.

....

Beauty is something we do regularly, not something we have permanently.

At one point or another in life we all fall prey to a fear that renders us immobile. However, allowing fear to rule our life is not how we win the game of life. We must remember that we have a choice. We choose between love and fear. We win the game of life by realizing that it is a game. You won that game a long time ago when you were conceived. If you don't believe me, think of Woody Allen's 1972 movie *Everything You Always Wanted to Know About Sex* but *Were Afraid to Ask*. If you haven't seen it yet, see it—it will give you a different perspective. I know it's just a funny movie, but with every joke there is a grain of truth that resonates with us. This movie will remind you of a divine reality— namely, that at the moment of conception, it could have been somebody else who won, but no, it was you. Think about it: you won the game of life a long time ago. Now it is up to you to make it worthwhile. Make it a masterpiece. The key lies in how you feel at every moment in your life; it lies in your ability to cultivate love versus fear. The alternative is much too gloomy. Let me illustrate this by giving you some statistical data about people who take themselves too seriously and unconsciously cultivate toxic emotions.

Think about it: is there anything more important in your life than the way you feel?

If your answer is no, then you are already doing what it takes to make you feel good most of the time and the next steps will simply be an additional reminder.

If your answer is yes, then I wonder what it is that is more important to you than your feelings. Is it your weight, your job, your financial situation, your child, your relationships, or your significant other? What is it that takes a higher priority in your life than your inner joy and happiness? Without knowing what your answer is I would like you to ask yourself *why* you want that particular thing? What will that thing (car, house, title, person, or job) give you when you get it? I bet that it is a certain *feeling* that you ultimately hope to get once you have that thing or person in your life.

Did you know?

Toxic emotions can *double* your risk of contracting a disease.

A mass analysis performed by Friedman and Boothby-Kewley, which combined 101 scientific studies, confirmed that **toxic emotions have colossal clinical importance for our overall health.** The renowned author of *Emotional Intelligence*, Daniel Goleman, summarizes it by saying that **"People who experienced chronic anxiety, long periods of sadness and pessimism, unremitting tension or incessant hostility, relentless cynicism or suspiciousness, were found to have double the risk of disease—including asthma, arthritis, headaches, peptic ulcers, and heart disease.** This order of magnitude makes **distressing emotions as toxic a risk factor as, say, smoking** or high cholesterol are for heart disease—in other words, a major threat to health."[145]

Now let me ask you another question: *Who or what created that feeling in your body?* Did your feeling of joy or happiness come from the outside or did you create it yourself? To find that out, I wonder if you can remember a time when you felt totally happy and fulfilled. Perhaps you were in love or you received a gift, a promotion, or simply a compliment from a total stranger. Is it possible that you made yourself feel good simply because you associated feeling good with the thing that you yearned for? This book looks at life through the prism of achieving and maintaining ideal weight—is it possible that you want that ideal weight because you associate good feelings with it?

It's Not About Your Weight, It's About Your Feeling

To underline the above statement, let me give you another statistic.

Did you know?

According to the *Handbook of Mental Control,*[146] women use eating three times more often than men as a way to comfort themselves. Men, on the other hand, tend to use drugs or alcohol five times more often than women when they are depressed.

In the previous chapter, we looked at the role of identity, beliefs, and values and how they affect our overall purpose in life, our weight, and our lifestyle. In addition, we defined a set of goals, including weight loss objectives, that would help us create a future in line with our life's purpose and that would bring us more happiness and fulfillment. But as fun and important as defining goals is, it is basically an intellectual exercise. As John Lennon famously said, "life is what happens when we're busy making plans." A good life is a life that makes us feel good. No matter what our plans are, we all know that as soon as our emotions come into play, we tend to forget about our intentions and become victims of some kind of automatic, thoughtless response over which we seem to have no control. Or do we? Before we search for an answer to that question, ask yourself first:

Why do I want to lose weight and keep it off?

Why do human beings want anything? What happens when we obtain our goals—the ideal weight, the partner, the house or the car of our dreams, the yacht, the plane, or the job?

Yet when was the last time you celebrated your success? How long did your happiness last? Successes come and go and so does happiness. It tends to last for a couple of hours or maybe days, weeks, or months, and then we get bored with the old and look for some new goal, some new excitement. The key word here is *excitement*, which is a feeling, an emotion. It's human nature—we all aim for happiness and a sense of fulfillment in life.

At the core of our being is the basic need to gain pleasure and avoid pain.

Our actions, our feelings, and our emotions drive us toward fulfilling that need. However, along the way most of us in the West have learned to associate material things or people with the feelings we have had in their presence. This is simply because we *allow* ourselves to feel happy when we achieve a certain goal, buy a certain thing, or fall in love with a certain person.

We often mistake the map for the territory.

The Power of Emotions

Have you ever wondered what causes a mother to walk into a burning house or lift a 2-ton car to save her child? It is unconditional love. Love is what breaks the barriers of everything, even the greatest fear. Like fear, love is a feeling.

Where there is love, fear disappears.

True love is unconscious, automatic, and instinctive. It is who we are at our core. If we are essentially love, why do we do things that are unloving and hurtful toward ourselves, such as overeating?

In order to understand such behavior, let's understand first what an emotion is. According to Stanford professor Philip Zimbardo, "An emotion is a complex pattern of changes including physiological arousal, feelings, cognitive processes, and behavioral reactions made in response to a situation perceived by an individual to be personally significant in some way."[147] In other words, emotions are a complex process that involves a physical but also an intellectual and a behavioral response.

As you can imagine, psychologists have numerous theories about how emotions develop and how we handle them individually based on our rational and emotional development. In his book *Emotional Intelligence*, Daniel Goleman has compiled the most prominent research on the power of emotions. He puts emotional mastery at "the center of aptitudes for living"[148] and encourages us to learn how to add "intelligence" to our emotions. Due to our ancient genetic inheritance, we may still sometimes be dominated by the emotional brain. However, to find happiness in life, we must hone the power of our rational mind, which resides in our higher brain and which can help us avoid emotional hijackings.

Let's take a look at a few principles that will help us address emotional responses in a more empowering way:

1. **We all have our dark sides.** An Indian Vedic aphorism says that a man blind from birth doesn't know what darkness is. In other words, we need to know the night in order to recognize the day; we need to know rain in order to appreciate sunshine. Under difficult circumstances and especially when we are challenged emotionally, we may move away from our core of unconditional love to conditional love or even fear. *Conditional love* means that in order to love ourselves or others, certain expectations have to be met. We give some situations a certain negative meaning *(negative cognitive appraisal)*, which triggers a certain negative behavior. If these expectations are not met, we withdraw our feelings of love. The great psychologist Carl Gustav Jung called this the *shadow*.[149] The sooner we learn to face and lovingly embrace the dark side of ourselves, the easier it becomes to integrate it and live with it. We no longer think we have to run away from it by covering it up with food, drugs, alcohol, or other things that hurt us even more.

2. **We don't know any better.** Depending on our upbringing and the habits we have developed over time, we have learned to respond with a certain behavior when particular cues occur. For instance, when we feel sad or depressed, we may have a piece of chocolate, smoke, or drink alcohol *(feelings precede cognitive appraisal)*. These things make

us feel better for the moment because they change our body chemistry. By doing something that changes the way we feel, we get a sense of connection with ourselves or others. But before we know it, we have developed a certain pattern of behavior such as eating, drinking, or taking drugs.

These routine answers may give us a feeling of certainty in the midst of change. However, if we don't pay attention, these behaviors may turn into addictions and ultimately take control of us. They can prevent us from pursuing our goals in life and impede us from being healthy and energetic, and living a life of meaning, generosity, pleasure, and excitement.

What are the emotions that trigger our habits? Where do they come from? Do they just attack us from out of nowhere? How can we change the habit of emotional eating or responding defensively to criticism, for instance?

••

Weight loss secret:
You can learn to choose your emotional response.

Scientists tell us we have not "evolved away from nonrational, primitive emotions as we evolved our superior brains."[150] As a result, we do not realize that the cognitive capacity of our higher brain can help us *choose* our response at any moment. We go on automatic pilot and respond to the current situation based on our habit or the memory of our past conditioning. To evolve emotionally, we have to learn to give up those automatic reactions that no longer serve us. Instead, we must learn how to choose consciously what we want to feel and how we want to respond. Unfortunately, most of us did not receive any   formal emotional training, but emotional maturity can be learned.

••

Similarly to how the clerk in the grocery store helped me change my focus from what I wasn't doing to what I could do, let me to share with you how you can learn to bring intelligence to your emotions so you can be the master rather than the slave of your emotional states.

The Psychology of Change

Without going into the various theories on the nature of emotions, let's assume that the root of any emotion is a thought. A thought is our *interpretation of reality*; it is our way of looking at the world. It is mostly based on our past experiences and on the state of mind at the moment we have the thought. In other words, reality may be and normally is totally different from our perception of it.

Therefore, we must stand guard at the door of our minds because the way we feel on a daily basis depends largely on our view of the world, the interpretations we have about what's happening, and the meaning we attach to it. Herein lies the key to changing anything in life including our weight.

"Your future does not depend on your past unless you live there"
—Tony Robbins

. . . .

Weight loss secret:
Do not go through life by looking into the rearview mirror.

How you feel at any moment is based on your interpretation of reality and is often determined by past experiences. To feel good and avoid emotional distress, learn to look at each new situation with an open and fresh mind. Are your current beliefs making you feel good or are they   reminding you of your negative past experiences? Remember that you are the only person thinking in your head. Choose thoughts that empower you.

. . . .

By assuming control of our thoughts we can take control of our emotions and change our responses. This is emotional mastery.

Cultivating Self-Awareness

> *"If you fill your heart with regrets of yesterday and worries of tomorrow, you have no today to be thankful for."*
> —Anonymous

At the foundation of emotional mastery lies the pain-and-pleasure principle, which acknowledges the fact that humans will do anything to gain pleasure and avoid pain. To create lasting change we must take conscious control over our thoughts as the basis of our emotions. To be able to do that we need to acknowledge that we can influence our thoughts but we cannot force our emotions.

However, we can make our emotions serve us rather than rule over us by:

1. **Becoming aware of and acknowledging our emotions.** This self-awareness enables us to identify the emotions as they happen and is the foundation of emotional intelligence.[152] Instead of being driven by them we are now in the driver's seat.

2. **Embracing, appreciating, and learning from our emotions** as the keystone to our ability to manage them.

3. **Consciously choosing the emotions** we actually want to experience as the premise for our ability to interact with ourselves but also relate to other people in our lives.

4. **Developing the ability to read other people's emotions**, as the foundation for healthy relationships. This ability is called *silent witnessing* and it can be learned. It is the key to changing any reactive response.

....

Weight loss secret:
Become the master of your feelings through quiet witnessing and mindfulness.

Take time every day to go for a walk in nature, breathe consciously, journal, meditate, pray, and contemplate what's going on in your life. Over time, you become the observer of your emotions, and in the words of eminent psychotherapist Mark Epstein, you adopt an "attitude of nonjudgmental awareness."[153] You realize that you are not your emotions. You begin to be more aware of what's going on in certain situations and you can choose how you want to respond rather than responding in a way that makes you feel sorry later.

....

By seeing ourselves from the outside, we can understand the situation much better and take control of our emotions rather than be enslaved by them. As with any training, however, we need to be very patient and stick to our intention until we achieve a higher level of emotional mastery. For there is nothing more rewarding in life than being happy and fulfilled.

> **We must become more mindful of our feelings every time we feel the impulse to eat, drink, smoke, or engage in a behavior that ultimately doesn't serve us.**

The Power of Focus

Let's say you would like to change the habit of overeating, heavy drinking, or smoking. By applying the power of mindfulness, your brain can begin to disengage from the desire to eat or drink too much or take a puff. Instead of grabbing for food or a drink or a cigarette every time you feel upset, take one moment and ask your body whether it really wants to eat, drink, or smoke. Your stomach, liver, or lungs will usually respond with a cringe or a cough. When you are then willing to consciously listen to your body, your brain will begin to associ-

ate more pain than pleasure with eating, drinking, or smoking. Instead of focusing on the addiction, you will now focus on your body's needs and on your
intention to support it to be healthy and vital. In doing so, you begin slowly to
change the old memory of, for instance, *pleasure of eating* (upon a certain cue),
to the *pleasure of supporting and loving your body* (upon that same cue). Even if
you still end up under those circumstances you will do it in full awareness of
what's going on. By practicing mindfulness and changing focus you take back
control over your emotions.

So can we actually develop a plan for emotional mastery? The answer is yes.
Every emotion we experience has a lesson embedded in it. Human beings have
the beautiful ability to apply the power of free will. We can decide to learn the
lesson and move on. If we don't learn, we will keep bumping into that emotion—which then truly controls us—over and over again until we finally get the
lesson. We can all learn to take a look at any emotion we experience, identify
what that emotion is trying to teach us, and choose—through the power of
thought—to interpret the emotion in a way that serves our well-being. This is a
very powerful technique because—remember—*it is the meaning we attach to a
certain emotion that creates our reality.* We get to choose the interpretation of the
world around us and the events in it.

To show you how you can hone your ability to change your focus, I would
like to share with you a simple but very powerful tool that I have learned from
my dear friend and teacher Tony Robbins. Tony, who has been instrumental in
my own personal growth since 1989, has developed some of the most powerful
techniques I know for creating lasting, life-transforming change. Although no
written words can replace experiencing Tony in a live event,[154] I would like to
share with you here the concept of the Triad. In summary, the Triad consists of
three steps that I would highly encourage you to use when you are feeling down
and want to change your mood and the way you feel:

1. **Manage your body posture.** The first thing you must do when you
   are sad or depressed and you don't like it is to change your body posture. Place yourself in front of a mirror and ask yourself, *Do I look up
   or down? Are my shoulders up or down? Is this who I am? Is this how I
   want to look? Is this the kind of energy that makes me feel good right now?*
   Then take a deep breath and just for the sake of experimenting, decide
   for no good reason to look at the sky, think of a funny situation, jump
   up and down, and tell yourself a few jokes for five minutes. Notice that
   you cannot get depressed when you laugh and look up instead of
   down. Look at the sky and feel in your body your gratitude for being
   alive and for all the wonderful people, pets, and other things in your
   life. Try it and you will be very surprised. By exerting conscious con-

trol over the way you *move* your body you can influence the way you feel. If you feel good in your body, you will feel good in your mind too. By intentionally changing how you look on the outside, you will change the way you feel on the inside.

2. **Control what you focus on.** You have lived long enough to know that we all eventually get what we focus on all the time. The emphasis here is *all the time*. If you truly want to lose weight and everything you do is focused on losing weight you will eventually lose weight, right? This is so because you will be driven to learn everything there is about weight loss, nutrition, exercise, and emotional mastery. You will try so many different things that you will have no choice but to achieve your goal if you are healthy. By focusing on what you want with total determination, you create the emotions that are necessary for you to achieve your ultimate outcome. The question is, what happens *after* you have lost your weight? This is, of course, what this book is all about, and according to Tony Robbins, 80 percent is about emotions/psychology and only 20 percent is about knowing what to do. Take charge of your emotions and you will succeed.

3. **Watch what you say**. How do you feel when you say *I am so happy! I am thrilled! I am so grateful! I am so much in love!* How do you feel in your body? Do you look up or down? Are your shoulders up or down? I imagine you feel wonderful and calm. Now let me ask you how you feel when you say *I am depressed! I can't stand this person! I hate my job!* How do you feel in your body? Do you look up or down? Are your shoulders up or down? I imagine you feel sad and depressed and your body shows it. This little exercise demonstrates that your thoughts and the language you use have immense power over you because they create the emotions that control how you feel. Therefore, you need to be very careful about the way you speak and the words you use. Tony calls this process "Watch Your TV." By "TV" he means your "Transformational Vocabulary"—that is, the empowering language you *must* use if you want to create the emotions and ultimately achieve the results you want in your life. In other words, when we use negative words they create in us feelings of helplessness and discourage us. However, if we use words that create hope and certainty in us we will ultimately feel good inside, which will show on the outside. Decide right now to purposely use empowering words that show gratitude and love for all the gifts in your life.

. . . .

Weight loss secret:
*To feel good, use only positive words, focus on the
good, and let your body move as if you were a queen
or a king.*

Changing your focus, language, or body posture will help you change
the way you feel in an instant. Research[155] performed by scientist
Richard Wenzlaff shows that you can change your mood by watching
a funny movie, reading an inspiring book, or going to a sports event.
Furthermore, Wenzlaff shows that heavy TV watching can cause and
increase depression.

. . . .

Mastering the Relationship with Yourself

"No one can make you feel inferior without your consent."
—Eleanor Roosevelt

Did you know?

Scientists at Stanford University Medical School[156] found that people
who had suffered a heart attack and continued to be angry, aggressive,
and hostile had the highest likelihood of having a second heart attack.
What this tells us is that harboring negative emotions hurts our bodies
in a significant way. And how we feel on a regular basis plays a significant role in predicting and possibly preventing health challenges.

Our ability to take control of our emotions and have them serve rather than
hinder us has to do in large part with the way we manage the relationship we
have with ourselves. The following questions will help you identify the quality
of your relationship with yourself:

1. Are you your best friend?
2. Do you like yourself? Do you love yourself?
3. Do you love to spend time with yourself meditating, praying, or
    contemplating?
4. Do you find yourself attractive? Which parts of yourself do you
    find attractive? Why? Which parts do you find less attractive?
    Why?

5.   Do you love your body and tell yourself regularly how much you appreciate your eyes, your ears, your hands, your feet, your heart, and every single organ in your body?

The answers you give to these questions are a direct reflection of the way you think and interpret the world inside and outside of you. The meaning you attach to your world has a major influence not only on the way you feel but also on the way you look, your weight, your overall health, and your well-being. Clinical research published in 1985 by Felten et al.[157] in the *Journal of Immunology* shows repeatedly that anxiety, depression, and anger are the most damaging emotions we can have because they cause stress, which in turn lowers our immune system response. Under stress, the endocrine system produces adrenaline, noradrenaline, prolactin, cortisol, beta-endorphin, and encephalin. These hormones affect the immune system.

Our weight is, of course, also affected because some of these hormones affect glucagon and the human growth hormones. Both these hormones counteract the effects of insulin, which leads to a deficiency of insulin in the body. Low insulin, in turn, negatively affects the digestion process, which leads to malnutrition, low levels of serotonin (the happy hormone), depression, insomnia, and overeating. With low insulin, blood sugar goes up until it spills into the urine. Over a long period of time this state can lead to numerous diseases including blindness, kidney failure, arteriosclerosis, heart disease, a weak nervous system, obesity, and diabetes. This is not a pretty picture. We create a vicious cycle that destroys us.

● ●

Weight loss secret:
Having a good relationship with yourself helps you reduce stress in your life, which if not addressed could make you gain weight.

Stress happens first in your head. In reality, nothing can truly affect you if you don't allow it to. By developing a good relationship with yourself, you are able to reduce significantly the stress in your life. As a result you will not only gain and keep your ideal weight, you will also increase your health, joy, and vitality.

● ●

It should be in your best interest to learn how to choose empowering thoughts and master your emotions before they hijack you. You can do that by having positive thoughts, cultivating awareness, and consciously deciding to see the good in everything. Having a good relationship with ourselves is the first step in the right direction.

Love Yourself

"As soon as you trust yourself, you will know how to live."
—Johann Wolfgang von Goethe

Much has been said and written about love. Jesus reminds us to "Love thy neighbor as thyself." But his statement presupposes that we have the ability to truly love ourselves, which is the premise for loving others. Being overweight and facing related health issues has a lot to do with our inability to feel love toward ourselves and our own bodies. In this context, loving ourselves includes understanding the messages our bodies send us and following them. If we loved ourselves unconditionally, we would rarely fall out of balance. Love is the antidote to fear, anger, depression, and all the other emotions that weaken us. As such, love creates a physiological response that is opposite that of stress. Love connects us with our heart and with the entire world. It reminds us who we really are.

Weight loss secret:
Love yourself unconditionally.

Self-love is the key to joy and happiness and to the body you desire. Show your self-love by

1.   thanking your body every day
2.   making yourself feel good
3.   moving your body regularly
4.   practicing gratitude and forgiveness
5.   rewarding yourself
6.   celebrating life and making it a masterpiece

The human body is the most magnificent and intelligent divine creation in the universe. If you cut your finger, the body's natural tendency is to heal itself right away unless it is prevented by external influences. When we have surgery, it is the surgeon performing surgery on us, but who heals the wounds? The body does it itself, right? It is not the doctor. It is not the medicine. It is the body itself coupled with our *belief* that we will be healed. As a matter of fact, scientific research shows that the more invasive the intervention, the higher the healing rate. This has to do with our faith in science, not with what the doctors really do. With that knowledge, you can learn to support your body's natural healing process by becoming more sensitive toward its signals. This means realigning yourself with infinite intelligence, the power that created you. I call this self-love, self-esteem, or self-confidence.

Here is more of what you can do to show love to yourself:

1. **Thank your body every day.** Take a moment, look in the mirror every morning, and show your appreciation to each and every one of your organs for serving you so wonderfully for so long. Thank your heart for beating 70 times per minute without interruption since you were born. Thank your brain for serving you without having to be told what to do. Thank your eyes and ears for showing you the beauty of life in all its colors and sounds. Thank your arms and legs for being there for you every time you need them.

2. **Make yourself feel good.** The skin is not only the largest organ in the body; it is also the greatest source of sensation. The experience of touch and sensation is really what an emotion is. You can influence your feelings, emotions, and desires through touching your skin, which feels good. Give yourself a massage followed by a mineral bath every day. If you wish, use warm sesame oil to enhance your sense of well-being and activate growth hormones. By stimulating the skin, you will automatically feel good and appreciate your body beyond measure.

3. **Move your body regularly.** Give your body the gift of exercise (walking, running, swimming, etc.) every day. Nature is healing and it will remind you that you are part of it. You will be amazed at how good you feel after being out in nature especially if it was difficult to get yourself to do it.

4. **Practice gratitude and forgiveness.** Think of all the people you love and who love you. Thank the universe for all the abundance in your life and simply for being alive. Allow the feelings of gratitude to flood your body with joy and happiness.

5. **Reward yourself with healthy things and celebrate** every single thing you are proud of. Develop a list of things you love to do and go out and do them. This could be listening to music (write down all the songs you like), meeting with a friend, watching movies (come up with a list of your favorite ones), painting, singing, reading, journaling, writing poetry or fiction, bowling, dancing, working out, (window) shopping, meditating, or taking a bubble bath. Collect jokes and read them regularly to make you laugh for no particular reason, and journal your magic moments daily.

Practice Forgiveness

"There is always a better way."
—Thomas Edison

At times, forgiving ourselves and others may be very difficult, especially when we sense injustice. And yet living with the burden of that injustice, hatred, anger, or disappointment is even more difficult because it keeps us locked in the past. Forgiving ourselves and others is actually very easy: it is only one decision away. It is one decision that separates us from being truly free and alive. Decide to let go and be free. There is always a new day and a new beginning. Gain emotional closure by journaling everything, learning from it, letting it go, and moving on. Do not allow the past to rule your future. You deserve better than that.

••

Weight loss secret:
Forgiveness helps unload the burden of emotional
suffering. By forgiving, you also unload the
overweight of your body.

In their book *Forgiveness: Theory, Research, and Practice,* McCullough, Pargament, and Thoresen have shown that current scientific research on forgiveness proves the significance of the gesture. The Stanford Forgiveness Project, for example, showed both emotional and physical benefits in people who learned how to decrease feelings of hurt, depression, and stress and increase their feelings of optimism and   willingness to forgive themselves and others. Within this context it is important to mention that people who were able to practice self-forgiveness without the ability to forgive others achieved the same positive emotional and physiological results.[158]

••

Manage Self-Talk

"We are what we repeatedly do.
Excellence, then, is not an act, but a habit."
—Aristotle

According to the National Science Foundation, the average person thinks about 16,000 thoughts and a deeper thinker thinks about 50,000 thoughts daily. Further research shows that more than 95 percent of the thoughts we think every day are the same thoughts we had yesterday. What is even more interesting is that most of the thoughts we have are not even ours. They originated in our childhood and during our education when we were more easily influenced by our parents, teachers, and the society in which we grew up. What the above research tells us, however, is that we keep thinking these old thoughts that are not even ours. We are the result of our social conditioning, which includes TV, radio, movies, newspapers, and other mass media. However, we can learn to make the mind an instrument that serves us rather than controls us.

Here is how you can make your inner dialogue an instrument of your inner peace:

1. **Use affirmations.** Simply decide to be the only person thinking in your mind. Begin to think only empowering thoughts that guide you toward a life of fulfillment, happiness, and meaning. For instance, you can use affirmations that support your weight loss goals, such as, "Every day and every way I am healthier and thinner" or "All I need is within me now." Create your own affirmations and post them in your car, on your refrigerator, or on your bathroom mirror so that you are reminded of them everywhere you go.

2. **Reduce TV or computer time**. If you are watching TV or spending too much time on the Internet, you may want to cut down and instead go for a walk, read a book on personal growth, or listen to empowering tapes. By refusing to become an instrument of the messages in the mass media you create a vacuum where your own wishes and ideas can come in to help you achieve your life's purpose.

3. **Be smart and raise your standards.** Become more selective about the newspapers, magazines, and books you read, the movies you watch, and the people you spend time with. Read books that support you in your current weight loss program as well as in your personal and spiritual growth, and spend time only with people you love, who love you, and who are willing to help you on your new path. Your self-speech will begin to manifest new friends and a higher standard in life. You will be transformed.

4. **Meditate, pray, or contemplate daily**. Ask the universe for support in your weight loss program. You will be amazed how coincidences will begin to happen in your life to support your new journey. Your inner talk will begin to be guided by the universe.

5. **Unleash your creativity**. Do something creative every day. Paint, sing, work with your hands. Listen to calming, uplifting, and empowering music to let your spirit speak through you. Your self-talk will begin focusing on how your creativity can be better expressed and will become more empowering and supportive of your new endeavors.

6. **Reframe your thoughts**. When something upsets you, make a conscious effort to look on the bright side of things. Ask yourself, *What's*

good in this? How will I look at this 10 years from now? Remember that you are the only person thinking in your head and that negative thoughts only bring more negative thoughts and eventually disease. Instead, choose health, love, and a life of meaning.

....

Weight loss secret:
Make your self-talk an instrument of inner peace.

1. Learn how to think consciously through the power of **affirmations.**
2. **Reduce your TV and computer time.**
3. **Raise your standards** about what you allow to influence you.
4. **Calm your mind** daily through meditation, contemplation, or prayer.
5. **Do something creative** every day.
6. **Reframe your thoughts** by looking at the bright side of things.

....

By practicing these tools, you will see many of your disempowering thoughts and inner monologues begin to shift and your entire attitude become much more positive and empowering. As a result, you will have much better control over your emotional life than in the past. Your whole reality will become a direct reflection of your peaceful inner self and you will experience much more love and fulfillment.

Reduce Stress

I don't know why, but driving a car continues to be stressful for me no matter how many years I've been driving. My husband, however, loves to drive and deal with unexpected traffic situations, which he perceives as exhilarating. For years he has attended special BMW driver training classes where he has learned how to get his car back under control after an unexpected spin. What means total stress for me is absolute pleasure for him. However, he tells me that he also feels stress, it's just that he wants to play with it and push his own limits.

Each of us may interpret the same situation in a totally different way. However, we all experience stress in our lives, and psychologists tell us that beneath stress lies fear at both the physical and psychological level. How we deal with stress has a lot to do with our *own interpretation* of what the stressor means for us at that particular moment in space and time. Stress is not done *to* us. It is not happening outside of us. It is *within* us. We *do* stress to ourselves by the way we give *meaning* to what is happening around us.

We must learn how to deal with stress because it is part of life. By training ourselves to handle stress in a better way, we increase our ability to respond appropriately when stress occurs. That way we can remind ourselves at the right moment that we always have a choice: we can perceive stress as a threat, which can make us angry, anxious, or hostile, or we can just crack a joke and walk away unaffected by it. We can take on the challenge and grow tremendously.

If we interpret a situation as threatening, we experience stress. If we interpret it as a challenge or an opportunity, it is no longer stressful.

Here are a few tools that may help you reduce stress in your life:

1. **Practice conscious breathing.** Take time to breathe consciously for one minute three times a day. Take a deep breath in for one count, hold it for four times that amount, and let it out for two counts. You will feel renewed with very little effort.

2. **Superhydrate.** Make sure to drink a minimum of eight glasses of water per day. To lose weight, drink one gallon (four liters) of green drink (water with SuperGreens in it) per day.

3. **Manage your sugar level.** Get enough nutrients (SuperGreens, essential fats, vitamins, and minerals) so your blood sugar has the right levels. This is the best way to maintain a high level of energy, cultivate self-awareness, and handle stress.

4. **Practice meditation, prayer, or contemplation.** Roger Walsh and Frances Vaughan[159] define meditation as a technique to "train attention in order to bring mental processes under greater voluntary control and to cultivate specific mental qualities such as awareness, insight, concentration, equanimity, and love. It aims for development of optimal states of consciousness and psychological well-being." Take time twice a day to go into silence for 20 minutes each time. If you want to learn how to meditate, there are an abundance of meditation centers where you could study. Taking a walk in nature, sitting by a lake or the ocean, looking deeply into someone's eyes, and hugging a tree are other ways of communing with your higher self.

5. **Write in a journal.** Journaling is a very powerful way to deal with stress. Write down what stresses you in order to get it out of your mind so it no longer preoccupies you.

6. **Exercise regularly** in order to generate "happy hormones." Other physical activities, such as going for a walk, mowing the lawn, walking the dog, gardening, and washing the car, are also helpful in reducing stress.

7. **Use HeartMath tools.** If you prefer a hands-on tool to help you relax and reduce stress while sitting in front of a computer, I would highly recommend the Freeze-Framer® from HeartMath. Researchers have

found that emotions are reflected in the patterns of our heart rhythms. The Freeze-Framer is a learning program that allows you to see your heart rhythms on a computer screen. It provides you with training on how to shift your heart rhythms from stress to relaxation on demand. Learning how to shift heart rhythms has a dynamic effect on your health and cognitive function as well and is key to achieving high-performance states. If you don't like to use a computer but still want the benefits of HeartMath technology, use another device called the emWave Personal Stress Reliever, which I highly recommend.[161]

Cultivate Happy Emotions

In 1974, psychologist Robert Ader discovered that, like the brain, the immune system possesses learning abilities.[162] The implication of this discovery is immense because for the first time, humans are recognizing the intimate connection between the body, the mind, and the emotions. In other words, the immune system is the "brain" of the body. Thus, by making sure the immune system is healthy, we ensure that the body is healthy. As we have seen, the immune system is deeply affected by the emotions. With our cognitive capacity as human beings, we are in a position to choose everything and anything in life, including the emotions we want to experience on an ongoing basis. By having the intention and putting our attention toward a set of positive emotions—such as determination, patience, laughter, and joy—we take control of our emotional life and experience more joy and fulfillment.

Weight loss secret:
Laughter is nectar for the soul and body.

Create rituals to experience more laughter and humor every day. By playing with children or laughing at yourself in the mirror for no reason whatsoever, you increase the joy in your life as well as in others'. By listening to music, going for a walk, doing aromatherapy, getting a massage, engaging in biofeedback, or practicing yoga, you can change your old thoughts and create happy new emotions. In addition, by practicing meditation, contemplation, and prayer you can reach a level of self-awareness or a state of consciousness without thoughts. This supports you in cultivating the silent witness technique, which takes you out of the automatic emotional response and into the desired emotional response. True freedom and joy are the results.

Changing Your Perception of Time

Those of us who have been in love know that when we are with our beloved, time falls away. Conversely, when we stand in line somewhere, such as at the supermarket, time seems to stand still. Thanks to Albert Einstein, we know that time is relative, and yet I for one never seem to have enough time to do all the things I want to do. This, of course, stresses me enormously. When this happens I have trained myself to remember to ask the following questions:

1. What would happen if I did not accomplish X?
2. What are some alternative and more productive ways to achieve X?
3. Who can help me achieve X?
4. Can I extend the deadline?
5. What can I do now to relax and be more productive?
6. Whom can I model who achieved the same results in a shorter period of time?
7. Is it worth ruining my day through the stress I generate?
8. What can I do to have fun in the process and still achieve my goal?

As I ponder these questions I become more aware of what's going on and remind myself of who I am and how I want to live. I remember that a rigid attachment to an outcome interferes with the process of creating it.

· ·

Weight loss secret:
Change your notion of time.

By asking yourself the above questions and practicing silent witnessing in the ways I have illustrated, you can learn to switch your orientation from the result to the process itself. By doing this, you can accomplish much more with much less effort because you are calmer and in line with nature, which has no notion of time. There is no such thing as time in the universe. Time is a human creation. As a result you can make time serve you rather than the other way around. By learning more about your inner thought process and about yourself and how you operate, you can create a greater sense of happiness and fulfillment. Greater health and ideal weight are the results.

· ·

Master Your Emotions by Treating Food and Chemical Imbalances in Your Body

Indigestion, food allergies, and food sensitivities can create biochemical and hormonal imbalances in the body. These imbalances can produce severe emotional disturbances, which in turn are caused by low levels of serotonin, the so-called happy hormone. Consult with your physician to make sure your nutrition and the absorption of nutrients is normal and do not trigger emotional imbalance.

• •

Weight loss secret:
Heal food allergies, sensitivities, and indigestion.

Make sure to address your allergies and food sensitivities. The result is increased production of serotonin, which in turn leads to overall well-being and healing. However, hormonal interactions in the body are extremely complex and difficult to address. I highly recommend consulting your physician for further information.

• •

How to Stop Emotional Eating

Did you know?

Approximately 2 percent of the population in the United States suffers from a disorder called binge eating. Furthermore, there are people who eat practically anything, including dirt, laundry starch, chalk, buttons, cigarette butts, matches, sand, soap, toothpaste, and so on.[163]

How often have you eaten when you felt bad, or good, for that matter? Under these circumstances, we often eat hoping it will make us feel better. And it does, doesn't it? By eating we add more blood to our stomach and that makes us feel better. Through food, drugs, alcohol, or smoking, we seem to be able to connect with ourselves when love and connection with the outside world seem out of reach. Of all things, food seems most comforting. It is there when other people or things are not available. It makes us feel good — at least for the moment. What we don't seem to realize, until it is too late, is that **food is only a symbol for love and not love itself.** So it is important to recognize and deal with our emotions rather than channeling them through substitute outlets. When we do, we gain control over our emotions rather than having them control us.

My dear friend and teacher Deepak Chopra explains that the easiest way to avoid a temptation is to give in to it. But we need to do this consciously, he recommends, with full awareness and lack of judgment. As we respond to our craving we become aware of the sensations in the body, which will send out signals of comfort or discomfort. We slowly start to respond to those signals and eventually lose the desire. A new habit has been created.

Losing weight and keeping it off means often learning new habits.

Clinical research shows that fear of consequences cannot motivate us permanently. As a result, we cannot permanently force ourselves into new habits because we are motivated mostly by the drive to gain pleasure and avoid pain. If happiness is the goal, then addiction is nothing else but the linking of certain stimuli with the interpretation of happiness or pleasure. Most overweight people eat automatically on a certain cue, in the same way smokers reach for a cigarette. We can identify what those cues are for us and observe ourselves. We can observe our behavior and disassociate eating from those cues.

The key to losing weight is identifying times when we are prone to overeating. When we eat, we should not do anything else but eat and do it consciously. Deepak Chopra recommends we gently put our awareness into the whole body and ask the body whether it needs to eat right now. The body will answer yes or no, but we have to be very careful not to go into the automatic behavior of eating without awareness. The challenge is that we have practiced this behavior unconsciously in the past and have gotten stuck with it. The key to change is to disassociate ourselves from the old behavior. We have to link pleasure to something else.

To be able to break emotional eating habits, we need to create better eating memories. Our genetic makeup, or DNA, changes every six weeks, but it remembers the diary of the evolution of mankind because our memory is nonmaterial. We change our physical body, but we keep the memory because the physical body is the result of that memory. In other words, when we sit in front of a chocolate cake, all we focus on is the memory of the last good chocolate cake we had. The cake in front of us can taste totally different, of course, but our body remembers the last taste. It is the memory of the last cake that drives us to eat *this* cake. We look in the rear view mirror but we drive forward. To cut into the habit of eating foods that make us fat, we need to create new memories of eating healthy foods that taste just as good or even better. We will never forget the old memories, but we will overlap them with better ones – create better eating memories.

To change old habits we need to learn how to create better eating memories.

We may want to eat not because we're hungry but because we're addicted to the past *memory* of eating. In such a case, just start eating, Dr. Chopra recommends, and do it very consciously. Don't interpret anything—just start being aware of your actions. If you do this every time you eat, you'll slowly see that the body keeps rejecting the food that is not good for it. By chewing very slowly we saturate the senses with the taste of the food and the experience of pleasure. We should be very aware of what we are doing because we want this experience to not be overshadowed by any other experience. Soon our sense of hunger will be gone and we will feel satiated and satisfied very quickly and without overeating.

••

Weight loss secret:
Stop emotional eating by creating better eating memories.

When you are about to eat a piece of chocolate cake or pizza, for example, notice how the memory of eating chocolate cake manipulates you into   eating this piece of cake. Become aware that this cake is not that cake you have in your mind. This is the key to changing the old memory into a new one. Push the plate away and walk away from it with a sense of celebration and pride. You did it! Your brain will begin to create a new, more pleasant memory that will support you next time you are tempted.

In summary, in order to stop emotional eating you must:

1. Learn to observe yourself. Give a name to your feeling.
2. Identify those times and activities when the urge to eat and overeat arises.
3. Look for those automatic cues that make you eat.
4. Control your impulses and delay your gratification— wait for five minutes before you consider eating something again.
5. Consciously disassociate from old cues.
6. Link pleasure with doing something else that supports you.

••

Now that we have analyzed the many aspects of how we can improve our relationship with ourselves as the foundation of a fulfilled life, let us look at how we can improve the relationship we have with others. Both are key to emotional mastery.

Master Your Relationships with Others

> *"For every minute you are angry with someone,*
> *you lose 60 seconds of happiness that you can never get back."*
> —Anonymous

Another important aspect of emotional mastery is the ability to build and maintain empowering relationships.

· ·

Weight loss secret:
Community is power.

The ability to relate to other people is not only important to our well-being and permanent weight loss; it is even lifesaving. According to research performed at Stanford University Medical School, women with breast cancer who joined support groups doubled their life expectancy compared with women who tried to cope on their own.[164]

· ·

Relating with other people begins by honoring gender differences, racial differences, and differences of opinion. Relating to other people begins with our ability to communicate with them in an empowering, compassionate, and solution-oriented way.

The Power of Clear Communication

"If I love the world as it is, I am already changing it:
a first fragment of the world has been changed,
and that is my own heart."
—Petru Dumitriu

Three years ago, my father-in-law was diagnosed with prostate cancer. A self-made man, he had survived World War II in Berlin and managed to leave East Germany right before the Berlin Wall was built. Having lived through tough times, he learned to appreciate food early on and was overweight most of his life. At the time of his cancer diagnosis in his late sixties, he was approximately 35 kg (78 pounds) overweight. When we learned about his disease, we knew that this kind of cancer could be taken care of quite easily and that it could be healed. We offered him our advice and support, which he was reluctant to accept. He was more trusting of his local doctor, who treated him through chemotherapy. Years passed and we trusted that his cancer had healed, until we received an emergency phone call. We were told that his cancer had metastasized to his bones, which had caused his hip to fracture. Immediate surgery was required, which posed an additional burden to his already weakened body. His health was deteriorating quickly.

Faced with this emergency situation, we all seemed to resort to old and deeply ingrained behaviors that allowed us to deal with our emotions. My husband went into what John Gray would call his "cave" and withdrew from the family. I wanted to support him by talking and by offering advice, the typical "female" reaction, which he could not relate to. Not realizing my husband's need for tranquility and solitude, I kept pushing and became quite defensive when he did not respond. I wanted to be close to him and criticized him for being so distant. Out of love and the need for connection, I allowed myself to become a victim. I felt angry and helpless.

It was not until I attended yet another Tony Robbins[165] event that I realized what was going on. As Tony shared with us his latest model of how to reduce stress, I realized that the real culprit of my unhappiness was my underlying fear. What I subconsciously had clearly seen was my husband's fear; what I could not allow to happen was the manifestation of my *own fear*. I did not know how to deal with it when it showed up, and I kept it hidden because I was frightened. Instead, I interpreted my husband's seclusion as his abandoning me. I gave him the space he needed but resented it. I continued to try to get close to him, but my approach was motivated by fear, not love. I continued to give him what *I* needed, not what *he* needed, for I did not understand his needs.

During the seminar, I realized that I wasn't able to follow my own advice—to transcend challenges that life posed rather than reacting to them and becoming a victim. My *own* fear of death prevented me from joining my husband in his pain. He was afraid of losing his father. My own emotions prevented me from sharing his suffering, and I could not bring him relief through my unconditional love. During that seminar, I realized I had treated my relationship like horse trading. Although I love my husband unconditionally, I could not give him all of my love regardless of what he did or did not do. My fear had prevented me from sharing his pain regardless of the consequences. In theory, my compassion was there, but when my husband went into his cave and I interpreted it as retracted love, I went and retracted my own love. Fear makes us settle for less of what we can be.

> Why did I react the way I did? What could I have done better
> to support my husband and prevent my own suffering?

Born and raised in communist Romania, I was brought up in an environment dominated by fear, insecurity, control, mistrust, struggle, and lack of basic needs such as food and clothing. Most of the people in my life, such as my parents, friends, and teachers, were fighting for survival. Some protected themselves by becoming overly aggressive, others by masking their fear and calling it discipline. This discipline was often enforced through physical abuse. It was normal for the teachers to smack their students to ensure their authority was observed. Although my teachers never spanked me in school, I grew up in fear of being the next one to be hit. When I was faced with a threat or what I perceived to be an unjust attack, I would become angry and combative rather than compassionate and understanding. In both cases, I had the impression of being a victim.

It wasn't until I left home at age 20 that I was able to embark on a healing process. I eventually became a student of psychoanalysis, human potential, and spiritual development. I began meditating on a regular basis and created a toolbox for healing interpersonal communication which I call *compassionate communication*.[166]

Compassionate communication is rooted in my innate belief that we are all connected with each other and with the world around us. I have learned that the more I support the needs of my environment, the more the universe supports me. Underlying this reciprocal relationship is my understanding that I need to connect with my inner self before I can serve the needs of others. By doing that I am able to attend to myself and take care of my own needs so that I am emotionally fulfilled and consequently become more open to the needs of others. Compassionate communication the becomes a natural process. Please refer to the poster below for an overview of the eight steps of compassionate communication.

COMPASSIONATE COMMUNICATION

"I open my heart to others in love and service"
~George Leonard

The mission of my life is to be joy and contribution. My awakening is the awakening and welfare of others.
~ Mariana Bozesan

HEART QUESTIONS

"Is this who I am?"

"What do I appreciate more than the current pain?"

"Who could be in more pain than I am right now?"

"Whom can I help?"

"Who am I?"

"What is my identity?"

"Who do I love and who loves me?"

"What am I grateful for in my life right now?"

I AVOID:

- Moralistic judgment or criticism.
- Victimizing words "abandoned, abused, rejected" making others responsible for my own feelings
- Offering solutions that serve only my own needs
- Demands such as "you should, you have to, you must...."

My identity:

- I live in the field of all possibilities
- I am joyful, feminine & passionate
- I am a healthy 62 Kg athlete
- I am playful, warm and caring
- I am humble and centered
- I am grateful and aware
- I am perseverance
- I am determination
- I am wise and courageous
- I am an outstanding wife, mother, daughter and friend
- I am a leader for Good
- I embrace all challenges of life with great excitement & optimism
- I am manifesting abundance in every area of my life for I am one with God and God is everything!
- I am totally committed to love, contribution, growing and learning.

1. STOP VICTIMIZATION: I give new meaning to current situation

2. DEEP BREATHING: I breath deeply to connect with my higher self and with infinite intelligence

3. HEART CONNECTION: I access the wisdom of my own heart and allow feelings of gratitude to flood my body

4. HEART TO HEART: I connect with the other person's heart

5. FEELINGS & NEEDS: I ask empowering questions to identify with my own and the other person's feelings and needs

6. VERBALISATION: I

- OBSERVE: "When I hear, see, perceive, note, remember ..."

- FEEL: "I feel excited, touched, concerned, angry, frustrated, afraid, alarmed, irritated, lonely..."

- NEED: "I need to be accepted, valued, loved..."

- REQUEST: "Would you be willing to...?"

7. ACTIVE LISTENING: I just listen

8. REALITY CHECK: I continue if successful and stop if not

Empowering Questions

How can I turn this situation around?

Who is in control of my feelings right now?

Do I miss the larger picture?

What else could this mean?

How can I make this work?

What's funny about this?

Why am I manifesting this in my life right now?

What can I learn from this?

What's most important right now?

How will I feel when I have accomplished what we all want out of this situation?

What can I do to support this person and myself?

What are this person's needs?

What's going on in this person's life?

What would improve this person's life right now?

What do I respect about this person?

Will this even matter five years from now?

Compassionate Communication

1. REFUSE TO BE A VICTIM — CHANGE THE MEANING

When you find yourself in a heated argument, simply stop and say silently to yourself, "I refuse to be a victim because I am more than this."

In his marvelous book *Nonviolent Communication: A Language of Life*, Marshall Rosenberg writes, "When we listen for their feelings and needs, we no longer see people as monsters." Seeing people as monsters happens only when we interpret someone else's "no" as a rejection. We then take the rejection personally instead of understanding what's going on within the other person. We need to realize that it is we who label what just happened as good or bad. The moment we change the interpretation of the situation and focus on the other person, everything around us changes.

This is the reason I call this process *compassionate communication*. Through compassion we focus on the other person rather than on ourselves.

Compassion enables us to be in the present moment and see what is.

When we open our hearts "in love and service,"[167] we are in a true position of support for ourselves and others.

2. DEEP BREATHING AND AWARENESS — CONNECT WITH YOUR INNER SELF

To connect with your inner self, close your eyes for a few seconds and take several deep breaths into the belly while counting very slowly from one to ten. Empty the mind of all thoughts and emotions. Envision yourself totally connected with infinite intelligence as a source of wisdom. Visualize a beam of pure light shining from the sun through your head into your body. Your body will feel warm, calm, serene, and absolutely loved.

3. HEART CONNECTION — ACCESS THE WISDOM OF YOUR OWN HEART

When you feel pain, ask your heart, "Am I this pain or is this just a feeling that was *initiated* by the thoughts I had about the outside world?" Remind yourself that others can be the *trigger* but not the cause of your feeling. Then reflect on the following:

"Who is in control of my feelings right now?"

"Is this who I am?"

"Can it be that I'm missing the larger picture?"

"What else could this mean?"

"What do I appreciate more than my current pain?"

"Who could be in more pain than I am right now?"

- *"Who can I help?"*

Now go deep down into your heart and ask:

- *"Who am I?"*
- *"What is my identity?"*
- *"Who do I love and who loves me?"*
- *"What am I grateful for in my life right now?"*

Allow all feelings of gratitude to flood your body. As you feel a sense of gratitude for being alive and for all the blessings Existence has bestowed upon you, visualize how rays of compassion and wisdom are flooding your body, dissolving the ego's clouds of selfishness and fear.[168] Realize you are able to take responsibility for your own feelings, knowing this is the only thing you can influence. You cannot take responsibility for the other person's behavior, which you can't control.

Now you are *one* with lovingkindness and infinite intelligence. You have empowered yourself to fulfill both your own and other people's needs.

4. HEART TO HEART — BUILD AN EMPATHIC RELATIONSHIP BY CONNECTING WITH THE OTHER PERSON'S HEART

Equipped with the wisdom and love of your own heart, visualize going right into the other person's heart. Have the honest intention to support that person in any way you can. Be determined to open up to this person's suffering by allowing yourself to feel connected with him or her and by becoming aware of all of his or her difficulties. Feel how a strong compassionate intention is rising within you to release the other person from their suffering and even its causes.

Visualize the other person's pain in the form of a dark cloud.[169] Then breathe in this cloud and visualize it coming into your heart center. Breathing out, visualize sending to the other person a beam of brilliant light along with love, warmth, energy, confidence, and joy.

By connecting with your own as well as the other person's heart, you can now move your attention from your head to your heart. In this empowering state, you are in a position to truly help and support yourself and the other person in coming up with a solution for the issue at hand.

5. FEELINGS AND NEEDS — ASK EMPOWERING QUESTIONS

Before beginning your verbal communication, silently contemplate a few empowering questions about the situation and the person. You will be able to find out what his or her needs are as well as change your focus toward solving the issues at hand. Empowering questions provide new understanding, help us focus on solutions rather than problems, move us to action, make us be *response-able*, give us the power to make a change by providing a deeper meaning, and help us and other people learn from any situation. You can ask yourself some of the following questions:

- *"How can I turn this situation around?"*
- *"How can I make this work?"*
- *"What's funny about this?"*[171]
- *"Why is this manifesting in my life right now?"*
- *"What can I learn from this?"*
- *"What's most important right now?"*
- *"How can I make this better?"*
- *"How can I utilize this?"*
- *"How will I feel when I have gotten what I want out of this situation?"*
- *"What do I need to do to support this person and myself?"*

In addition, become curious about the other person rather than angry at them, by asking:

- *"What are this person's needs?"*
- *"What's going on in this person's life?"*
- *"What can I do to improve this person's life right now?"*
- *"What do I appreciate and respect about this person?"*
- *"Will this even matter five years from now?"*

The more clearly we know what our needs are, the easier it is fulfill them or ask someone else to help us fulfill them. There are various ways to classify human needs. Tony Robbins has identified six human needs: certainty, variety or uncertainty, significance, love and connection, growth, and contribution. Deepak Chopra distinguishes four basic needs—attention, affection, appreciation, and acceptance—along with the following hierarchy of needs, beginning with the simplest: survival, safety, achievement, belonging, creative expression and renewal, self-esteem, and self-actualization.

No matter how we classify human needs, it is important that we know what they are and know how to express them. I call this process compassionate verbalization.

6. COMPASSIONATE VERBALIZATION
OBSERVING VS. JUDGING OR CRITICIZING

Equipped with the love in your heart, you are now in a position to express candidly and in a compassionate way what you are observing in your world. Please be aware that it is your own reality that you are describing. This might be—and more often than not is—different from the other person's reality. The language applied at this point is of crucial importance because the language we are using creates our reality.

Express candidly what is happening to you and describe what the present-moment observation is, using words such as "When I hear, see, perceive, note, remember...."

AVOID moralistic judgment, evaluation, or criticism. Never use words that make you seem like a victim, such as abandoned, abused, rejected, or unwanted.

DESCRIBE FEELINGS IN THE BODY VS. EXPRESSING THOUGHTS IN THE MIND

Now proceed to give details about how you feel. To express your feelings, which ultimately describe whether your needs have been met or not, use words such as "I feel excited, touched, proud, relieved, grateful, inspired, moved, cheerful, angry, frustrated, afraid, alarmed, irritated, lonely, concerned, scared, nervous, mad, overwhelmed, disappointed...."

AVOID expressing the thoughts in your *head*. Instead let the love in your compassionate *heart* speak. Expressing your thoughts creates arguments, fuels criticism, and prevents others from listening to what you have to say. Under all circumstances, avoid words that imply victimization and evaluation based on the past, such as "I feel abandoned, abused, misunderstood, unwanted, threatened." These words imply that the other person did something on purpose to hurt you. By using such words, you are actually making the other person responsible for your own feelings.

The only person responsible for your feelings is you. Through this process, you become *response-able*. Take charge. Herein lies your true power. Do not give it to someone else. Speak from the heart.

EXPRESSING YOUR NEEDS

By talking honestly about your needs, you show your true vulnerability. Accepting and showing your weakness is the greatest strength of all. Soviet President Mikhail Gorbachev supposedly told President Reagan during one of their meetings that he would deprive the American president of his "greatest enemy by letting down all of our defenses." This is what eventually led to the fall of the Iron Curtain.

An Indian proverb says, "When we are established in nonviolence, our environment ceases to feel hostility." This principle led Gandhi to free India from British occupation. Gandhi said, "There is no such thing as defeat in nonviolence."[173] Living this principle eventually leads to absolute freedom and the end of suffering. And this is what your ultimate goal is, isn't it?

To show your needs, use words such as "I need to be accepted, valued, loved, appreciated, cared for, protected, safe, joyous, close, intimate...."

AVOID offering solutions or strategies as to how things should be done to serve your needs. Remember that the other person's needs are to be valued just as much as your own.

ASK AND YOU SHALL RECEIVE

Now you have the great opportunity to ask for what you want. The language you use here is again of major importance. To be successful, your request has to be stated in a positive way, has to be very specific, and has to be expressed from a position of equality and willingness to connect with the other person. You can say, "Would you be willing to...?" or "Now I need you to help me with..." or "Would you be willing to tell me how you feel?"

AVOID making demands like "You should, you have to, you must...."

To illustrate how compassionate verbalization works, I would like to give you an example of how I could have communicated with my husband in a much more successful way when his father was ill. For instance, I could have said to him:

"When I see you so quiet, I perceive you as detached and feel very lonely and helpless because I love you and need to be close to you. I have the urge to help you, especially if you are worried about your father's health situation. Would you be willing to let me know if there is anything bothering you? If so, let me know how I can assist you, because I want you to know that I am always there for you no matter what."

7. ACTIVE AND COMPASSIONATE LISTENING

After making your request, listen actively to the other person's response while keeping your focus on his or her heart. Go deeply into the other person's heart to get a sense of what is there. You will be amazed at what you will *feel* regardless of what the other person is *telling* you. If you feel pain there, use the technique of breathing in the other person's suffering and breathing out relief as described in Step 4. This will make you empathize more with the other person even if he or she is still in his or her head and not yet in a position to express his or her feelings. Through active listening, you will be able to see what is *behind* the uttered words, especially if you are able to interpret the other person's body language. It will tell you in an instant more than a thousand words.

Active listening also means paying attention to what the other person is saying without preparing to answer before he or she has finished speaking. Make sure not to interrupt the other person.

8. REALITY CHECK

If you were successful with your *compassionate verbalization*, you will feel the tension loosen at some point. You will notice that the two of you (yourself and your partner) are beginning to communicate with your hearts. Negativity and anger will give way to warmth, love, and understanding. Both conversation partners will feel good, and the energy—and sometimes also tears—will start flowing. Even if you don't come to a solution to the issue, you will see that harmony and friendship have taken over and you have come closer than ever to addressing this challenge.

If, however, you or the other person are not responding to love and compassion and continue to be negative, blaming, and judgmental, you have three choices:

One: Blame the other person.

Two: Blame yourself and feel guilty or offended.

Three: Go back into your own heart and release the person and the current situation into love. Wes Taylor,[174] an excellent trainer in nonviolent communication, calls this process "refusing to be a doormat." Refuse to be either your own or someone else's doormat. You can excuse yourself and ask for an opportunity to get back to this conversation later. Then you can remove yourself from the scene and get a fresh perspective on the situation.

In this chapter, we have addressed one of the most important aspects of human existence: the ability to master our emotions. The way we feel at any moment is influenced by the way we think, perceive, and interpret reality. By taking responsibility for our thoughts, we empower ourselves to feel more happiness and joy every day. By managing the thoughts in our head we manage not only our relationship with ourselves but also our relationship with our environment and the people around us. Using that power has never been more important in our society, where massive research "shows a worldwide trend for the present generation of children to be more troubled emotionally than the last, more lonely and depressed, more angry and unruly, more nervous and prone to worry, more impulsive and more aggressive."[175]

• •

THREE SECRETS TO REMEMBER:
At the foundation of winning the game of life lies your emotional mastery and your ability to

1. **Be grateful.** Go into your heart and appreciate all of the people and things you are grateful for. This will fill your heart with love for yourself and others.

2.   **Be happy most of the time.** If you are not happy most of the time then know that you are challenging your health and sooner or later you will feel sorry for missing out on your beautiful life. Remember that happiness is a choice and only one decision away.

3.   **Relate to other people in an empowering way.** Make a point of telling people around you regularly how much you love and appreciate them. Show empathy and compassion to others and you will receive it back a thousandfold. Stay away from people who don't share your goals and your values. Remember the idiom that says that "people who don't go with you hold you back."

• •

As Helen Keller said, *"Keep your face to the sunshine and you cannot see the shadows."* This means you have to make the conscious decision to face the light. It is your choice.

Part 3

Creating Lasting Change

Step 6: Conditioning for Success – Make It a Habit

"We are what we repeatedly do.
Excellence, then, is not an act, but a habit."
—Aristotle

It was on a winter day in 1955 that a seamstress in Montgomery, Alabama, violated a city ordinance by refusing to give up her bus seat to a white passenger. Her act of defiance started the modern civil rights movement in the United States, which ended legal segregation in America. The name of this brave woman was Rosa Parks, and her decision to exercise her free will changed the course of history and made her an inspiration to people worldwide.

Free will is a divine gift. Even in the most oppressive societies and in the most depressing situations we all have the opportunity to make choices—about our actions and our attitudes—at every moment. Our life and our future are shaped at the moment we make a decision. But despite this gift of free will, we sometimes take the wrong decision because we are afraid of the pain the "right" decision implies—even if we know that the right decision would result in achieving the desired goal. Rosa Parks, Mahatma Gandhi, Nelson Mandela, Mother Theresa, Martin Luther King Jr., and everybody else who has ever exercised their free will were perhaps afraid to take a chance but did it anyway. They did it because they realized that not stepping up would create even more pain. Their desire for peace and freedom helped them overcome their fears.

According to the Vedas, the primary texts of Hinduism, desires are nothing less than "pure potentiality seeking manifestation." This 5,000-year-old quote tells us that along with our desires, the universe is already providing us the full plan for their manifestation, just as it did so for Rosa Parks, Gandhi, and others. Deep down inside, we already know the answer to our problems and we generally have the means to fulfill our desires. It comes down to trusting our instincts and deciding to follow through with our decision to act despite the potential discomfort, embarrassment, or pain.

In other words, the simple fact that you want to lose weight permanently is already leading you toward your weight success. You have decided to acknowledge your desire to change. You have decided to read this book. You may have already started to formalize how you will implement the behavior changes discussed in earlier chapters.

In addition to exercising your right to decide whether or not to execute a particular action, such as eating a healthy diet, you have control over your *attitude* toward a decision or situation. For example, you may choose to follow a healthy diet plan, but unless your attitude is one of pride and optimism for the fitness goal you will achieve down the road, resentment for having denied yourself the food you once regarded as pleasurable may make your efforts feel like torture or punishment and you may not be able to remain committed to your nutrition regime over the course of your life.

Our life and our future are shaped at *each moment* we make a decision. Each moment we allow ourselves to eat an unhealthy meal we lose some ground in achieving our goals and we weaken our resolve to face the next temptation, thus compounding the risk for failure. And a positive, congratulatory attitude toward our "good" decisions can make all the difference in the world between success and failure.

The last three steps of this program will not only demonstrate how you can take concrete action to reach and maintain your weight loss goals but will also show you how to create a life of meaning, fulfillment, and contribution beyond yourself, which is the true secret of lifelong health and happiness—the ultimate goal of any generation or culture of people.

Harness the Power of Attention and Intention

Like training your fingers to hit the right keys when you play the piano, training yourself to make good choices may feel forced until it becomes second nature and you no longer have to think consciously about it. The ability to consistently make good choices in the face of constant challenges or temptations takes two very important and powerful personal attributes—you must harness the power of intention and attention. So first, we must have the *intention* to make good choices—to acknowledge a particular desire and decide to achieve a particular goal like serious weight loss. Then we must have the *conviction* to follow through with our intent, our decision. Then we must be vigilant, paying *attention* to what it is we do, in order to catch ourselves in the act of performing a "bad habit."

To illustrate the power of attention and intention to manifest our desires, I would like to share with you a little story. The other day, I had a project meeting at my house. My team and I had worked hard all day and at around 7 p.m. we decided to call it a day. To celebrate our outcomes for the day, I offered a glass of champagne to the group. When I asked my dear friend Tisha whether she wanted a glass, she smiled at me and said with the sweetest voice, "Thank you, but I don't drink and drive." As she spoke, it dawned on me how tightly her identity is connected with the fact that she doesn't drink and drive. Tisha desires to respect the law by avoiding behaviors that might put her, and others, in danger. This is not to imply that Tisha never drinks champagne, because she enjoys champagne as well as any other champagne lover. But she will not drink and drive—under any circumstance—because each time she might do so, she knows she would lower her resistance to repeating it and risking the ugly consequences.

This is the kind of conviction we need to achieve permanent weight success. We have to truly *want* it. We have to *decide* once and for all to be slim, healthy, and vital. Then we must not sabotage our efforts. This state of mind has to become one with our identity, the manifestation of our desire to be thin, healthy, and happy; otherwise we will not achieve it. Life will throw at us all kinds of challenges. The only way we will be able to handle them successfully is through the power of intention, conviction, and attention to follow through with our decision. We have to know what we want (our *intention*) and then go after it by focusing (our *attention*) on it like a laser beam. Our habits must be congruent with who we really are—congruent with our identity, the self-manifestation of our desires.

Identity also means knowing ourselves. Knowing what prevented us from reaching our goals in the past is part of the process of becoming who we want to be in the future. We may find this process quite challenging since often our behaviors are so habitual that we do not stop to ask ourselves why we do things in the first place. We often forget that our habitual behavior *is* our identity. We *are* what we repeatedly *do*, as Aristotle reminded us. And if we don't like what we see when we look in the mirror we must be willing to change it. No one else can do it for us. It is in this willingness to break old habits—despite the perceived pain, despite the self-imposed shame—that our healing exists. If deep down inside your identity is that of a person who is unhappy being fat, heavy, and overweight because of detrimental behavior that you are unwilling to acknowledge and reform, then fat and unhappy is what you will manifest and remain. As Henry Ford expressed in a very empowering way,

**"Whether you think you can or whether you think you cannot,
you are right."**

••

Weight loss secret:
Harness the power of your attention and intention

By knowing your goal in its smallest detail and by having the intention and the conviction to focus your attention on its fulfillment, the entire universe conspires to help you achieve it. With attention and intention, the behaviors and good choices that lead you to your goal become second nature—become habit—as part of your identity and the manifestation of your truest desires.

The smaller the difference between your own true self and your habitual behavior is, the more fulfilled and healthier you are overall.

••

It is wise to revisit goals and question habits on a regular basis. Periodically, ask yourself, is it still my desire to achieve a healthy weight? Do my habits and behaviors still serve this goal? Asking and answering these questions is key to eliminating those compromising behaviors and habits that no longer serve to help you achieve your desired weight loss.

Action 1: Reasons why I failed in the past

Please go back to your journal or the Permanent Weight Success Worksheet provided in Appendix 5 and revisit the weight loss goal you have identified for yourself. Write down all the pertinent details of your goal. For instance:

"By <date>, I weigh x pounds (y kg) and fit with ease into my favorite <brand name> dress/pants (size x!). Everyone tells me how great I look, and <name of significant other> says I'm really awesome. I feel better than ever before."

Action 2: Reasons why I will succeed this time

Next, write down all the reasons you were not able to follow through with other weight loss programs in the past. Give answers to questions like the following:

- *What were the beliefs that prevented me from achieving and maintaining my ideal weight?*
- *Did I think of myself as an inherently fat person with little chance of becoming slim or as a dynamic and vibrant person with the potential to be thin and healthy?*
- *Did being overweight serve me in any way in the past?*
- *Did I feel in control of my emotions or did I let my emotions control me?*
- *Did I see myself as a victim of something or someone, or was I the captain of my life ship?*

Now write down all the reasons why this time you will succeed with your weight loss goal. Answer questions like the following:

- *Do I now have the intention and am I willing to do anything it takes to change my old conditioning, form new habits, and live a life of fulfillment and joy?*
- *Do I now have the conviction to follow through and make this lifestyle change work?*
- *How will this time be different from the past?*
- *Whose help am I going to enlist?*
- *Do I respect myself and desire this goal enough to commit to achieving healthy and sustained weight loss on a lifelong basis, no matter what?*

Now Let's Get Motivated!

Human nature is driven by two very basic instincts: the tendency to avoid pain and the drive to gain pleasure. To lose weight, we need to look into the basic assumptions of our own psyche that control the associations we have with food and with being slim, healthy, and vibrant. To lose weight, we need to associate massive pain with being overweight, overeating, and unhealthy behaviors, so that we will want to avoid this pain. And we need to associate massive pleasure with being at our ideal weight, healthy, and vibrant so that we will strive for this pleasure. Even if you consider this a mind trick, the reality is that mental motivation is everything. If we define enough reasons to lose weight and make it fun and enjoyable, we will endeavor to live in that modus operandi, or method of operation, all the time. Then, attaining an athletic body that we love—one that is healthy and vibrant—becomes a reflection of our true nature. Let's take a look at all the reasons that would motivate you to be slim.

Action 3: What are my motivations for attaining a healthy weight?

Please go back to the journal or worksheet and make your weight loss goals so compelling that they will drive you and give you a sense of fulfillment, fun, and pleasure. Give answers to the following questions:

- *What exact action or thing will get me out of my current painful situation of being overweight and catapult me into massive pleasure?*
- *What will give me more joy, happiness, and connectedness with my higher self than eating?*
- *What exactly will help me make my behavior congruent with my identity?*

- *What would motivate me to truly follow through this time around? Is it my own sense of pride? My willingness to be a teacher and role model for weight loss and vitality for my children, family, or friends?*
- *Would I be motivated by the vision of growing old enough to hold my great-grandchildren in my arms, or the vision of attending their weddings?*
- *What difference could I make in the world if I had more energy to devote to my local community or my favorite charity?*
- *How much more connected would I be to my significant other if I felt better about my own body?*
- *How much more passion would I have in my intimate relationship if I were more confident about the way I look?*
- *How would my sense of self improve if I achieved and permanently maintained my ideal weight?*

How to Break Hurtful Habits

Losing weight is about initiating and managing the change from one physical and psychological state to another. Psychologists call the phase of transition from one state to another "destabilization." We go through this destabilization phase several times per day, such as when we get out of bed and get ready for the day, when we go to bed at night, and when we go to work or come back home from work. Destabilization in the context of going to bed at night means that we interrupt our ordinary activities in order to wind down and relax, brush our teeth, read something that calms us down, and prepare to go to sleep. In short, we do something different from what we were doing before; we interrupt the old pattern and create a new one that prepares us and takes us to the state of body and mind where we want to be next.

With respect to weight loss, we have to harness the power of destabilization in the same way. The first step is often the realization that we have come to an intersection in life, a place where things have turned for the worse and action must be taken. At that point, we decide that we have suffered enough with the old pattern and want to change. We want to go from being fat, tired, and depressed to slim, energized, and enthusiastic. We need to decide to let go of the old behavioral patterns that made us gain weight and replace them with new, more empowering patterns that will put us, and keep us, in the state of being slim.

Everyone who has tried to lose weight knows that this is easier said than done. We all know that permanent change doesn't happen overnight and certainly not by forcing emotions that often lead us to overeat or eat the wrong thing.

. . . .

Weight loss secret:
Use the power of your brain to your advantage.

Change happens by addressing the *memory* we have attached to certain events and emotions. Research indicates that it is impossible for us to forget memories in their entirety. In other words, the memories of eating a pizza or a chocolate cake stick with us forever. Attempting to get rid of those memories is a nuisance, especially if there is a strong emotional association involved with the experience, be it good or bad. If we want to disassociate from old memories we must consciously interrupt the old behavior and *replace* it with a new one that serves and supports us better. By doing that and by rewarding ourselves each time we land on the better side of the destabilization process, we begin to change in the desired direction. This is how the brain works, and this is the power that we must use to our advantage.

. . . .

There are several techniques we can use to achieve the goal of destabilization. One of the most powerful ones is to cultivate awareness, which means focusing on the goal of losing weight and keeping it off permanently. This involves practicing the power of intention and attention mentioned before. Every time we find ourselves going back to some old behavior that doesn't serve us, such as overeating, we need to notice what we are doing—the cue that triggered the old behavior—gently let go, and perform the new, healthy behavior like playing the piano or going for an evening walk after dinner when we would normally be having dessert. We then acknowledge ourselves for becoming aware of the old behavior and thwarting it. And we can reward ourselves with a relaxing walk or exchanged massage with a partner, for example, each time we make a good choice and exhibit a healthy behavior.

In his tapes, books, and seminars,[176] Tony Robbins teaches several very powerful NLP (neurolinguistic programming) techniques to induce destabilization and interrupt disempowering patterns by replacing them with new, more empowering behaviors. Tony has further developed these NLP techniques and coined the term NAC® (neuro-associative conditioning®), a method that supports the brain in quickly learning new patterns. Based on personal experience, I can tell you that both NLP and NAC can make change happen in the fastest possible way. Check them out.

No matter what technique we apply, however, it is important that we decide to change. In doing so, we become more and more aware of what we are actually doing. Our behavior begins to change to support our new goals.

Action 4: What am I willing to do to change my life for the better?

Now go back to your journal or the worksheet and look into what you are willing to do to interrupt your disempowering habits for the purpose of achieving your permanent weight goals. Ask yourself the following questions:

- *What am I willing to do to destabilize my old destructive habits?*
- *What will I do the next time I find myself overeating?*
- *What am I willing to do so my brain links pain to eating everything on my plate and pleasure to pushing the plate away?*
- *How am I going to celebrate every time I succeed with eating right, exercising, etc.?*
- *What powerful visual images of myself am I willing to create and envision daily that will help my brain want to go there more often?*
- *Whose support (friend, child, partner, other relatives) will I enlist to support me in my process of leaving behind old habits and creating new ones?*
- *What am I willing to do to keep on my new path when I feel overcome by distress, chaos, or insecurity?*

Restructuring – Creating Healthy Habits for Permanent Weight Loss

Major change, such as weight loss, is always challenging and can be scary because it takes us into the unknown. No matter how bad we felt doing the same old thing, we still had a sense of certainty, because we knew what the result would be. So to make change easier, we have to slowly interrupt old and destructive patterns that no longer serve us and develop new, more empowering habits. The best way to change old habits is to feed the brain with new and more pleasurable experiences and to reward ourselves, on the spot if possible, whenever we make a "good choice."

- **Eat organic food**. Consume mostly organic produce and foods whenever possible. Make sure that more than 70 percent of what you eat still remembers Mother Earth. Consume high-water-content foods, such as salad, fruits, and vegetables, in an unaltered state.
- **Eat moderately**. Deepak Chopra recommends.[177] taking two cupfuls of food for the first helping. He then advises waiting five minutes before getting more. Don't go beyond the feeling of discomfort. As a rule of thumb, in the beginning of the program, eat only *half* of what is in front of you.
- **Consume fewer acid-forming foods** such as processed white carbohydrates, processed fats, dairy products, meat, caffeine, and desserts in-

cluding all sugar-laden foods. Also eliminate negative thoughts and emotions, alcohol, drugs, and smoking.

· ·

Weight loss secrets for healthy eating habits

- **Make it an evolution, not a revolution.** Start where you are. Use the information in this book to make intelligent choices and trust your intuition. Your increased level of energy and well-being will be a steady confirmation that you are on the right track. Just imagine where a 1-percent-per-day shift in your knowledge, attitude, and motivation will take you in 180 days. It is important that you come up with a diet for yourself that serves you, makes you happy, and fits your body type, needs, and overall lifestyle. Be smart and have fun with it.

- **Apply the 70-30 rule.** To function properly and lose weight, the body needs to be fed what it is actually made of. Before eating your next meal, remember to match your body structure of 70 percent water with what is on your plate. About 70 percent of your food should be vegetables (but not potatoes) and leafy green salads.

- **Combine foods properly.** If you're not vegetarian, decide upfront whether to have a protein-based (meat or fish) or carbohydrate-based (noodles, rice, potatoes) meal. Avoid mixing the two in the same meal. Either the protein or the carbohydrate you have chosen for the particular meal should represent less than 30 percent of your meal. **Eat fruits (especially melons or citrus fruits such as oranges or grapefruits) alone or at least 20 minutes before a meal. Do not mix fruits with each other, especially sweet fruits, such as bananas, with acid fruits such as oranges.**

· ·

- **Eat more green vegetables** such as green salads, cucumbers, and zucchini, and consume essential oils found in avocados, olive oil, flaxseed oil, and other oil blends such as Udo's Oil. In addition, eat a variety of food colors and tastes to make sure you get all possible nutrients, vitamins, and minerals directly from the food.

More weight loss secrets for healthy eating habits

- **Refuse to be a garbage can.** After a meal, never eat the leftovers (yours, your children's, or your partner's) when cleaning up the table.
- **Practice eating awareness:**
  ‡ *Sit down to eat.* Don't drive or walk or speak on the phone while eating.
  ‡ *When eating, just eat.* Make eating a meditation. Don't talk, read, or watch TV. Maximize the experience of taste and listen for the body to signal that it is satiated. Become a gourmet.
  ‡ *Eat only when you're hungry* and when the stomach is empty. This is usually three to four hours after your last meal depending on your body type and metabolism. Ask the stomach if it wants food. This way, you maximize your enjoyment of food.
  ‡ *Chew food thoroughly* for 30 times before swallowing.
  ‡ *Take a fresh bite* only after the previous one has reached your stomach.
  ‡ *Do not speak* while food is still in your mouth. That takes away the enjoyment of the taste of the food and makes you overeat because you are not aware of what you are actually eating.
  ‡ *Eat a varied diet.* Your food should activate all the taste buds you have in your mouth so you have a sense of fulfillment while eating. These taste buds are sweet, sour, salty, bitter, pungent, and astringent, which have few receptors on the tongue but lots of effect.
- **Alkalize and energize.** Consume at least one gallon of green drink throughout the day to alkalize and energize your body. By drinking this much, your body can release its stored fats and toxins because it doesn't need to compensate for an acidic lifestyle.

- Reduce intake of toxins. Ensure that the food you consume is from the best possible source and free of chemical pollutants such as preservatives, additives, herbicides, pesticides, hormones, and irradiation. Make it a habit to read labels and eat low on the food chain, such as live, uncooked, and unaltered foods.
- Eat the right fats. Be sure to consume essential fats, such as those in avocados, cold-pressed extra-virgin olive oil, flaxseed oil, or perfected oil blends.

- Take supplements. For proper digestion and absorption and to make sure you have enough means to alkalize and energize your body, I recommend supplementing your daily nutrition with vitamins, minerals, and enzymes. In Step 1 you'll find a list of recommended daily allowances for vitamins and minerals.
- Take digestive enzymes. Take enzymes with meals to ensure proper digestion, assimilation of nutrients, and fast elimination of waste from your system.

· ·

Even more weight loss secrets for healthy eating habits

- **Use water to your advantage:**
  - ‡ *Before* **each meal drink a glass of water at room temperature** or preferably a green drink. By doing that you will tend to eat less while you get the best alkalizing nutrients and energy.
  - ‡ **Refrain from drinking ice water.** Room-temperature water saves energy for weight loss.
  - ‡ **Never drink water with or after a meal** because that will slow down the digestion and the weight loss process.
- **Cleanse and detoxify twice a year to address your cravings.** Food cravings are often associated with food allergies and food sensitivities that may come from your inability to digest and assimilate foods properly. Food cravings are also often linked with emotional issues. By cleansing and detoxifying twice a year you have the opportunity to address your cravings. Make sure to get professional support and the support of a group when you detox.
- **Don't blame yourself for relapsing.** When you relapse, notice it, learn from it, and remember there is always another day and another meal ahead of you during which you can apply your newly learned lessons.

· ·

- **Have fun**. Learn how to make healthy eating fun, and don't take anything too seriously.

- **Celebrate**. Every time you realize that you are satiated and manage to stop eating by pushing your plate away, celebrate like crazy. Celebration and the feeling of pride will send your brain the empowering signal that you are committed to changing your disempowering eating habits and you are ready to adopt a higher standard.

- **Reward your successes in weight loss.** Associating pleasure with your new habits is key to replacing the old and disempowering ones. Put a smiley face sticker on your notebook or agenda when you've had a good day.

Healthy Exercise Habits

"Those who think they have no time for bodily exercise will sooner or later have to find time for illness."
—Edward Stanley

Human beings were made to move. This is why we have such beautiful long legs and arms. Honor this gift by exercising daily, keeping in mind the following secrets:

- **Begin where you are.** It is never too late to begin with physical activity. Say yes to life, be open to new things, and follow your heart. Decide today that you are totally committed to your health and well-being and begin to move. Move your body regularly and commune with nature daily by walking, gardening, biking, or washing your car.

- **Hydrate and drink green drink.** Moderate exercise in a temperate climate can result in the loss of half a gallon of water per day, so be sure to drink enough water throughout the day and during your workout. Consume one gallon (4 liters) of green drink throughout your training to keep yourself hydrated and alkalized.

- **Take the time to stretch and to warm up and cool down.** Always begin and end your workout with stretching to prevent muscle injuries and ensure your muscles don't shorten. The best way to learn how to stretch properly is to take a yoga class, where you will also learn how to breathe consciously.

- **Combine cardio and flexibility training.** For optimal results, perform the cardio and flexibility training together in one and the same workout, three to five times a week, no matter where you are: at home, at the gym, or on a trip.

- **Get additional benefits while moving your body.** To maximize the use of your time, listen during your workout to empowering tapes that support your new lifestyle. Use tapes by Deepak Chopra, Tony Robbins, Wayne Dyer, Ram Dass, Louise Hay, or any other inspiring person who will help you along the way. You can also make your own tapes containing your own affirmations and goals. These tapes will help tremendously in conditioning you to new habits and behaviors.

Weight loss secrets for healthy exercise habits

- **Start small and be kind to yourself.** If you've been sedentary for a long time, start your new exercise program by walking three times a week. I would caution against diving headfirst into a vigorous exercise regimen without giving the body an opportunity to adapt to a new routine—that's a setup for failure. Remember, exercise is a lifestyle change, so it's important to adjust gradually. For the first week, you may want to walk for only 15 minutes at a time at a slow pace. Gradually extend your workout time from 15 to 45 minutes. Finally, pick up the pace! After eight weeks, you should be able to walk 45 minutes, five days a week, at a fairly brisk pace.

- **Fake it until you make it: call yourself an athlete.** Link your identity to that of an athlete. If you want to make exercise an integral part of your life you need to attach athleticism to your identity. Seeing yourself as a fat person who hardly moves will not get you into your running shoes, but visualizing yourself as a beautiful and happy athlete will. To have your brain support you while working out, say to yourself over and over again, "I am a beautiful, happy, and healthy athlete." This will soon become part of who you are, I promise you.

- **Be steadfast and committed.** Stick to your exercise routine religiously no matter where you are: at home or on the road. Get yourself a buddy or someone you will work out with regularly. This way you will ensure that you stick to your commitment to that person even when you may not feel like working out. Remember that your body is the foundation of everything you want to achieve in life and that it must always come first.

- **Don't worry about relapse.** Should you neglect your exercise routine for a while, simply resume it and refrain from beating yourself up for it. Remember there is always another day and you can embark on your new journey right here and now.

- Have fun. The most important thing is that you have fun while exercising every day. Do anything it takes to make it as enjoyable as possible so you will want to go out and exercise. Listen to music, sing, and dance along the way, and feel proud of yourself.

- **Celebrate after each workout.** Thank your heart, legs, arms, skin, and your entire body for supporting you so well. Jump up and down a couple of times to give your brain this pleasurable message so it will want to remind you to exercise again tomorrow.

Lifestyle Habits for Permanent Weight Loss

In addition to cultivating good nutritional and exercise habits, take care of your emotional fitness to achieve lasting weight success:

••

Weight loss secrets for emotional fitness

- **Cultivate empowering emotions** such as love, generosity, cheerfulness, passion for life, determination, flexibility, understanding, tolerance, curiosity, a sense of wonder, and any other emotion that makes you feel happy and fulfilled.
- **Make yourself feel good** by giving yourself regular massages and mineral baths. The skin is not only the largest organ in the body but also the greatest source of sensation and the richest source of growth factors that keep us healthy and make us feel good. By stimulating your skin you will automatically feel good and appreciate your body beyond measure. As a result, watch your stress level decrease dramatically.
- **Care for your soul and cultivate your spirituality.** Meditate, pray, or contemplate daily, listen to music, meet with a friend, watch empowering movies, paint, sing, read inspiring literature, write poetry or fiction, go bowling, dance, go (window) shopping, collect jokes and read them regularly to make you laugh for no reason, and journal your magic moments daily.
- **Practice gratitude and forgiveness.** Learn to forgive yourself and others and thank Existence for keeping you alive. Honor each moment because this is all there is: life is a collection of moments.

I-CAN-TATION: *I am grateful to those I love and those who love me. I am grateful for my open heart, deep love, compassion, and absolute faith as the guiding forces in my life. I am grateful for my vibrant health, intelligence, and beauty. I am grateful for absolutely everything in my life right now—the abundance as well as the things that have been challenging but have changed my life for the better. I am grateful to everyone and everything. I am grateful for all things that are happening from now on. I am grateful for my life. I love life!*

••

- **Allow yourself to be childlike**. Follow your inner voice, higher self, soul, and spirit, and allow yourself to be happy and joyous for no good reason. Be as you were as a little baby when you had no teeth, no hair, were chubby, and peed in your pants. Begin jumping up and down every time you remember that this is your true nature.

- **Collect magic moments every day**. You will be astounded at the beauty that surrounds you now that you are aware of it. You will begin to live in awe of the beauty and the miracle that life truly is.

- **Keep a journal**. In the journal write down every day how you feel, how you spend your time, and how you are progressing. Be kind and loving to yourself by acknowledging the fact that you are on the right track and that the universe is conspiring to help you succeed.

I-CAN-TATION: *I have an open and compassionate heart. I have within me the light of love as my universal source of faith, intelligence, and compassion. I am divinely guided. I am one with my creator and a force for good. I am humble, grateful, and aware at every moment of my life. I have an outstandingly healthy and vital body that I exercise daily with joy. I eat only healthy foods that give me life force, heal my body, reinforce my vibrant health, and give me energy and strength. I always have my ideal weight. I let go of old hurts and I am free. I have a healthy and loving family life that is enhanced by influential, smart, and successful friends and business associates. I empower people to create a life of true fulfillment for themselves and others. All I need is within me NOW!*

- **Honor the call of nature** and go to the bathroom when asked to do so by your body. Make sure you have at least one bowel movement per day. Preferably you should have one bowel movement 30 minutes after each meal.

- Be smart about food shopping. Don't shop for food when you are hungry. Eat some fruit before going to shop for food. Always purchase organic foods whenever available: you will need to eat less to feel satiated, will be better nourished, and will have the satisfaction of having contributed to a healthier planet. In the long run, you will save money by having fewer doctor bills, which might compensate you for the possible higher prices of organic foods. Also, reduce your purchase and consumption of prepackaged and processed foods. Make a habit of reading labels. Use the rule of thumb that says that if you cannot read or understand it, it is not good for you. Remind yourself that your body is part of nature and that these foods are treated so that nature cannot break them down. Therefore, do not put these foods in your body. Leave them on the shelf where they belong. Your body is not some shelf in a store.

- **Eat healthy snacks**. Don't eat prepackaged snacks unless they are made of raw foods. Instead, make a habit of carrying with you soaked raw nuts and seeds, carrots, celery sticks, or other fruits and vegetables that you can eat when you need to snack during the day.

....

Weight loss secrets for lifestyle changes

- **Choose supportive peers.** We become like our environment. To make sure you achieve your weight loss goals, surround yourself with people who will support you 100 percent on your new path. Stay away from those who drag you down, are jealous, or are afraid of losing you because you may change and be different from them. Remember the old adage "people who don't go with you hold you back." There are more than 6 billion people on this planet, so if one of them doesn't like you, you can easily choose new friends.

- **Make no exceptions.** Until you have achieved your goal of losing weight by adopting new habits, make no exceptions in anything you do until new habits have been established in your life.

- **Cultivate flexibility.** Change doesn't happen overnight. It takes time to define your journey. Stay focused on your goals and be flexible in your approach. Make adjustments to your weight loss program until you find the right path for you. Be open and have fun with it.

....

- **Learn how to listen to your body.** After a meal, if you feel tired, heavy, bloated, or have reflux, take it as a sign that you have eaten the wrong foods. Next time avoid these foods until you desensitize your body through cleansing and enzymes.

- **Commit yourself to lifelong learning and growing.** Continue to grow by attending seminars, reading inspiring literature, listening to tapes, and belonging to a peer group that supports you. Get a life coach to help you stay focused on creating a life of meaning and fulfillment where having a healthy and vital body is a natural by-product.

A Typical Day in the Diet for a New Life

*"There is no passion to be found in playing small
—in settling for a life that is less than what you are capable
of living."*
—Nelson Mandela

From my personal experience I know that when I develop a plan upon which I can easily act, I can accomplish anything I want. As an example, I would like to share my daily routine with you. Please feel free to use it in creating your own schedule, because as Tony Robbins reminds us,

"What you talk about is a dream. What you envision is exciting. What you plan becomes possible. What you schedule is real."

Now you have the opportunity to make your dream a reality by scheduling your weight loss plan. Here is my daily routine, which you can use a model:

5:00 a.m.	**Wake** up and take my friendly bacteria—probiotic—with a large glass of water.
5:00–5:20 a.m.	**Personal morning hygiene and breathing exercise** while drinking hot water with ginger and lemon.
5:20–6:10 a.m.	**Yoga, visualizations, Transcendental Meditation.**
6:10–7:00 a.m.	**Prepare agenda and outcomes for the day.**
7:00–8:00 a.m.	**Breakfast** with family: raw food smoothie, enzymes, greens, supplements. Establish the family goals for the day.
8:00–8:40 a.m.	**Commune with nature and condition for personal success** while running outdoors (4–5 miles), listening to empowering tapes, and reciting my affirmations.

Figure 8: Mariana's Daily Health Routine

A morning person, I usually get up around 5:00 a.m. Before doing anything else I drink a large glass of water at room temperature and take my probiotic intestinal-friendly bacteria[180] to protect my intestinal flora. In addition, I boil and drink a cup of hot water. The water has several advantages. It flushes my body and helps rid it of toxins accumulated during the night. It gives me the feeling of being satiated. It warms me up during the cool morning hours and facilitates a bowel movement within less than five minutes.

8:40–9:00 a.m.	**Take a shower and get dressed.**
9:00–9:30 a.m.	**Listen to empowering tapes/CDs while commuting to work.**
9:30–6:30 p.m.	**Office hours,** which includes a lunch break (organic salad with enzymes), one pot of green tea, six glasses of water at room temperature, green drinks, breathing exercises, fruit for snack (with enzymes), and 20 minutes of afternoon meditation.
6.30–7:00 p.m.	**Listen to empowering tapes/CDs while commuting home.**
7:00–9:00 p.m.	**Dinner** with family: daily review of magic moments of the day. Every day during our meals together we cultivate consciously the feeling of gratitude for life's gifts while realizing that every day above ground is a great day. In addition, we have an outcome each day. For instance, Monday we practice the Law of Giving as taught by Deepak Chopra in his book *The Seven Spiritual Laws of Success*. We learn how to give and to receive gracefully.
9:00–10:00 p.m.	**Bedtime** routine including breathing exercises, journaling, massage with warm sesame oil, soothing music, calming literature or poetry, as well as giving thanks for and celebrating the day.

Figure 8: Mariana's Daily Health Routine

While I perform my morning hygiene and breathing exercises, I keep sipping hot water, which I sometimes enhance with minced ginger and lemon. The hot water continues the flushing of toxins and gives me a wonderful sense of warmth and well-being at that early hour. The ginger has astonishing properties: it energizes the body, enhances and supports the immune system, and acts as a wonderful antibiotic fighting anything with which the body might be struggling. The lemon alkalizes the body.

After that I begin my morning contemplation with 15 minutes of yogic stretching exercises while I listen to tapes.[181] I then spend 10 minutes visualizing every single personal and professional intention and aspiration I have. This includes connecting with my creator and giving thanks to Existence for all the manifestations of love and abundance in my life, including my family members (even the cats!), friends, teachers, and spiritual guides. Also, I intentionally let go of all grievances, regrets, resentments, and other negative emotions I might have by forgiving myself and all the people who might have caused me harm in the past. After that I practice Transcendental Meditation for about 30 minutes.

Following my meditation I prepare for the day by formulating my daily outcomes along with an action plan to achieve those results. I usually have breakfast with my family. Thirty minutes later I go for a run outdoors. On my runs I listen to empowering tapes, affirmations, or music. Home again, I take a shower and brush my skin intensely with a loofah bath pad[182] to remove dead skin cells, increase the amount of oxygen in the skin, and facilitate new skin building. On my way to work I listen to audio books on personal growth or something else I find interesting.

My meals generally consist of raw or vegan foods, which I always consume sitting down at a table. I take a digestive enzyme and eat without drinking water to avoid diluting the gastric juices. Normally, I have three larger meals and two vegetables or fruit snacks every day and take my last meal usually more than two hours before I go to bed. Most of the time, I spend my evenings with my family, sharing the events of the day and giving thanks for all blessings.

These are the simple guiding principles that provide the foundation for everything I do on a daily basis. This kind of routine continues to remind me what a miracle life is. Every day I can't thank Existence enough for the blessings I have been given since I was born in communist Romania. If I get upset, I simply take a deep breath and look at photos of my loved ones and at my life poster, which I shared with you in Step 4 and which you can find in the appendix of this book. By doing this I am reminded of who I am and why I am here—namely, *to love and to contribute*. Usually this small cue is enough to get me back on the track of love and gratitude so I can move on with my daily activities and focus on *"How I can serve?"*[183] as my daily mantra.

Your Daily Schedule and Rituals

If we want intended habits to become second nature so they bring about permanent weight management, then an *intellectual* understanding of what to do is not sufficient. The nervous system—specifically, the brain—has to be "rewired" through *physical action* in order to link pleasure with being fit and thin and pain with being heavy and overweight. Psychologists call this process *restructuring and stabilization* of new formative patterns. This rewiring is nothing more and nothing less than learning a new behavior. We need to allow ourselves the *time* to learn a new pattern of being, a new behavior that is more empowering. In order for this new behavior to become part of our daily life, we have to condition it until it becomes second nature, pretty much in the same way we learned the disempowering habits of the past. We all learn new habits through the power of rituals, which help the seed of change to grow. Like any seed of a tree planted in the ground, this seed needs to be watered, nourished, given light, protected, and loved before it can turn into a tree that gives shade and shelter to other people.

Now it's your turn to plant your own seeds for permanent weight loss and well-being. Begin by scheduling your own rituals.

Action 5: Morning rituals

- **Bowel care.** Upon waking up, take your friendly bacteria (probiotic, acidophilus bifidus, etc.), which often needs to be taken on an empty stomach. In addition, drink a large glass of water at room temperature to get the bowels moving.

- **Personal hygiene.** Brush your skin intensely with a loofah bath pad to remove dead cells, support and encourage the detoxification process, and enable new skin building. To stimulate the natural production of human growth hormones as healing agents, self-administer a massage with sesame oil before taking a shower. While performing personal morning hygiene, drink a cup of hot water with ginger and lemon.

· ·

Weight loss secret:
Sip hot water every 30 minutes throughout the day.

In Ayurveda, this simple technique has been successfully used to support effortless weight loss and healing for thousands of years. The results can be astounding.

· ·

- **Mind-body success.** Spend at least 10 minutes every morning in meditation, prayer, or contemplation. Before doing that, bring weight loss and all other goals into your awareness. Close your eyes and visualize having accomplished all of them. See yourself healthy and vibrant in a favorite outfit. Visualize yourself with your dream mate and accomplishing all of the successes you ever wanted. Ask yourself, *"How would that make me feel? How proud would I be?"* Put as many feelings of happiness and fulfillment as you possibly can into these visualizations. See them as if they were already part of your life. In addition, cultivate daily the power of gratitude and forgiveness by thinking of all the people in your life whom you love and who love you. Think of all the things you are grateful for and forgive all of those people—including yourself—who have caused you harm in the past. Decide to let go of all negative feelings in your life. Remember that you are the master of your feelings and not the other way around. Realize that compared to most people on earth you are very blessed.

- **Breathing awareness.** Before your daily exercise, perform your breathing routine. Count breathing in (for example, up to 8), hold the breath for four times that count (32), and breathe out for twice the breathe-in count (16). This ensures that your body has enough oxygen to help you in your detoxification process and to create the health and energy you need for the day.

- **Daily exercise.** Go for a brisk walk, swim, or jog, and use your rebounder to support your immune system. Do whatever works best for you, but make sure to do it for at least 30 minutes daily. Exercising in the morning ensures that your metabolism stays high throughout the day. This way your body consumes more calories and deposits less fat. Exercise outdoors so you can connect with nature. If indoors, read some inspiring literature or listen to empowering tapes.[185]

- **Set yourself up to win.** Prepare for your day by formulating outcomes and scheduling an action plan for your goals. Achieving the scheduled outcomes will provide a sense of accomplishment and fulfillment at the end of the day.

- **Green drink.** Have one teaspoon of green drink mixed with one teaspoon of essential fatty acids (oils)[186] in a glass of water. This will energize and alkalize your body and ensure weight loss. This habit will ensure that you will have already had a huge "salad" no matter what else the day brings.

- **Breakfast.** For breakfast, as with everything you put into your mouth from now on, remember the 70-30 rule, which reflects the content of your own body. This means that 70 percent of the food on your plate has to be high-water-content, high-fiber-content, unaltered, alkalizing natural food. Alternatively, you can have a raw food smoothie[187] or one type of fruit if you are not too hungry. Make sure to take digestive enzymes and daily supplements.

Action 6: Lunch rituals

- **Breathing awareness.** Before lunch, perform your breathing routine. Count breathing in (for example, up to 8), hold the breath for four times that count (32), and breathe out for twice the breathe-in count (16). This ensures that your body has enough oxygen to help you in your detoxification process and to create the health and energy you need for the day.

- **Green drink.** Have one teaspoon of green drink mixed with one teaspoon of essential fatty acids (oils)[186] in a glass of water before your meal. This will energize and alkalize your body and speed up weight loss.

- **Lunch.** Have the heaviest and largest meal of the day at lunchtime. This will ensure you use up all of the calories you have eaten during the day by the time you go to bed. Again, follow the 70-30 rule for all the foods on your plate (70 percent water-rich foods and 30 percent the rest). Remember to take your digestive enzymes with your meal. Practice proper food combining: decide ahead of time if you want to have more protein or more carbohydrates for that meal and eat either of them with vegetables or salad. Eat moderately and continue to ask your body if it is still hungry. Follow the eating awareness exercises outlined previously.

- **Go for a walk.** Make sure you go for a walk in nature after lunch even if it is only for 10 minutes. Let go of all of your regular thoughts and focus your attention on the nature around you: the sky, trees, grass, birds, and children. Cultivate gratefulness and bring into your awareness the fact that you are actually very fortunate to live the wonderful life you have, while every 20 minutes a child starves in some part of the world.

Action 7: Evening rituals

- **Breathing awareness.** Before dinner, perform your breathing routine. Count breathing in (for example, up to 8), hold the breath for four times that count (32), and breathe out for twice the breathe-in count (16).

- **Evening meditation.** Meditate or contemplate for 20 minutes before you eat dinner. Cultivate daily the power of gratitude and forgiveness by thinking of all the people in your life whom you love and who love you. Think of all the things you are grateful for and forgive all of those people who have caused you harm in the past, including yourself.

- **Green drink.** Have one teaspoon of green drink mixed with one teaspoon of essential fatty acids (oils)[188] in a glass of water before your meal.

- **Dinner.** Make sure you have your last meal at least two hours before bedtime. Eat a light meal following the 70-30 rule (70 percent water-rich food and 30 percent the rest). Remember to take your digestive enzymes with your meal. Take the second half of your supplements if needed. Practice proper food combining: decide ahead of time if you want to have more protein or carbohydrates for that meal and eat either food type with vegetables or salad. Eat moderately and continue to ask your body if it is still hungry. Follow the eating awareness exercises outlined previously.

- Before bedtime. Cut down TV time significantly. Instead, spend time with your family or friends, read something empowering, and journal the magic moments of the day while you cultivate gratitude. If any challenge showed up, spend 20 percent on the problem and 80 percent on its solution. Be willing to learn the lessons of each experience and move on. Self-administer a sesame oil massage and take a mineral bath to wind down. Listen to quiet, beautiful music and read some love poems or literature. Read inspiring literature right before bed, something that will soothe both your body and your soul so you will get a good night's sleep and recover quickly from the stress of the day. Go to sleep with the intention to remember your dreams and receive answers to the questions you have.

With this list of rituals in hand, go back to your journal or worksheet and identify what additional actions you are committed to do today to support your weight loss program. Give answers to the following questions:

- *Which actions am I committed to performing today to embark on the program that will support me in losing weight permanently as well as in creating a life of meaning?*
- *What are the three most important principles I want to apply when I have my next meal (separate protein and carbohydrates, 70-30 rule, no water, digestive enzymes, etc.)?*
- *Which daily exercises (walking, swimming, yoga, etc.) am I committed to performing, starting today?*
- *Which gym will I call today to set up an appointment?*
- *What are the top 10 things (music, dancing, painting, singing, prayer, etc.) I am willing to do to make myself feel good every day from now on?*
- *Which tape program will I buy/order today to support my weight loss process?*
- *Which friends will support me on this journey?*
- *Which friends will I openly commit to and ask for support?*
- *What else can I do today to show my full commitment to myself and my new life of meaning and contribution?*

Now you know what to do, and it is up to you to follow through. If you are still reluctant to take your destiny into your own hands, I would like to remind you that

Success builds on success and every journey begins with the first step.

Also, I would like to conclude this portion of the program with a quote from Thomas Edison:

"Many of life's failures are people who did not realize how close they were to success when they gave up."

I know that you are not one of those people.

Step 7: How to Close the Gap between Where You Are and Where You Want to Be

"He who gains victory over others is strong.
He who gains victory over himself is all-powerful."
—Lao-Tzu

No matter how successful you are in life, I dare say you want more. How do I know? I know because growing is the first law of nature: we either grow or die. So if you want more, and I suppose you do—otherwise you would not still be reading this book—I want to welcome you to the club. It is the club of people who want to make a difference in the world, who want to grow and contribute beyond themselves, who want to be today more than they were yesterday. It is the club of people who are conscious about the fact that they are unique and yet by being who they really are participate in the evolution of all of us.

So how can you close the gap between where you are today and where you want to be tomorrow? How can you kick your old habits and develop good new habits to continue to lose weight, gain health, contribute beyond yourself, and keep growing as an emotional and spiritual human being? How can you win the "inner game" with yourself?

The answer is simple: continue your journey trusting that you are divinely guided at every step of the way. As Louise Hay says, continue to assume that "everything you need to know is revealed to you and everything you need comes to you in the perfect time-space sequence." But you have to listen to your instincts. You have to allow yourself to be guided by the instinctual survival mechanisms that have evolved in the human race over thousands of years.

• •

Weight loss secret:
You can only achieve what you can measure.

All too often in life we do the right thing but we don't notice it because we don't measure it. As a result, we keep raising the bar of our accomplishments without stopping to acknowledge ourselves for a job well done. To prevent us from frustration and in order to notice consciously that we have indeed achieved what we want, we must measure it. However, keep in mind that success is, of course, an inside job. Nobody can tell you whether you are successful with your program or not. To succeed you must create your own measurement chart. This is the key to every successful person who is also fulfilled in life.

• •

For example, in Step 6 you created a concrete list, a scheduled daily plan of action, and daily rituals for permanent weight loss—actions and rituals that you might instinctively know would be beneficial for your health but that you have been avoiding or denying out of convenience or fear of failure. So to ensure weight loss success, Step 7 will show you how to keep yourself accountable so you know you are on track and will succeed. You will be guided to test your plan in the real world and see what works and what doesn't. Where needed, you will learn how to make the necessary adjustments so your plan is sound and supports you, rather than frustrates you, on your journey of more health and fulfillment.

Real-Life Testing

The best way to test a new plan is to have your first meal in the real world, your normal environment. However, to make sure you succeed, you will have to prepare.

Visualization Exercise:

1. Sit down in a comfortable position, close your eyes, and take 10 deep breaths. Fill your heart with love, gratitude, and appreciation for all the gifts in your life right now. Honor the beauty and opportunity this day has provided for you. Remind yourself of your beauty and uniqueness. Know that you are supported by the universe in anything you do.
2. Visualize going out with friends or family and successfully applying all of the new tools you have decided to use to achieve permanent weight success.

    ‡ See yourself wearing your favorite outfit and being totally fulfilled, proud, and happy.

    ‡ See yourself suggesting a dynamic activity, like walking and going to the park, instead of sitting at the pastry shop.

    ‡ See yourself tell your friends how much you appreciate them and their friendship.

    ‡ See yourself smile often and remember to breathe deeply because you know how relaxed and happy that makes you feel and how it makes others feel happy and relaxed as well.

3. Visualize yourself going into a restaurant and ordering your food following proper food combining (animal protein separate from carbohydrates).

    ‡ Choose room-temperature water or herbal tea over alcohol.

    ‡ Ask the waiter to replace the side of starch with a side of steamed vegetables.

    ‡ Resist the temptation to eat the bread provided.

4. Visualize yourself ordering and eating 70 percent high-water-content veggies and salads.

5. Visualize yourself enjoying your new eating habit because you know it will help you achieve and maintain your weight loss goals for the rest of your life.

6. Chew thoroughly, eat slowly, and see yourself pushing your plate away as soon as your body gives you the signal of being satiated.

7. Celebrate your new way of eating along with the fact that you skipped dessert.

8. Imagine yourself walking out of the restaurant full of energy and the pride of following through with your program.

9. As you sit in your chair, feel all of these emotions deeply, smile to yourself, and watch how your mood improves.

10. Visualize your friends complimenting you and asking you to be their coach in achieving the same results you have achieved.

Do this visualization exercise every day for at least five minutes. This is a proven neuro-linguistic programming (NLP) technique that will guarantee success if it is done regularly and with full emotional intensity because the brain doesn't make the difference between visualization and real life.

Real-Life Exercise

Now, let's do real-life testing. Let's say you meet with friends and go to a restaurant. Given the knowledge you now have about which foods make you gain weight, which restaurant would you choose? Let's say your friends want to go to a pizzeria and you go along because you don't dare tell them yet that you have embarked on a new life program. Once at the restaurant, what can you do to still be part of the group and yet keep to your new commitment?

First of all, remember that the moment you decided to go to a pizzeria you chose to have a carbohydrate meal. That means that when you order pizza, make it very light on cheese, order a thin crust, and stay away from meat, fish, or any other kind of animal protein. In addition, order lots of vegetables on the pizza and a large salad on the side.

Make sure to take a digestive enzyme before or with your meal. Drink water at room temperature—preferably bottled and without bubbles—before your meal and none during or less than one hour after the meal. Eat all of your salad and veggies but only a few slices of pizza and not more than half of it. Listen to your body and at the first signal of satiation push your plate away; do it with a gesture of pride and success. If you feel strong enough, you can share your new program with your friends. If not, don't say anything. Eventually, they will ask you what you are doing that is helping you lose so much weight. Then they will be truly motivated to listen, for you have proven to them that your program works. Once back home again, drink a glass of green drink to alkalize and energize your body.

Measure Weight Success

Here are some indicators for weight success:

- **Your level of motivation.** Once you have committed yourself to achieving your weight loss goal, you will have to make sure you revisit again and again the reasons why losing weight is so important to you. You will also need to reexamine what you have already lost and will continue to *risk losing* in your life if you *don't* follow through.

- **Your body-size measurement.** The simplest way to measure your body size is to see how loose your clothing gets before you feel the need to buy a new pair of pants or a new dress.

- **Your energy level.** As your body has less work to do digesting, you will have significantly more energy than before. You will begin to need less sleep and have more hours to yourself during the day.

- **Your weight.** As you begin eliminating reactive foods from your diet, you will begin losing significant pounds of "false fat" (water tissue and bloating) very quickly. In addition, through the process of the detoxification/cleanse and after eliminating mucoid plaque, you will have lost at least 10 pounds of garbage that will never return if you stick to your new, healthier lifestyle. Your bathroom scale and your BMI scale (use mine at www.SageEra.com) will show you the difference. However, if you did not exercise before and have only begun now, you need to take into consideration that muscle mass weighs approximately 30 percent more than fat. You will feel better than ever and more energized although you may not be able to see an immediate and direct reflection on your scale.

- **Your increased level of awareness.** As soon as you set your mind to something, the universe conspires to help you make it happen. For example, you will miraculously begin to remember to do the things you want to do at the right time. For instance, you know you are succeeding in achieving your goal when you notice you remember to practice proper food combining, separate protein from carbohydrates in one meal, drink water at room temperature before your meal and not during, etc. And you will be doing all of this at the perfect time and on a consistent basis. In addition, you will be able to become the observer of your disempowering habits. As a result, you will be able to catch yourself at the right time and stop before you overeat, you will be guided to seek support from the right people, and you will begin to feel much healthier and more energetic.

- **Your competency.** You will no longer feel like a victim of food cravings and compulsive eating because you will remember at the right time to use all the tools made available through this program. You will know what to do when relapse happens.

- **Social proof.** As you begin to lose weight and look better, you will also feel better and be happier. You will receive more compliments and social feedback for your achievements. This recognition will validate your success and your new lifestyle.

- **Role modeling.** As you move on with your program, you will be able to support others with your newly acquired knowledge and become their coach and teacher. In the beginning, you may notice that your old friends may not like the new you. They may fear losing their connection to you. They may want you to be your old self because if you change they may have to change and they are afraid to do that. However, if you stick to your commitment to living a healthier life of meaning and fulfillment, you will be able to help those friends who want to change and you will attract new friends people who truly love you and are willing to support you on your journey.

- **Your emotional mastery.** Your ability to have better control of your feelings will increase as you succeed in bringing your body back into balance. Your emotional life, your self-talk, and your relationship with yourself and others will become more satisfying as you begin to digest your food better and are less stressed.

- **Your physical mastery.** Through your improved physical condition, you will learn to read and understand your body and soul better. You will be able to let them guide you and you will learn to trust them. You will learn how to listen to your body as to what you can eat and what you should avoid eating.

- **Your improved relationships.** As you begin to feel better in your body, your relationship to yourself and others will improve significantly. You will have more understanding, love, and compassion for yourself and the people around you.

- **Your overall satisfaction and fulfillment.** As you feel better, you will be much more satisfied with your life, friends, family, and work. If not, you will have the power, energy, and determination to replace what is not rewarding and fulfilling with what is.

Creating your own Weight Success Chart will help you validate your weight success progress. Here's how.

Creating Your Own Weight Success Chart

A Weight Success Chart is available in Appendix 6. By filling it out once per week for 12 consecutive weeks—preferably before each weekend—you can get a simple overview of your current weight success status and allow for possible relapses—most likely on weekends—to be fixed before the next measurement. Where necessary, please fill out a number between 1 and 10, where 10 would be the best possible valuation.

Evaluating Your Weekly Chart and Closing the Gap

After completing your weekly Weight Success Chart, make sure you look at each and every one of the measurement points and evaluate them. If your meter has improved, celebrate by doing something you really enjoy such as calling a friend to share your success, going shopping for new clothes, buying a new book, or going dancing or to a movie (but do not eat anything while watching the movie and banish soft drinks from your life!). Even simply jumping up and down like an excited little kid and praising yourself for your milestone achievements is effective, not only for your soul but more importantly for your brain that needs positive reinforcement to condition the new behavior.

If your meter has remained the same or is lower than before, don't be disappointed. Give thanks for the opportunity to grow and for your ability to identify the specific factors that need adjustment. For you have already succeeded at the first step to permanent weight loss—acknowledging your intent to lose weight and being committed to making the new behaviors a habit—and now, after reading about all the good habits identified in Step 6, you know *what* behaviors to look at and what to change.

For example, let's say your weight has gone up one or two pounds. Revisit the healthy eating habits you identified for yourself in Step 6 of this program and see if anything else is missing or has dropped from your daily routine. Add these missing rituals to your program and move on without beating yourself up.

....

Weight loss secret:
Stop beating yourself up.

Remember that relapse is part of life and of any process of change. Beating yourself up will only discourage you and will not help anything or anybody. Rewarding yourself for catching yourself in a relapse is a   better response than beating yourself up. Catching yourself in a relapse is positive reinforcement of good behavior and should be celebrated and not rebuked.

....

Another example of a possible disappointment with your weight loss progress could be that you may have continued to lose weight but you feel lousy. Whether it's because you had a fight with your significant other or a friend or some other reason, you now have the opportunity to journal exactly what drags you down so you can release it from your brain and move on to a place of happiness and well-being. Let's say your emotional upset is related to a person. Do the following to release it and regain your joy and happiness:

- Identify and witness your feelings, as if you were someone else looking at yourself.
- Take responsibility and realize, without any judgment, that these are your feelings based on the interpretation you gave to what happened. Note that your feelings are separate from the actual event or the other person's behavior. The event occurred; feeling bad about it or another person's behavior does not change the event or make things better. Feeling bad only hurts you and wastes energy that you could be using to boost your happiness and exercise that weight off.
- Release your feelings and consciously let them go.
- Journal exactly what happened and what you could have done differently to help the situation; express all of your feelings.
- Re-channel your energy and release the tension in your body through some physical exercise like walking, jogging, or dancing.

- Review the Compassionate Communication poster from Step 5 of this program and use the tools to help you move on.
- Share your experience, ideally with the person with whom you co-created the emotional upset. Talk about the way you feel by using the tools of compassionate communication.

To keep yourself more accountable and better on track, you can also hire a life coach or get a buddy or friend to guide and accompany you. No matter what, stay open, loving, and flexible in your approach. If you relapse, notice it, refrain from beating yourself up, and remember that you can always go back to your plan at any moment. Decide to do it now. Take action, keep your sense of humor, and celebrate!

Gandhi said,

**"Strength does not come from physical capacity.
It comes from an indomitable will."**

You have that indomitable will. It is at the core of who you are. Use it to your advantage.

Step 8: Nobody's Perfect — Celebrate Your Life and Make It a Masterpiece

*"The way to achieve success is first
to have a definite, clear, practical ideal
—a goal, an objective.
Second, have the necessary means to achieve your ends
—wisdom, money, materials and methods.
Third, adjust your means to that end."*
—Aristotle

Relapse happens. And in a destabilizing situation where we must make a choice—about food, exercise, our emotional response to an upsetting situation—we sometimes fall back on our old bad choices out of fear, doubt, laziness, or whatever the reason may be. But if instead of beating yourself up for a relapse you reward yourself for catching yourself in the act and correcting the behavior, you are well on your way to lifelong satisfaction and health.

One way to feel better about rewarding yourself for catching and correcting a relapse in behavior is to remember that life is all about change—and change is a beautiful thing. Change is the result of a destabilized situation, and as was explained earlier, destabilization is the only way an undesirable situation can have a chance to be improved. So the sooner we acknowledge the power of change and celebrate our smart choices when encountering each moment of change, the better.

And yet it seems many of us have a hard time accepting and adopting change. This explains why psychologists tell us that about 80 percent of any successful program depends on the participant's ability to properly manage the psychology of change. Knowing *what* to do consists of only 20 percent of the total effort. This is the 20 percent that reading this book will bring you. With this knowledge in mind, you can now embrace and celebrate change because you know that from now on you are in charge of your choices. After reading what the top experts in this area have to say, losing weight and keeping it off is no longer a mysterious black box.

However, in order to succeed, it is not enough to *know* what to do—you have to *do* what you know. Learning how to associate massive pain with not losing weight and massive pleasure with achieving your ideal weight is the single most important method of psychological reinforcement you could apply. Therefore, it is imperative that you learn how to saturate your senses with the experience of pleasure and celebration within the context of weight loss and that you forgive yourself for relapses and praise and reward yourself for catching and correcting old undesirable behaviors.

There are several ways to reward and make yourself feel good every time you do something right in your weight loss program. Below you'll find some ideas. However, please let your imagination go wild and show the love you have for yourself at every possible occasion.

- **Get a massage**. Celebrate this body that has served you so well thus far by treating yourself to a glorious massage. Remember that your skin is the greatest source of sensation. Make yourself feel good either by getting a professional massage once a week or by self-administering a massage every day. If you want to, you can use warm sesame oil to enhance your well-being and activate your growth hormones. By stimulating your largest organ, the skin, you will automatically feel good and appreciate your body beyond measure.

- **Give yourself a reward for reaching every milestone**. Get yourself a new outfit every time you become one size smaller. Or buy yourself something you've always wanted.

- **Take more vacations.** Take a long weekend every time you manage to lose 20 pounds or less, depending on your time availability or financial situation.

- **Attend inspiring seminars**. Reward yourself for your conviction to stick with your goal by attending a personal growth seminar or a one-week fasting retreat with Gabriel Cousens, David Wolfe, or another inspirational life coach.

- **Train your friends to give you surprise compliments; give yourself surprise rewards**. Ask a friend or your buddy to reward you with a compliment any time they see you doing something right, such as pushing your plate away while it still has food on it, passing up dessert, and taking the stairs instead of the elevator. In addition, begin putting money ($5 or $10 or more) in a box every time you catch yourself doing something supportive with your weight loss program. After four weeks or three months, open that box and surprise yourself with a big reward by going to a concert, flying to New York to see a play on Broadway, visiting a friend, or going on an extended vacation. Do whatever feels right or appropriate.

- **Celebrate your existence.** Follow your inner voice, your higher self, your soul, and your spirit, and allow yourself to be happy and joyous for no good reason. Be as happy as you were as a little baby, when you had no teeth, no hair, were chubby, and peed in your pants. Celebrate every time you remember this is your true nature and that you don't have to do anything in particular in order to love and be loved.

- **Collect and celebrate every magic moment**. You will be astounded at the beauty that surrounds you once you become aware of it. Just look out the window and notice the sky, the bark of a tree, or the bird that just came into your awareness. You will begin to live in awe of the beauty and the miracle that life truly is.

- **Open your heart and practice gratitude and forgiveness.** Take a moment and look in the mirror every time you go to the bathroom. Become aware of and thank each and every one of your organs for serving you so wonderfully for so long. Think of all the people you love and the people who share their love with you. Thank your friends and your enemies because they allowed you to grow. Forgive yourself and others for all transgressions that may have ended in pain. Let it all go and be free to celebrate what is; your life is a gift.

- **Cultivate emotions that serve you.** Love, generosity, cheerfulness, passion for life, determination, flexibility, understanding, compassion, empathy, tolerance, curiosity, and a sense of wonder are emotions that make us feel happy and fulfilled. Celebrate your new sense of self by using these words regularly; you will be amazed at the results.

To support you in this process, I would like to share with you what I call my Weight Management Poster. If you feel that it would help you, create your own poster, print it, put it on your desk or refrigerator, or carry it with you as a supporting tool on your weight loss journey.

How can I lose weight, sustain it and have great fun in the process?

"Pain is part of life. Suffering is an option"
~Anthony Robbins

When tempted to eat I FOCUS on the PAIN of the results instead of pleasure!!!

If I don't achieve this goal, what will it cost me?

- My health & vitality
- My eyes & vision
- My joy & fulfillment
- My marriage
- My well-being
- My pride
- My self-respect
- My identity
- My mission in life

My identity is:

- I am one with God, calm and centered
- I live in the field of all possibilities
- I am a daily meditator
- I am a wise & guided leader for Good
- I am joyful, feminine & passionate
- I am a beautiful 62 Kg athlete
- I am playful, warm and caring
- I am humble, grateful and aware
- I am perseverance & determination
- I am intelligent, wise & courageous
- I am an outstanding wife, mother, daughter, friend and leader for Good
- I embrace all challenges of life with great excitement & optimism
- I am manifesting abundance in every area of my life for I am one with God and God is everything!
- I am totally committed to love, contribution, growing and learning.

My Weight Success Formula

- When tempted, I visualize myself in my coolest outfit and CHANGE my FOCUS from food to my goals in life. I take action right away.
- I eat a balanced diet of 80% alkaline foods
- I take my enzymes religiously to ensure digestion
- I chew on each bite 30 times
- I drink one gallon alkalizing green drink daily
- I have one goodies meal (cake) once weekly
- I rely on my buddy and life coach for support
- I celebrate every little success on the way!!!!
- I exercise daily for the Big Sur Marathon
- I snack on fruit, veggies & raw nuts
- I measure and celebrate success daily
- I remember who I am and what I really want

POWER QUESTIONS

Am I satisfied now?

Is this food empowering me?

What can I do & enjoy even more than eating?

What are other options & resources? Water, ten deep breaths, work out, read this, read a book, sing, talk, meditate.

Figure 9: Weight Success Chart

We have come to the end of the 8 Steps for Weight Loss and Well-Being. You had the opportunity to learn about nutrition, exercise, detoxification, emotional mastery, setting weight loss goals and measuring them, as well as how to celebrate weight loss successes. Now it is up to you to apply the knowledge you have learned so it serves and supports you on the journey you are about to begin. However, in the words of Ken Wilber, let's keep in mind that

> "In the end we will find, I believe, the inherent joy in existence itself, a joy that stems from the great perfection of this and every moment, a wondrous whole in itself…one with the All in this endless awareness that holds the Kosmos together kindly in its hand. And then the true Mystery yields itself, the face of Spirit secretly smiles, the Sun rises in your very own heart and the Earth becomes your very own body, galaxies rush through your veins while the stars light up the neurons of your night, and never again will you search for a mere theory of that which is actually your own Original Face."

Remember, you are a leader in the field of all possibilities, and I wish you good luck.

Conclusion

"The day that hunger is eradicated from the earth,
there will be the greatest spiritual explosion the world has ever
known."
  —Federico García Lorca

After all is said and done, we need to remind ourselves of the beauty and the miracle that life truly is. In light of the environmental degradation, global warming, wars, and injustice our planet is facing, let's acknowledge how fortunate we actually are to live in a society where having the problem of overweight is possible. In the larger scheme of things, the challenge of losing weight is a good one. It actually means that we do not belong to the one-seventh of the human family, or 840 million people, who, according to the World Food Summit, "live in the condition of chronic, persistent hunger."

A few years ago I received an email from one of my friends[189] with the following content:

"If we could shrink the earth's population to a village of only 100 people, it would look something like this:

There would be:

57	Asians
21	Europeans
14	North and South Americans
8	Africans
30	white
70	nonwhite
6	people would possess 59 percent of the world's wealth and all 6 would be from the United States of America

80   would live in substandard housing
70   would be unable to read
50   would suffer malnutrition
1   would have a college education
1   would own a computer."

I don't know about you, but when I read this, I feel endlessly grateful. It puts things in perspective for me. It reminds me that we are perfect the way we are at this point in time and space. We are whole and complete and, most of all, we are "sufficient," as my dear friend Lynne Twist puts it in her beautiful book *The Soul of Money*. In the book, Lynne, an anti-hunger activist who over 30 years has achieved great success in the fight against starvation with the Hunger Project, reminds us how much our social conditioning and the media manipulate us.

We are bombarded with messages telling us we are not beautiful enough until we buy this particular cream, or that we smell bad until we buy that particular deodorant, or that we are not eating right until we buy that particular type of food. We are too tall, too short, too thin, too fat, or too poor.

Consciously or not, we have become part of a culture that is out of control. It is out of our *own* control. We live in a society where *we* allow ourselves to be manipulated to consume—at the cost of our health, happiness, and environment. We seem to no longer know how to *stop* and ask ourselves why we wanted these things in the first place.

We seem to have forgotten that all we actually wanted was to love and to be loved. We wanted a little fulfillment and instead we have learned to settle for material gain. The *symbols* of love—status symbols such as jewelry, cars, and houses—have become more important to us than the real thing: unconditional love. The results are obvious: disease, endless addictions and, most common of all, unhappiness and dissatisfaction. However, most of us arrive at some point in our lives where we realize that the pleasure of having achieved a certain material gain is not lasting. So we want *more*, believing that the new *thing* will finally bring us long-sought fulfillment.

It is time we wake up and notice the messages our bodies and souls are sending us. It is time we realize that many of us have been living our lives facing the wrong way. We need to get back in touch with our core, our hearts, and our love for ourselves and others. Independently of what's happening around us, we have to begin reevaluating our *needs* and ask ourselves which ones are actually *wants*. We ought to find out for ourselves how much personal freedom and moment-to-moment happiness we are willing to give up in exchange for achieving those wants. As Lynne Twist puts it, we need to make a conscious decision about how much pain we are willing to accept in order to accomplish unnecessary things just because someone else told us to. It is time to stop this downward spiral and go for true fulfillment and happiness in life.

When we realize that we are perfect the way we are, our heart begins to open and we make *giving* and *contributing* our main goals in life. The moment we put our love, time, and money toward truly serving ourselves and humankind, we notice how rich, wealthy, and prosperous we actually are no matter what our bank account looks like. A life of meaning and fulfillment begins. The moment we let go of what we don't *need*, we get what we actually *want*, Lynne suggests.

As soon as we change the focus from serving ourselves to serving others—while continuing, of course, to take care of our own basic needs—our whole life changes. We are now in the flow of life. We feel that our life has meaning. All of our concerns drop away from us. And along with them disappear very naturally those extra pounds, because we have found the most precious thing of all: ourselves.

Welcome home!

Namasté! (The Light in Me Salutes the Light in You)

Appendices

Appendix 1:
A Delicious Two-Week Healthy Eating Plan

Week One

SUNDAY

Breakfast: Sliced Cantaloupe

Lunch: Vegetable roll: avocado, daikon, peppers, cucumbers wrapped in rice paper

Snack: Raw cashews (soaked)

Dinner: Roasted eggplant in a pesto sauce

Alternative Option: Lemon chicken (organic), steamed asparagus, avocado, yellow pepper, tomatoes, and cucumber salad

MONDAY

Breakfast: Fruit smoothie: banana, strawberries, mango, dates, raw cashews (soaked), vanilla extract, cayenne pepper, and cinnamon

Lunch: Caesar's salad (thinly sliced smoked salmon optional), no crouton's, use sprinkled granulated pine nuts (soaked)

Snack: Hummus and vegetable crackers (no yeast)

Dinner: Stir fry: tofu, broccoli, red peppers, mushrooms, red onions, and tomatoes lightly sautéed in sesame oil

TUESDAY

Breakfast: Tomato Soup: pine nuts or cashews (soaked), cherry tomatoes, sun dried tomatoes soaked/ marinated in olive oil, capers, herbs, salt, pepper, olives, basil and dates (or raisins)

Lunch: Thinly sliced roasted eggplant, yellow squash, sprouts, and Falafel on sprout whole wheat pita bread

Snack: Raw almonds (soaked)

Dinner: Taco salad: pinto beans, guacamole, soy-based sour cream, tomatoes, cilantro, onions, on a bed of romaine lettuce

Alternative Option: Grilled halibut in pesto sauce and mixed green salad

WEDNESDAY

Breakfast: Cucumbers, yellow peppers, tomatoes, avocado salad tossed with Udo's Oil and lemon juice

Lunch: Mediterranean Salad: Moroccan Olives (pitted), sliced apples and pears, cut bok choi, lettuce, lots of sliced basil, shredded dill and parsley, sliced red onions and soaked cashews

Snack: Sliced watermelon

Dinner: Vegetable fajitas on sprouted tortillas with guacamole & mango salsa with mixed green salad

THURSDAY

Breakfast: Steamed broccoli & cauliflower tossed with olive oil and lemon juice

Lunch: Tofu cubes (organic chicken strips optional) with mixed baby greens salad - feta cheese and black olives (pitted)

Snack: Cucumbers sprinkled with lemon juice & pepper

Dinner: Three bean (green beans, yellow beans and kidney beans) salad on a bed of romaine lettuce

Alternative Option: Salmon in a dill sauce with kale and spinach (both lightly sautéed)

FRIDAY

Breakfast: Berries galore: strawberries, red raspberries, and blue berries fruit salad

Lunch: Wild rice and vegetable medley

Snack: Celery sticks and hummus

Dinner: Coconut pad Thai noodles with a spicy peanut sauce

Alternative Option: Grilled tuna, sun-dried tomatoes with mushrooms and olives

SATURDAY

Breakfast: Hot chocolate: soaked hazelnuts, milk with warm water, cocoa powder (optional) little cinnamon to taste; Avocado sandwich on focaccia bread with alfalfa sprouts

Lunch: Veggie burger on sprouted wheat bun and fruit smoothie with shot of wheat grass

Snack: Raw almonds (soaked) and freshly cut honey dew melon

Dinner: Hummus filled beef-steak tomatoes or red bell peppers sprinkled w/ finely chopped green onions

Alternative Option: Barbeque chicken breast (organic), Sweet potatoes, and collard greens

W e e k   T w o

SUNDAY

Breakfast: Sliced honey dew melon

Lunch: Miso soup with mixed green salad and no yeast crackers

Snack: Vegetable sticks with raw cashew/ macadamia butter

Dinner: Vegetable/tofu shish-kabob

Alternative Option: Lamb w/ ginger, onions, garlic, orange peel, salt, pepper, cayenne, sauce topped w/ garlic butter, mango salsa, baby spinach salad w/ pine nuts (soaked) & apples

MONDAY

Breakfast: Steamed artichoke with olive oil and lemon juice

Lunch: Sliced cubes of cucumbers without seeds, sea salt and mint leaves sliced

Snack: Passionfruit

Dinner: Thai coconut soup with avocado, cayenne/chili pepper oil and pumpkin seed oil; Pad Thai rice noodles

TUESDAY

Breakfast: Smoothie: macadamia nuts (soaked), dates, shredded flax seeds, lecithin, raw honey, bee pollen, fresh coconut with flesh, water, Udo's oil

Lunch: Avocado sandwich (tuna optional) with romaine lettuce, tomatoes, and olive oil and lemon juice and side of green beans

Snack: Sesame crackers (no yeast)

Dinner: Spelt pasta with pesto sauce and a side of cabbage (lightly steamed)

WEDNESDAY

Breakfast: Brown rice, mushrooms, peppers, and onions
Lunch: Roasted eggplant and bell peppers – red, green and yellow shish-kabob (salmon/halibut optional) with tomato and cucumber salad
Snack: Healthy date filled oatmeal cookie
Dinner: Lentil soup with beets and mixed green salad

Thursday

Breakfast: Kiwi and strawberries mixed with blackberries
Lunch: Caesar's salad (large prawns optional) – no crouton's – use chopped pine nuts (soaked) instead
Snack: Tabbouleh and grape leaves
Dinner: Broth-based soup and California rolls (veggie)

FRIDAY

Breakfast: Sprouted whole wheat toast and raw almond butter with hot chocolate
Lunch: Grilled vegetable: eggplant, roasted peppers, onions, chestnuts (soaked), garlic on whole wheat foccacia bread
Snack: Citrus smoothie with shot of spirulina
Dinner: Stuffed portabella mushrooms: sliced scallions, olive oil, finely granulate pine nuts (soaked), fresh sage, tomatoes, and vegetable broth

**Alternative
Option:** Blackened red snapper with capers and black bean & bell pepper salad: chopped onions, yellow, orange, and red bell peppers

SATURDAY

Breakfast: Apple, celery, cucumber and raisin smoothie
Lunch: Chinese salad (organic chicken optional) with sesame seeds in lieu of rice noodles
Snack: Sun-dried tomatoes, avocado and cucumber tossed with olive oil and lemon juice
Dinner: Vegetarian burrito: pinto beans, guacamole, soy-based sour cream, cilantro, salsa, lettuce, peppers wrapped in a sprouted whole wheat tortilla

Appendix 2: Exercise Plan

MONDAY
(Gluteus/Quadriceps/Triceps)

One-Minute Workouts

Warm-up:

- Take deep concentrated breaths. Inhale counting to four — hold it for 16 counts, then exhale counting to eight. Repeat this step three times.
- Make quarter-circles with your head. Start with your ear near your shoulder on one side, rotate your head around to the front, ending with your ear near the shoulder on the other side. Roll your head back to the other side. Repeat five to 10 times.

Strengthening:

- Lunges (quadriceps/gluteus): Stand upright, lift one knee in a forward motion (as if you're taking a giant step) — in this motion place your foot (knee bent) 90 degrees in front of you slowly kneeling down into a lunge with knee directly aligned with the hip and back leg extended in a full bent knee stretch at a 90-degree angle. Then gently raise yourself up both feet in a grounded position. Then step front foot back to original upright position. Repeat exercise with opposite foot. Perform 10 reps per leg for one set. Weights are optional — you can also use one-gallon jugs of water in each hand.

Cool-down:

- Take deep concentrated breaths. Inhale counting to four — hold it for 16 counts, then exhale counting to eight. Repeat this step three times.
- Hip Stretch: Stand up, take a half-step back with your right foot. Bend your left knee and shift your weight back to your right hip. While keeping your right leg straight, bend forward more and reach farther down your right leg. Hold for seven seconds. Switch sides and repeat.

Five-Minute Workouts

Warm-up:

- Take deep concentrated breathes. Inhale counting to four — hold it for 16 counts, then exhale counting to eight. Repeat this step five times.

- Make quarter-circles with your head. Start with your ear near your shoulder on one side, rotate your head around to the front, ending with your ear near the shoulder on the other side. Roll your head back to the other side. Repeat five to 10 times.
- Jog in place for 45 seconds.

Strengthening:

- Bent Kickback (triceps): Use a bench or sturdy chair. Bend over bench on one knee with one palm flat on surface while the other hand holds the dumbbell in the starting position curled up parallel to your chest. Extend the weight out, moving in a controlled movement for 180 degrees. Repeat 15 reps for four sets.

Cool-down / Flexibility:

- Take deep concentrated breaths. Inhale counting to four — hold it for 16 counts, then exhale counting to eight. Repeat this step five times.
- Sit on the floor with legs extended in front of you. Bend one knee out to the side with your heel resting by your hip so that you are sitting in a runner's stretch. Gently lower your back to the floor keeping your bent knee as close to the floor as possible. Hold this stretch for 30 seconds. Then repeat stretch on the opposite leg.

10-Minute Workouts

Warm-up:

- Take deep concentrated breaths. Inhale counting to four — hold it for 16 counts, then exhale counting to eight. Repeat this step five times.
- Make quarter-circles with your head. Start with your ear near your shoulder on one side, rotate your head around to the front, ending with your ear near the shoulder on the other side. Roll your head back to the other side. Repeat five to 10 times.
Jog in place for one minute.

Cardio:

- Use a small step pedestal or sturdy chair and step up (one foot at a time), then down (one foot at a time) smoothly increasing your pace to a jogging motion. Repeat 15 reps for three sets.

Strengthening:

> Seated Overhead Press (triceps): Sit in a sturdy chair — feet firmly planted on the ground. Grasp a dumbbell in both hands and carefully lift overhead, keeping elbows slightly bent. Slowly bend your elbows and lower weight behind your head — hold for one second. Then carefully raise weight to starting position. Repeat 15 reps for four sets.

Cool-down / Flexibility:

- Take deep concentrated breaths. Inhale counting to four — hold it for 16 counts, then exhale counting to eight. Repeat this step five times.
- Sit on the floor with legs extended in front of you. Bend one knee out to the side with your heel resting by your hip so that you are sitting in a runner's stretch. Gently lower your back to the floor keeping your bent knee as close to the floor as possible. Hold this stretch for 30 seconds. Then repeat stretch on the opposite leg.

45-60 Minute Workouts

Warm-up:
- Take deep concentrated breaths. Inhale counting to four — hold it for 16 counts, then exhale counting to eight. Repeat this step five times.
- Make quarter-circles with your head. Start with your ear near your shoulder on one side, rotate your head around to the front, ending with your ear near the shoulder on the other side. Roll your head back to the other side. Repeat five to 10 times.
- Jog in place for one minute.

Cardio:

- Take a walk or run around your neighborhood or on the treadmill for 30 minutes.

Strengthening:

> Standing Squats (quadriceps/gluteus): Perform squats with your feet hip-width apart, bending your knees until your torso is parallel with your bent knees; then slowly raise your body up to the starting position. Repeat this exercise for 15 reps at four sets.
> Downward Dog (arms and legs): Perform the downward dog yoga pose: Stand erect, bend torso forward placing your hands palms side down on the floor while keeping you knees slightly bent and heels up.

Place one foot at a 90-degree angle behind you, then the other foot so that your body is in an upside down "V" stance. Slowly lower heels to the ground — hold for 30 seconds.

- Crunches (stomach/oblique muscles): Lie on your back and bend knees, raising your upper torso to a 90-degree angle. Repeat exercise for 20 reps. Then working the oblique muscles, do crunches at a 90-degree angle to the right, then to the left, for 20 reps on each side. Repeat four sets of each suggested rep.

Cool-down / Flexibility:

- Take deep concentrated breaths. Inhale counting to four — hold it for 16 counts, then exhale counting to eight. Repeat this step five times.

- Sit on the floor with legs extended in front of you. Bend one knee out to the side with your heel resting by your hip so that you are sitting in a runner's stretch. Gently lower your back to the floor, keeping your bent knee as close to the floor as possible. Hold this stretch for 30 seconds. Then repeat stretch on the opposite leg.

TUESDAY

(Back/Hamstrings/Shoulders)

One-Minute Workouts

Warm-up:

- Take deep concentrated breaths. Inhale counting to four — hold it for 16 counts, then exhale counting to eight. Repeat this step three times.
- Dance in place for 15 seconds.

Cardio:

- Jumping Squats (hamstrings): Think of a frog leaping from lily pad to lily pad. At one side of a large room, stand erect with feet shoulder-width apart. Slowly lower your body so that your thighs are parallel to the floor, then leap up and forward as if you've been stung by a bee. As you are coming down keep knees bent, allowing your body to continually lower itself into the original squatting position — thighs parallel to floor. Repeat five reps.

Cool-down / Flexibility:

- Take deep concentrated breaths. Inhale counting to four — hold it for 16 counts, then exhale counting to eight. Repeat this step three times.
- Sky-Reaching Pose (shoulder and spine): Stand tall and reach both hands toward the sky, slightly elevated on your tip-toes. Hold for 10 seconds.

Five-Minute Workouts

Warm-up:

- Take deep concentrated breaths. Inhale counting to four — hold it for 16 counts, then exhale counting to eight. Repeat this step five times.
- Dance in place for one minute. Turn the music up loud, flail your arms and have fun with it!

Strengthening:

- Hamstring Lift: Lie on floor with feet elevated on a sturdy chair. Slowly raise your pelvis with slightly bent knees until you are in a diagonal position — hold for one minute. Lower your pelvis to starting position. Repeat three times.

Cool-down / Flexibility:

- Take deep concentrated breaths. Inhale counting to four — hold it for 16 counts, then exhale counting to eight. Repeat this step five times.
- Ardha Matsyendrasana — The Half Twist Posture (lower back): Sit on the floor bending both knees. Slide your left foot under your right leg until left foot reaches right hip. Step the right foot over left leg with the right knee pointing straight up. Gently twist the torso to right placing the right palm on the floor. Place the left arm over the right knee further extending the torso right. Turn your head to the right. Hold this pose for one minute. Then counter twist with torso to the left. Right foot by left hip. Step left foot over right leg with left knee pointing straight up. Gently twist torso to the left placing left palm on floor. Place right arm over left knee further extending the torso to the left. Turn head to the left. Hold for one minute.

10-Minute Workouts

Warm-up:

- Take deep concentrated breaths. Inhale counting to four — hold it for 16 counts, then exhale counting to eight. Repeat this step five times.

- Dance in place for one minute. Turn the music up loud, flail your arms and have fun with it!

Strengthening:

- Overhead Press (shoulders): Sit in a sturdy chair. Use two dumbbells, one in each hand. Make sure your back is straight and abs are tight. With bent elbows, hold dumbbells facing outward around ear level. In a smooth motion raise your arms over your head (arms should be parallel to floor) — hold for one minute — then slowly lower arms to starting position. Repeat 15 reps for four sets.
- Inverse Leg Lifts (lower abdomen): Lie flat on your back with your legs lifted at a 90-degree angle. Gently raise your pelvis in a upward motion pointing your toes to the ceiling — hold for five seconds. Then gently lower yourself to beginning position. Repeat 10 reps for four sets.

Cool-down / Flexibility:

- Take deep concentrated breaths. Inhale counting to four — hold it for 16 counts, then exhale counting to eight. Repeat this step five times.
- Ardha Matsyendrasana — The Half Twist Posture (lower back): Sit on the floor bending both knees. Slide your left foot under your right leg until left foot reaches right hip. Step the right foot over left leg with the right knee pointing straight up. Gently twist the torso to right placing the right palm on the floor. Place the left arm over the right knee further extending the torso right. Turn your head to the right. Hold this pose for one minute. Then counter twist with torso to the left. Right foot by left hip. Step left foot over right leg with left knee pointing straight up. Gently twist torso to the left placing left palm on floor. Place right arm over left knee further extending the torso to the left. Turn head to the left. Hold for one minute.

45-60 Minute Workouts

Warm-up:

- Take deep concentrated breaths. Inhale counting to four — hold it for 16 counts, then exhale counting to eight. Repeat this step five times.
- Dance in place for one minute. Turn the music up loud, flail your arms and have fun with it!

Cardio:

- Elliptical machine: Use for 30 minutes or walk up and down the bleachers at your neighborhood school's football field.

Strengthening:

- Lateral Raise (shoulders): Sit in a chair with your back firmly straight. Take two dumbbells — one in each hand with the palms facing down at your sides. Exhale as you slowly lift the weights out to the side until they are slightly above shoulder level — make sure your elbows are slightly bent. Hold for one second. Then inhale as your slowly lower your arms back to your sides. Repeat 15 reps for four sets.
- Squats (hamstrings): Using an inflated workout ball, place it against the wall and between your lower back. Slowly bend your legs and lower your body so that your knees travel forward over your toes. A full squat position is reached when your upper legs are parallel with the floor. Without bouncing, slowly push up to starting position. Repeat 10 reps for three sets.
- Crunches (stomach/oblique muscles): Lie on your back and bend knees. Raise your upper torso to a 90-degree angle. Repeat exercise for 20 reps. Then working the oblique muscles, do crunches at a 90-degree angle to the right, then to the left, for 20 reps on each side. Repeat four sets of each suggested rep.

Cool-down / Flexibility:

- Take deep concentrated breaths. Inhale counting to four — hold it for 16 counts, then exhale counting to eight. Repeat this step five times.
- Ardha Matsyendrasana — The Half Twist Posture (lower back): Sit on the floor bending both knees. Slide your left foot under your right leg until left foot reaches right hip. Step the right foot over left leg with the right knee pointing straight up. Gently twist the torso to right placing the right palm on the floor. Place the left arm over the right knee further extending the torso right. Turn your head to the right. Hold this pose for one minute. Then counter twist with torso to the left. Right foot by left hip. Step left foot over right leg with left knee pointing straight up. Gently twist torso to the left placing left palm on floor. Place right arm over left knee further extending the torso to the left. Turn head to the left. Hold for one minute.

WEDNESDAY
(Biceps/Calves/Chest)

One-Minute Workouts

Warm-up:

- Take deep concentrated breaths. Inhale counting to four — hold it for 16 counts, then exhale counting to eight. Repeat this step three times.
- Jump in place while shaking your arms out in front of you then to your sides for 15 seconds.

Strengthening:

- Push-ups (chest): Facing the floor, arms are extended with elbows slightly bent — balancing on your palms and toes (for modified version bend at knees). Arms should be shoulder-width apart and your head should be up. In a controlled motion, lower yourself to just above the floor's surface — hold for 10 seconds. Then lift yourself to the starting position. Repeat eight reps.

Cool down / Flexibility:

- Take deep concentrated breaths. Inhale counting to four — hold it for 16 counts, then exhale counting to eight. Repeat this step three times.
- As you are doing your breathing exercises, stand tall and pivot up on your tip-toes, working your calf muscles with arms out parallel to shoulders.

Five-Minute Workouts

Warm-up:

- Take deep concentrated breaths. Inhale counting to four — hold it for eight counts, then exhale counting to 16. Repeat this step five times.
- Jump in place while shaking your arms out in front of you, then to your sides for 15 seconds.

Strengthening:

- Seated Raise (calves): Sit in a sturdy chair with soles of feet flat on the ground. Use two dumbbells in each hand resting on each knee — forearms facing down. Raise your heels, keeping toes on floor — hold one second — then release to starting position. Repeat 10 reps for four sets.

Cool-down / Flexibility:

- Take deep concentrated breaths. Inhale counting to four — hold it for 16 counts, then exhale counting to eight. Repeat this step five times.
- Supta Padangusthasana — Reclining Big Toe Pose (calves, hamstrings, hips and groin): Lie supine (on back) on the floor. Legs must be strongly extended — using a long scarf or strap, grasp it at both ends and secure around the arch of your right foot. Then slowly raise leg to a 90-degree angle — hold it for one minute. As you're holding, walk hands up strap until arms are fully extended. As you feel comfortable, pull the foot closer to the head — hold 30 seconds then slowly lower leg to starting position. Perform stretch on opposite leg.

10-Minute Workouts

Warm-up:

- Take deep concentrated breaths. Inhale counting to four — hold it for 16 counts, then exhale counting to eight. Repeat this step five times.
- Jump in place while shaking your arms out in front of you then to your sides for 15 seconds.

Strengthening:

- One-Arm Curl (biceps): Sit in a sturdy chair — feet firmly on ground. Hold a dumbbell in one hand and raise forearm so that elbow is pressed against the inner thigh. Bring palm toward your chest — hold for one second — then in a controlled motion, release to starting position. Repeat 15 reps for four sets.

Cool-down / Flexibility:

- Take deep concentrated breaths. Inhale counting to four — hold it for 16 counts, then exhale counting to eight. Repeat this step five times.
- Supta Padangusthasana — Reclining Big Toe Pose (calves, hamstrings, hips and groin): Lie supine (on back) on the floor. Legs must be strongly extended — using a long scarf or strap, grasp it at both ends and secure around the arch of your right foot. Then slowly raise leg to a 90-degree angle — hold it for one minute. As you're holding, walk hands up strap until arms are fully extended. As you feel comfortable, pull the foot closer to the head — hold 30 seconds then slowly lower leg to starting position. Perform stretch on opposite leg.

45-60 Minute Workouts

Warm-up:

- Take deep concentrated breaths. Inhale counting to four — hold it for 16 counts, then exhale counting to eight. Repeat this step five times.
- Jump in place while shaking your arms out in front of you then to your sides for 15 seconds.

Cardio:

- Stairmaster: Perform 30 minutes of cardio or hike one of your neighborhood trails (preferably a hilly trail, if possible).

Strengthening:

- Standing Curl (biceps): Take two dumbbells (use a weight comfortable for you), one in each hand. Stand with feet shoulder-width apart, placing palms upright at your side. Breathe out as your lift the dumbbells toward your biceps. Keep elbows close to your sides. Hold for two seconds, then as you gently lower the dumbbells back to your original position in a controlled motion, inhale slowly until you are at the starting point. Repeat 10 reps for four sets.
- Push-ups (chest): Facing the floor, arms are extended with elbows slightly bent — balancing on your palms and toes (for modified version, bend at knees). Arms should be shoulder-width apart and your head should be up. In a controlled motion, lower yourself to just above the floor's surface — hold for 30 seconds. Then lift yourself to the starting position. Repeat eight reps for three sets.
- Crunches (stomach/oblique muscles): Lie on your back and bend knees. Raise your upper torso to a 90-degree angle. Repeat exercise for 20 reps. Then working the oblique muscles, do crunches at a 90-degree angle to the right, then to the left, for 20 reps on each side. Repeat four sets of each suggested rep.

Cool-down / Flexibility:

- Take deep concentrated breaths. Inhale counting to four — hold it for 16 counts, then exhale counting to eight. Repeat this step five times.
- Supta Padangusthasana — Reclining Big Toe Pose (calves, hamstrings, hips and groin): Lie supine (on back) on the floor. Legs must be strongly extended — using a long scarf or strap, grasp it at both ends and secure around the arch of your right foot. Then slowly raise leg to a 90-degree angle — hold it for one minute. As you're holding, walk

hands up strap until arms are fully extended. As you feel comfortable, pull the foot closer to the head — hold 30 seconds, then slowly lower leg to starting position. Perform stretch on opposite leg.

THURSDAY
(Gluteus/Quadriceps/Triceps)

One-Minute Workouts

Warm-up:

- Take deep concentrated breaths. Inhale counting to four — hold it for 16 counts, then exhale counting to eight. Repeat this step three times.
- Standing in place with feet shoulder-width apart, raise knee to a 90-degree angle and hold one second. Repeat five reps on each leg.

Strengthening:

- Pelvic Raise (gluteus): Lie on your back with knees bent at a 90-degree angle. Arms should be by your side with palms facing down. Gently raise your midsection and buttocks six inches, keeping upper torso firmly on the ground. Hold lift for one second, then lower four inches — hold for another second. Repeat 10 reps for two sets.

Cool-down / Flexibility:

- Take deep concentrated breaths. Inhale counting to four — hold it for 16 counts, then exhale counting to eight. Repeat this step three times.
- Child's Pose (back, hips, thighs, ankles): Kneel on your knees. Exhale and tuck your chin to your chest while lowering your torso between your thighs — keep palms face up on the floor while resting your buttocks on your heels. Your forehead should be gently placed on the floor. Hold pose for 10 seconds.

Five-Minute Workouts

Warm-up:

- Take deep concentrated breaths. Inhale counting to four — hold it for 16 counts, then exhale counting to eight. Repeat this step five times.
- Sprint to the end of the hallway and back raising your knees as high as you can while extending your arms in a forward and backward motion with a bent elbow. Repeat this exercise for one minute.

Strengthening:

- Standing Knee Lift (quadriceps): Stand with feet shoulder-width apart, arms resting at your sides. Lift knee to a 90-degree angle — hold one second, then extend foot forward until it is parallel to hip — hold one second. Return foot to starting position. Repeat 15 reps for four sets on both legs.

Cool-down / Flexibility:

- Take deep concentrated breaths. Inhale counting to four — hold it for 16 counts, then exhale counting to eight. Repeat this step five times.
- Moving Child's Pose (back, hips, thighs, ankles): (a) Kneel on all fours, slightly arching the lower back, palms lying flat with knees positioned under hips. Slightly raise the back into a cat position — tip pelvis forward forming a slight arch in the stomach — inhale as you move your pelvis forward. Lower back to the starting position. (b) Kneel on your knees. Exhale and tuck your chin to your chest while lowering your torso between your thighs — keep palms face up on the floor while resting your buttocks on your heels. Your forehead should be gently placed on the floor. Continue alternating between steps (a) and (b) for three reps.

10-Minute Workouts

Warm-up:

- Take deep concentrated breaths. Inhale counting to four — hold it for 16 counts, then exhale counting to eight. Repeat this step five times.
- Sprint to the end of the hallway and back raising your knees as high as you can while extending your arms in a forward and backward motion with a bent elbow. Repeat this exercise for one minute.

Strengthening:

- Dip (triceps): Sit on the floor with arms behind you about 12 inches apart — palms flat with bent elbows and fingers facing toward your body. Gently raise your body with your palms and feet as support — hold for one second. Then gently lower your body but your buttocks should not touch the floor until set is completed. Repeat 10 reps for four sets.
- Leg Lifts (lower abdomen): Lie flat on your back with your legs extended straight out — lift legs to a 90-degree angle — hold for 30

seconds. Then release hold slowly, lowering legs in a controlled movement to just above ground level — hold for 30 seconds. Then slowly raise legs in a controlled fashion to a 90-degree angle again — hold for 30 seconds. Repeat 15 reps for three sets.

Cool-down / Flexibility:

- Take deep concentrated breaths. Inhale counting to four — hold it for 16 counts, then exhale counting to eight. Repeat this step five times.
- Moving Child's Pose (back, hips, thighs, ankles): (a) Kneel on all fours, slightly arching the lower back, palms lying flat with knees positioned under hips. Slightly raise the back into a cat position — tip pelvis forward forming a slight arch in the stomach — inhale as you move your pelvis forward. Lower back to the starting position. (b) Kneel on your knees. Exhale and tuck your chin to your chest while lowering your torso between your thighs — keep palms face up on the floor while resting your buttocks on your heels. Your forehead should be gently placed on the floor. Continue alternating between steps (a) and (b) for three reps.

45-60 Minute Workouts

Warm-up:

- Take deep concentrated breaths. Inhale counting to four — hold it for 16 counts, then exhale counting to eight. Repeat this step five times.
- Sprint to the end of the hallway and back, raising your knees as high as you can while extending your arms in a forward and backward motion with a bent elbow. Repeat this exercise for one minute.

Cardio:

- Bicycling (stationary or outdoor cycling): Perform 30 minutes of cardio.

Strengthening:

- Triceps Pressdown: Take a bar(bell) in both hands (or dumbbells in each hand). Palms should face torso; bend elbows at chest level. Slowly lower bar in a concentrated, controlled movement until arms are fully extended. Then raise arms — elbows out to the side — in a controlled movement to the starting position. Repeat 10 reps for four sets.
- Kick-up (gluteus): Kneel on all fours with palms facing down — hands shoulder-width apart. Raise your leg until thigh is same level as torso. Bend knee as you push your leg toward the ceiling. Keep head up through exercise. Repeat 15 reps for four sets.

Crunches (stomach/oblique muscles): Lie on your back and bend knees, raising your upper torso to a 90-degree angle. Repeat exercise for 20 reps. . Then working the oblique muscles, do crunches at a 90-degree angle to the right, then to the left, for 20 reps on each side. . Repeat four sets of each suggest rep.

Cool-down / Flexibility:

Take deep concentrated breaths. Inhale counting to four — hold it for 16 counts, then exhale counting to eight. Repeat this step five times.

- Moving Child's Pose (back, hips, thighs, ankles): (a) Kneel on all fours, slightly arching the lower back, palms lying flat with knees positioned under hips. Slightly raise the back into a cat position — tip pelvis forward, forming a slight arch in the stomach — inhale as you move your pelvis forward. Lower back to the starting position. (b) Kneel on your knees. Exhale and tuck your chin to your chest while lowering your torso between your thighs — keep palms face up on the floor while resting your buttocks on your heels. Your forehead should be gently placed on the floor. Continue alternating between steps (a) and (b) for three reps.

FRIDAY
(Back/Hamstrings/Shoulders)

One-Minute Workouts

Warm-up:

- Take deep concentrated breaths. Inhale counting to four — hold it for 16 counts, then exhale counting to eight. Repeat this step three times.
- Jump rope in place for 15 seconds.

Strengthening:

- Single Leg Curl (hamstrings): Support yourself up, resting one knee and foot on the floor and both hands slighter wider than shoulder-width apart, palms facing forward. Keeping one leg off the floor at about shoulder height, bend at the knee bringing your foot up toward- your buttocks. Throughout the exercise aim to keep your back straight, and look down toward the floor at all times. Repeat seven reps on both sides.

Cool-down / Flexibility:

- Take deep concentrated breaths. Inhale counting to four — hold it for 16 counts, then exhale counting to eight. Repeat this step three times.

- Hurdler's Stretch (hamstrings, lower back): Sit on floor, legs fully extended straight out. Keeping lower back flat, gently lean forward reaching the fingertips towards your toes — hold for 10 seconds.

Five-Minute Workouts

Warm-up:

- Take deep concentrated breaths. Inhale counting to four — hold it for 16 counts, then exhale counting to eight. Repeat this step five times.
- Jump rope in place for one minute.

Strengthening:

- Wall Push-ups (lower back, shoulder, triceps): Use an open doorway. Evenly place your hands (arms fully extended) slightly above chest level on each side of door frame. Position your feet 90 degrees out from the door opening. In a controlled motion, bend your elbows, bringing your upper torso in so that your face is directly between the door frame. Gently extend your arms back to the starting position. Repeat 10 reps for three sets.

Cool-down / Flexibility:

- Take deep concentrated breaths. Inhale counting to four — hold it for 16 counts, then exhale counting to eight. Repeat this step five times.
- Bharadvaja's Twist (lower back, spine and abdomen): Sit with your legs straight out in front of you. Shift onto right buttocks, bend your knees. Then lift buttocks and slowly reposition your torso to rest evenly on or hover over the soles of your feet. Gently twist your torso to the right side, placing both hands (and palms) on the floor next to your right thigh. Then softly counter twist to the left side, placing both hands and palms near your left thigh. Hold this pose for one minute on both sides.

10-Minute Workouts

Warm-up:

- Take deep concentrated breaths. Inhale counting to four — hold it for 16 counts, then exhale counting to eight. Repeat this step five times.
- Jump rope in place for two minutes.

Strengthening:

- Lying Lateral Raise (shoulders): Lie on your right side, right arm bent supporting the head, dumbbell in left hand fully extended so that the arm is in line with shoulder. Gently lower dumbbell to the side. Continue 12 reps for four sets on each side.

Cool-down / Flexibility:

• Take deep concentrated breaths. Inhale counting to four — hold it for 16 counts, then exhale counting to eight. Repeat this step five times.

• Bharadvaja's Twist (lower back, spine and abdomen): Sit with your legs straight out in front of you. Shift onto right buttocks, bend your knees. Then lift buttocks and slowly reposition your torso to rest evenly on or hover over the soles of your feet. Gently twist your torso to the right side, placing both hands (and palms) on the floor next to your right thigh. Then softly counter twist to the left side, placing both hands and palms near your left thigh. Hold this pose for one minute on both sides.

45-60 Minute Workouts

Warm-up:

• Take deep concentrated breaths. Inhale counting to four — hold it for 16 counts, then exhale counting to eight. Repeat this step five times.

• Jump rope in place for two minutes.

Cardio:

• Swim for 30 minutes.

Strengthening:

• Pull-ups (arms, back, shoulders): Use a pull-up machine or bar that will support your weight. Grasp bar with palms facing out — hands should be positioned wider than shoulder-width apart. Allow your lower body to dangle with bent knees. Gently pull yourself up until your chin is level to the bar. Then lower your body to the starting position. Repeat 10 reps.

• Crunches (stomach/oblique muscles): Lie on your back and bend knees. Raise your upper torso to a 90-degree angle. Repeat exercise for 20 reps. Then working the oblique muscles, do crunches at a 90-degree angle to the right, then to the left, for 20 reps on each side. Repeat four sets of each suggested rep.

Cool-down / Flexibility:

• Take deep concentrated breaths. Inhale counting to four — hold it for

16 counts, then exhale counting to eight. Repeat this step five times.

- Bharadvaja's Twist (lower back, spine and abdomen): Sit with your legs straight out in front of you. Shift onto right buttocks, bend your knees. Then lift buttocks and slowly reposition your torso to rest evenly on or hover over the soles of your feet. Gently twist your torso to the right side, placing both hands (and palms) on the floor next to your right thigh. Then softly counter twist to the left side, placing both hands and palms near your left thigh. Hold this pose for one minute on both sides.

SATURDAY
(Biceps/Calves/Chest)

One-Minute Workouts

Warm-up:

- Take deep concentrated breaths. Inhale counting to four — hold it for 16 counts, then exhale counting to eight. Repeat this step three times.
- Arm Circles (arms and chest): Start with your arms at your sides — fists clenched. Continue to keep arms at your side, swing your arms in a clock-wise motion for five reps, then in a counter-clockwise motion for another five reps.

Strengthening:

- Calf Pivot: Stand upright with back erect. Place hands on your hips. Gently pivot forward onto your tip-toes and hold for one second. Release the hold, bringing your soles back to the ground — as you are flattening out your feet extend the release out to your heels so that you are performing a rocking motion — tip-toes to heels. Repeat for 20 reps.

Cool-down / Flexibility:

- Take deep concentrated breaths. Inhale counting to four — hold it for 16 counts, then exhale counting to eight. Repeat this step three times.
- Dhanurasana — Bow Pose (chest, back, abdomen, ankles, groin): Lie on your stomach with knees bent in a 90-degree angle with soles of feet facing ceiling. Exhale, stretching heels close to your buttocks, and bring back your hand to grasp ankles, lengthening the pull to the buttocks as far as you can. Hold pose for 10 seconds — continue breathing throughout hold.

Five-Minute Workouts

Warm-up:

- Take deep concentrated breaths. Inhale counting to four — hold it for 16 counts, then exhale counting to eight. Repeat this step three times.
- Arm Circles (arms and chest): Start with your arms at your sides — fists clenched. Continue to keep arms at your side, swing your arms in a clock-wise motion for 10 reps, then in a counter-clockwise motion for another 10 reps.

Strengthening:

- Rubberband Press (chest): Use a large strength- resistant rubberband (specifically designed for workouts).Lie on your back holding the band in each hand loosely. Fully extend the rubberband — hold for five seconds, then release. Repeat for 15 reps.

Cool-down / Flexibility:

- Take deep concentrated breaths. Inhale counting to four — hold it for 16 counts, then exhale counting to eight. Repeat this step five times.
- Dhanurasana — Bow Pose (chest, back, abdomen, ankles, groin): Lie on your stomach with knees bent in a 90-degree angle with soles of feet facing ceiling. Exhale, stretching heels close to your buttocks, and bring back your hands to grasp ankles, lengthening the pull to the buttocks as far as you can. Hold pose for 30 seconds — continue breathing throughout hold.

10-Minute Workouts

Warm-up:

- Take deep concentrated breaths. Inhale counting to four — hold it for 16 counts, then exhale counting to eight. Repeat this step five times.
- Arm Circles (arms and chest): Start with your arms at your sides — fists clenched. Continue to keep arms at your side, swing your arms in a clock-wise motion for 10 reps, then in a counter-clockwise motion for another 10 reps.

Strengthening:

- Seated Curl (biceps): Sit on the edge of a sturdy chair. Two dumbbells

— one in each hand — palms facing upward parallel with the thighs. Curl dumbbells up toward biceps (extend to 90 degrees) — hold for one second. Return to starting position. Repeat 15 reps for four sets.

Cool-down / Flexibility:

- Take deep concentrated breaths. Inhale counting to four — hold it for 16 counts, then exhale counting to eight. Repeat this step five times.
Dhanurasana — Bow Pose (chest, back, abdomen, ankles, groin): Lie on your stomach with knees bent in a 90-degree angle with soles of feet facing ceiling. Exhale, stretching heels close to your buttocks and bring back your hand to grasp ankles, lengthening the pull to the buttocks as far as you can. Hold pose for 30 seconds — continue breathing throughout hold.

45-60 Minute Workouts

Warm-up:

- Anjali Mudra (Salutation Seal): Sit down with both legs outstretched. Bend the left knee and place the sole of the left foot against the right thigh so that the heel touches the perineum. Bend the right knee and put the right heel against the public bone. Keep hands with palms open if done between sunrise and sunset; otherwise reverse the palms. The spine should always be held erect. Practice the "perfect pose" for five minutes.
- Arm Circles (arms and chest): Start with your arms at your sides — fists clenched. Continue to keep arms at your side, swing your arms in a clock-wise motion for 10 reps, then in a counter-clockwise motion for another 10 reps.

Cardio:

- Dumbbell Press (chest): Lie on your back with knees bent at a 90-degree angle. Holding dumbbells in each hand, lower your arms leading with your elbows forming an arch — elbows should be in line with shoulders. Then slowly extend your arms and press dumbbells toward the ceiling. Repeat 12 reps for four sets.
- Hammer (biceps): Stand with your feet shoulder-width apart holding dumbbells in each hand by your side — palms should be facing in. Slowly curl your arms up to a 90-degree angle — hold for one second. Then return to starting position. Repeat 15 reps for four sets.

Strengthening:

Lower Leg Lifts (lower abdomen): Sit on the floor and bend knees at 90-degree angle. Raise knees to your chest, then extend legs straight out in front of you — hold for one second. Then return knees to your chest. Repeat exercise for 20 reps.

Cool-down / Flexibility:

- Take deep concentrated breaths. Inhale counting to four — hold it for 16 counts, then exhale counting to eight. Repeat this step five times.
- Dhanurasana — Bow Pose (chest, back, abdomen, ankles, groin): Lie on your stomach with knees bent in a 90-degree angle with soles of feet facing ceiling. Exhale, stretching heels close to your buttocks and bring back your hand to grasp ankles, lengthening the pull to the buttocks as far as you can. Hold pose for 30 seconds — continue breathing throughout hold.

SUNDAY

Celebrate!! You have just completed a week's worth of extensive exercise. Do something very special for yourself!! And get some rest — this is the first week of the rest of your life!

Appendix 3: Cleanse Menus

A Delicious Healthy Pre-Cleansing One-Week Program

SUNDAY

Breakfast: *Green drink* (before meal); *Steamed broccoli:[1]* with 1 red pepper; ½ cup of chopped onion and tossed with olive oil or Udo's oil

Morning Snack: *Edamame* (fresh peas)

Lunch: *Vegetable Nori roll:* 1 avocado, sliced; 1 Nori sheet; 1 red bell pepper, sliced; 1 cucumber thinly sliced; alfalfa sprouts; 1 scallion, slivered. Wrap in Nori sheet and cut in equal portions.

Snack: *Green drink*

Dinner: *Steamed zucchini, sun dried tomatoes, and red bell pepper tossed with a Pesto sauce* made of garlic, fresh basil, parsley, dill, soaked pine nuts, olive oil, sea salt, and pepper.

MONDAY

Breakfast: *Green drink* (before meal); *Banana smoothie*: 1 banana, 1 inch chopped ginger, ½ cup soaked nuts, 1 Tsp. green drink power, all blended; mix in by hand (not in the blender because it gets bitter) 1 Tsp. Udo's oil before serving.

Snack: *1 cucumber, sliced; 1 tomato, chopped*; Tossed with lemon/lime juice

Lunch: *Vegan Caesar's salad* made with romaine lettuce tossed with a dressing made of garlic, lemon, avocado, olive oil, sea salt, and pepper; no crouton's - instead sprinkle on flax or sesame seeds

Snack: *Green drink*

Dinner: *Stuffed Tomato*: 1 beef-steak tomato filled with hummus and sprinkled w/ finely chopped scallions and parsley.

TUESDAY

Breakfast: *Green drink* (before meal); *Cucumber Smoothie*: 1 cucumber, sliced; 1 yellow bell pepper, large slices; 1 tomato, chopped; 1 med. avocado, sliced; handful of sprouts, salt & pepper;

*For all the recipes in this cleansing menu, the heating temperature should be no higher than 118º Fahrenheit.

blend it all and add at the end Udo's Oil and fresh lemon juice to taste.

Snack: ***Sliced red, yellow and green bell peppers***

Lunch: ***Organic Mixed Green Salad*** with 1 avocado, sliced; ½ cup radishes, sliced; 1 sliced zucchini; 1 chopped tomato; alfalfa sprouts. Toss with Sesame seed oil, lemon juice, salt and pepper.

Snack: ***Green drink***

Dinner: ***Butternut Squash Soup***: 1 butternut squash & zucchini chopped; 1 Tsp. raw almond milk; ½ tsp. of ginger root, slivered; sea salt, cayenne pepper to taste; blend in food processor until creamy; Heat bowl in microwave and serve after decorating it with 1 Tbs. of pumpkin seed oil and a handful of pine nuts.

WEDNESDAY

Breakfast: ***Green drink*** (before meal); ***Raw Chocolate Smoothie***: 1 banana, 2 apples sliced, 1 inch chopped ginger, ½ cup soaked nuts, 1 Tsp. green drink power, 2 Tsp. minced raw chocolate beans all blended; mix in by hand (not in the blender because it gets bitter) 1 Tsp Udo's oil before serving.

Morning
Snack: ***Celery sticks and raw almond butter***

Lunch: ***Spinach Salad***: 2 cups spinach; ½ cup broccoli, cut in small pieces; 1 stalk celery, chopped; 1 red bell pepper chopped; 2 shallots, chopped, 2 slices of apple chopped; Toss mixture in large bowl with olive oil, Udo's oil, lemon juice, sea salt and pepper. Garnish with sunflower seeds.

Snack: ***Green drink***

Dinner: ***Raw Minestrone***: 1 red, 1 yellow, 1 green bell pepper sliced; 1 zucchini, sliced; 1 onion, chopped; 1 garlic clove; 1 organic salad, 1 ripe avocado; sea salt, cayenne. Blend all ingredients with warm water. Serve in a microwave heated bowl and garnish with 1 tsp. pumpkin seed or truffle oil and pine nuts.

THURSDAY

Breakfast: ***Green drink*** (before meal); ***Apple Smoothie***: 2 apples sliced, 1 ripe avocado, 1 inch chopped ginger, ½ cup soaked

---

For all the recipes in this cleansing menu, the heating temperature should be no higher than 118° Fahrenheit.

nuts, 1 Tsp. green drink power, ½ tsp. cinnamon; blend it all; mix in by hand (not in the blender because it gets bitter) 1 Tsp Udo's oil before serving.

Morning
Snack: *Broccoli florettes with raw almond butter*
Lunch: *Steamed asparagus* tossed with 2 minced garlic cloves; 1 chopped red bell pepper; 2 diced scallion stalks, sesame seed oil, lemon juice, salt and pepper. Decorate with parsley and pine nuts.
Snack: *Green drink*
Dinner: *Raw Tomato Soup*: 1 ripe avocado; 1 cup fresh organic tomatoes; ½ cup sun dried tomatoes in olive oil; 1 red chili pepper, seeded; sea salt, cayenne pepper, ½ cup raw soaked macadamia nuts. Blend it all until smooth, decorate with basil leaves and 1 tsp. of pumpkin seed oil, and serve in preheated bowl.

FRIDAY

Breakfast: *Green drink* (before meal); *Bell Pepper/Zucchini Smoothie*: 1 red, 1 yellow, 1 green bell pepper sliced; 1 zucchini, sliced; 1 onion, chopped; 1 garlic clove; 1 organic salad, 1 ripe avocado; sea salt, cayenne. Blend all ingredients and mix with 1 Tsp. Udo's Oil by hand.
Morning
Snack: ½ cup soaked raw almonds
Lunch: *Steamed broccoli* tossed with 2 minced garlic cloves; 1 chopped red bell pepper; 2 diced scallion stalks, sesame seed oil, lemon juice, salt and pepper.
Snack: *Green drink*
Dinner: *Rainbow Cabbage with Jicama:* 1 cup red & 1 cup green cabbage, thinly sliced; 1 red bell pepper, slivered; ½ jicama tiny sliced; 1 inch. ginger, minced; 1 apple chopped; 4 Tbs. parsley and dill, minced; ¼ cup lemon juice; 1 Tbs. oil (each Extra Virgin Olive, Flax Seed or Udo's Choice); sea salt, dash of cayenne pepper; 1 Tsp. Ground Cumin or Curry, Nama Shoyu or Organic Soy Sauce. Combine a large bowl and toss – let stand for half-hour before serving.

*For all the recipes in this cleansing menu, the heating temperature should be no higher than 118° Fahrenheit.

SATURDAY

Breakfast: *Green drink* (before meal); ***Mango Smoothie***: 1 ripe mango, inch chopped ginger, ½ cup soaked nuts, 1 Tsp. green drink power, dash of orange flavor; blend it all; mix in by hand (not in the blender because it gets bitter) 1 Tsp Udo's oil before serving.

Morning Snack: ***Organic Baby Carrots with raw cashew butter***

Lunch: ***Cucumber Salad:*** 2 cups cucumbers, sliced; 2 Tbs. parsley and dill, chopped; 1 Tbs. lemon juice; 1 Tbs. Flax Seed Oil or Olive Oil; salt and pepper to taste.

Snack: *Green drink*

Dinner: *Avocado salad*: Avocado on bed of organic mixed greens, kale, tomatoes, dressed with olive oil, lemon juice, salt and pepper, and a handful of sun flower seeds.

A Delicious Healthy Post-Cleansing One-Week Program

SUNDAY – Breaking the Cleanse

Breakfast: *2 slices organic apples* – chew them very well and very slowly

Morning Snack: *Green drink*

Lunch: *Organic romaine lettuce*

Snack: *Green drink*

Dinner: *Green Raw Soup*: 1 avocado; ½ green bell pepper, ½ head of organic red-leaf lettuce, lemon juice; 1 Tbs. fresh cilantro mixed with dill and parsley; 1 chopped carrot, olive oil, salt, cayenne pepper. Blend all ingredients with warm water and serve in a microwave-heated bowl.

MONDAY

Breakfast: *1 grapefruit*

Morning Snack: *Green drink*

Lunch: *Stuffed Tomato*: 1 beef-steak tomato, seeded (or use a hallowed out red bell pepper); Fill with avocado paste made from 1 avocado, 1 tomato diced, cilantro, I scallion chopped, salt & pepper to taste. Sprinkle w/ finely chopped parsley.

*For all the recipes in this cleansing menu, the heating temperature should be no higher than 118° Fahrenheit.

Snack: *Green drink*

Dinner: *Rainbow Salad*: Fresh organic mixed greens, grated beets, grated carrots, grated yellow bell pepper, grated jicama, sprouts, sun flower seeds. Toss with dressing made from fresh lemon juice, olive oil, ½ avocado paste, sea salt, cayenne pepper.

TUESDAY

Breakfast: *Bell Pepper/Zucchini Smoothie*: 1 red, 1 yellow, 1 green bell pepper sliced; 1 zucchini, sliced; 1 onion, chopped; 1 garlic clove; 1 organic salad, 1 ripe avocado; sea salt, cayenne. Blend all ingredients and mix with 1 Tsp. Udo's Oil by hand.

Morning Snack: *Green drink*

Lunch: *Spinach Salad*: 2 cups spinach; ½ cup broccoli, cut in small pieces; 1 stalk celery, chopped; 1 red bell pepper chopped; 2 shallots, chopped, 2 slices of apple chopped; Toss mixture in large bowl with olive oil, Udo's oil, lemon juice, sea salt and pepper. Garnish with sunflower seeds.

Snack: *Green drink*

Dinner: *Steamed zucchini & kale*: 1 fresh beefsteak tomato chopped, ½ cup sun dried tomatoes diced, and 1 red bell pepper. Toss all with a Pesto sauce made of garlic, fresh basil, parsley, dill, soaked pine nuts, olive oil, sea salt, and pepper.

WEDNESDAY

Breakfast: *Steamed Broccoli Stir-fry:* 1 broccoli crown, chopped; 1 red bell pepper, chopped; 2 green onions, chopped; (low heat with 1 tsp. of water); Garnish with avocado and red bell pepper slices and taste with sea salt, cayenne pepper and Udo's oil.

Morning Snack: *Green drink*

Lunch: *Organic Mixed Green Salad* with 1 sliced avocado; ½ cup sliced radishes; 1 sliced zucchini; 1 chopped tomato; alfalfa sprouts. Toss with Sesame seed oil, lemon juice, sea salt and pepper.

Snack: *Green drink*

*For all the recipes in this cleansing menu, the heating temperature should be no higher than 118º Fahrenheit.

Dinner: *Raw Tomato Soup*: 1 ripe avocado; 1 cup fresh organic toma-toes; ½ cup sun dried tomatoes in olive oil; 1 red chili pepper, seeded; sea salt, cayenne pepper, ½ cup raw soaked macadamia nuts. Blend it all until smooth, deco-rate with basil leaves and 1 tsp. of pumpkin seed oil, and serve in preheated bowl.

THURSDAY

Breakfast: *Banana smoothie:* 1 banana, 1 inch chopped ginger, ½ cup soaked nuts, 1 Tsp. green drink power, all blended; mix in by hand (not in the blender because it gets bitter) 1 Tsp Udo's oil before serving.

Snack: *Green drink*

Lunch: *Steamed broccoli* tossed with 2 minced garlic cloves; 1 chopped red bell pepper; 2 diced scallion stalks, sesame seed oil, lemon juice, salt and pepper.

Snack: *Green drink*

Dinner: *Raw Gazpacho Soup:* 4 cups fresh diced tomatoes with their juices; 1 cup chopped cucumber; ½ chopped green bell pepper, ½ chopped red bell pepper; 1 Tbs. olive oil; ½ tsp. cayenne pepper; ¼ cup. basil; 3 minced garlic cloves. Combine all ingredients. Cover and chill overnight.

FRIDAY

Breakfast: *Bell Pepper/Zucchini Smoothie:* 1 red, 1 yellow, 1 green bell pepper sliced; 1 zucchini, sliced; 1 onion, chopped; 1 gar-lic clove; 1 organic salad, 1 ripe avocado; one handful of macadamia nuts, sea salt, cayenne. Blend all ingredients and mix with 1 Tsp. Udo's Oil by hand.

Snack: *Green drink*

Lunch: *Vegan Caesar's salad* made with romaine lettuce tossed with a dressing made of garlic, lemon, avocado, olive oil, sea salt, and pepper; no crouton's - instead sprinkle on flax or sesame seeds

Snack: *Green drink*

Dinner: *Vegetable Nori Roll* (15 mins. to prepare): 1 avocado, sliced; 1 nori sheet; 1 red bell pepper, chopped; 1 cucumber, thinly sliced; ½ cup alfalfa sprouts; 1 scallion, sliv-ered. Wrap in Nori sheet and cut in four equal portions.

*For all the recipes in this cleansing menu, the heating temperature should be no higher than 118° Fahrenheit.

SATURDAY

Breakfast: *Raw Chocolate Smoothie:* 1 banana, 2 apples sliced, 1 inch chopped ginger, ½ cup soaked nuts, 1 Tsp. green drink power, 2 Tsp. minced raw chocolate beans all blended; mix in by hand (not in the blender because it gets bitter) 1 Tsp Udo's oil before serving.

Snack: *Green drink*

Lunch: *Cucumber Salad:* 2 cups cucumbers, sliced; 2 Tbs. parsley and dill, chopped; 1 Tbs. lemon juice; 1 Tbs. Flax Seed Oil or Olive Oil; salt and pepper to taste.

Snack: *Green drink*

Dinner: *Butternut Squash Soup:* 1 butternut squash & zucchini chopped; 1 Tsp. raw almond milk; ½ tsp. of ginger root, slivered; sea salt, cayenne pepper to taste; blend in food processor until creamy; Heat bowl in microwave and serve after decorating it with 1 Tbs. of pumpkin seed oil and a handful of pine nuts.

*For all the recipes in this cleansing menu, the heating temperature should be no higher than 118° Fahrenheit.

Appendix 4: Creating a Life of Meaning Worksheet

This process is an immense opportunity for personal growth. Be honest and write down everything about how you perceive yourself and what drives you in life.

Who are you? What is your identity? Write down every thought (good or bad) you have about your own identity that enhances or limits your choices in life. How do you see yourself in general as a human being, a parent, a partner, a businessperson, a friend, a contributor to the world?

_____

_____

_____

_____

_____

What are your beliefs about yourself, life in general, relationships, money, career, food, dieting?

How do you see yourself with respect to your weight? Do you see yourself as a beautiful, smart, athletic person who is a go-getter and achieves anything and everything you ever wanted in life? Or do you feel sorry for yourself and perceive yourself as a victim of self-pity and depression?

_____

_____

_____

_____

_____

What do you value most in life and why? Develop a list of the values that you treasure and that have guided your life so far. Make sure you list them in the order of importance for you. For instance, being a good parent might be more important for you than being a successful businessperson. Are health and vitality on that list? At what rank?

_____

_____

_____

_____

_____

Are you currently living your highest potential? If yes, why — and if not, why not? What could you do differently today to prevent regrets later? What would you want to accomplish that would make you very proud at the end of your life? How could you live the life that you envisioned as a teenager? How could you create your dreams? What could you do to reach your highest potential? How can you give to life all you have to give? What would you have to change today to live differently and more in line with who you are? What would give you more satisfaction? How could you live with no regrets later?

_____

_____

_____

_____

_____

What are you grateful for in your life right now? How can you thank your eyes, nose, ears, heart and all of your organs for serving you so well? What is great in your life right now? Who do you love? Who loves you? What are you proud about in your life now? What about that makes you proud? How does that make you feel? What are you happy about in your life now? What are you enjoying most in your life right now? What are you excited about in your life now? What about that makes you excited? How does that make you feel?

_____

_____

_____

_____

_____

Who do you have to forgive today? Who do you have to let go of to be free to implement your life goals including losing weight and keeping it off forever?

_____

_____

_____

_____

_____

What is the meaning and purpose of your life? What is the vision and mission of your life? Why are you here? Write down everything that comes to mind without being censored. What do you want to be, do and create? Who do you want to serve?

_____

_____

_____

_____

_____

What are your goals in life? What do you want to accomplish at the personal, professional, financial and relationship level? Write everything that comes to your mind as if you were a child making a list for Santa Claus. Prioritize the goals you have for the next 12 months and pick the top three.

_____

_____

_____

_____

_____

Why do you want to achieve the top three goals within the next 12 months? What will that give you? How would it make you feel if you achieved them?.

_____

_____

_____

_____

_____

_____

_____

_____

What are your goals for losing weight? How much weight do you want to lose and in what time frame? Give exact (daily, weekly, monthly and quarterly) milestones for action items and goals you want to achieve. Make everything very specific in terms of time and exact weight including a vision of the clothing you want to wear, the place you want to wear it at and the compliments people are paying you.

_____

_____

_____

_____

Why do you want to lose all that weight? What will that give you? How would that make you feel?

_____

_____

_____

Why have you failed to follow through in the past? What will be different this time? What are you willing to do to follow through and make this work now? Whose help are you going to enlist?

_____

_____

_____

_____

_____

_____

_____

Which concrete actions are you going to take today to show your total commitment to losing that weight this time around? Whose help will you enlist? Who will you call to get support from? What gym will you join? Which books will you buy and read? What will achieving that weight loss goal give you? How would that make you feel? How do you want to measure your success along the way? How do you want to stay on track?

_____

_____

_____

_____

_____

Appendix 5: Permanent Weight Success Worksheet

> *"The significant problems we face cannot be solved by the level of thinking that created them."*
> — Albert Einstein

Action 1: What are my weight loss goals?

How much weight do I want to lose and in what time frame? Give exact (daily, weekly, monthly and quarterly) milestones for action item and goals you want to achieve. Make everything very specific in terms of time and exact weight including a vision of the clothing you want to wear, the place you want to wear it at and the compliments people are paying you. For example, "By <date>, *I weigh x pounds (y kg) and fit with ease into my favorite <name> dress/pants (size z!). Everyone tells me how great I look and my <significant other> says I'm really "awesome." I feel and look great as never before."*

_____

_____

_____

_____

_____

_____

Action 2: Why have I failed to follow through in the past?

What was my belief system that prevented me from achieving my ideal weight in the past?

Do I think of myself as a fat or a slim, dynamic and vibrantly healthy person? Did being overweight serve me in any way in the past? Do I feel in control of my emotions or do I let my emotions control me? Do I see myself as a victim of something or someone or am I the captain of my life ship? Am I willing to decide to do anything it takes to change the old conditioning and to live a life of fulfillment and joy? What will be different this time than in the past? What am I willing to do to follow through and make this work now? Whose help am I going to enlist? To whom will I state my commitment to achieving this goal, no matter what, this time?

_____

_____

_____

_____

_____

Action 3: What is my own motivation for losing weight?

What will achieving this goal give me? How would that make me feel? What would motivate me to truly follow through this time around? Is it my own sense of pride, my willingness to be a teacher and role model for weight loss and vitality for my children, co-workers or family members? Would I be motivated by the vision of growing old enough to hold my great-grandchildren in my arm or attending their weddings? What difference could I make in the world if I had more energy to serve my local community or my favorite charity? How much more connected would I be to my significant other if I felt better about my own body? How much more passion would I have in my intimate relationship if I were more self-confident about the way I look? How would my sense of self improve if I achieved and permanently maintained my ideal weight?

_____

_____

_____

_____

Action 4: What am I willing to do to stop and change my old disempowering habits?

What will I do next time I find myself overeating? What am I willing do so my brain links more pain to overeating and much more pleasure to pushing the plate away? How am I going to celebrate every time I succeed with eating right, exercising, pushing my plate away, etc.? What powerful visual image of myself am I willing to create and envision daily that will help my brain want to go there more often? Whose support (friend, child, spouse) will I enlist to support me in my process of giving up the old and creating new habits? What am I willing to do to keep on my new path when I feel distress, chaos or insecurity?

_____

_____

_____

_____

_____

Action 5: Which concrete actions am I going to take today to show my total commitment to losing weight and keeping it off permanently?

What are the three most important things I want to apply when I have my next meal (separate protein and carbohydrates, 70-30 rule, no water, digestive enzymes, etc.)? Which daily exercises (walking, swimming, yoga, etc.) am I committed to perform starting today? Which unhealthy foods will I discard from my refrigerator and never buy again? Which gym will I call today to get an appointment? What are the top 10 things (music, dancing, painting, singing, prayer, etc.) I am willing to do to make myself feel good every day? Which tape program will I buy/order today to support my weight loss process? Which trustworthy friends will I choose to support me on my weight loss journey? Which friends will I openly commit to and ask for support? What else can I do today to show my full commitment to myself and my new life of meaning and contribution? What will doing all the above give me? How would that make me feel? What else would give my life more meaning and would easily get me out of bed every morning?

_____

_____

_____

_____

_____

_____

Appendix 6: Weight Success Chart

Week number	1	2	3	4	5	6	7	8	9	10	11	12
Weight												
Clothing Size												
Number of Cravings												
Level of Bloating (1–10)												
Overall Satisfaction (1–10)												
Loving Myself (1–10)												
Relationship Meter (1–10)												
Feelings of Gratitude (1–10)												
Number of Workouts												
# of Affirmation Exercises												
Overall Stress Level (1–10)												
Number of Compliments												
Level of Motivation (1–10)												
Level of Awareness (1–10)												
Ability to Correct (1–10)												
Number of Celebrations												
Emotional Stability (1–10)												
Energy Level (1–10)												
Food Combining (1–10)												

Appendix 7: Inspirational Movies

1. Antoine Fisher
2. Babette's Feast
3. Being There
4. Brave Heart
5. Brother Sun, Sister Moon
6. Chariots of Fire
7. Dances With Wolves
8. Field of Dreams
9. Forrest Gump
10. Fahrenheit 9/11
11. Gandhi
12. Gone With the Wind
13. Groundhog Day
14. Harold and Maude
15. Hearts and Souls
16. The Last Temptation of Christ
17. Like Water for Chocolate
18. Love Jones
19. Midnight Express
20. Mindwalk
21. Out of Africa
22. Philadelphia
23. Remember the Titians
24. The Razor's Edge
25. Resurrection
26. Schindler's List
27. The Shawshank Redemption
28. Super Size Me
29. The Aviator
30. Benny & Joon
31. Bliss
32. The Fischer King
33. The Birdcage
34. Awakenings
35. I am Sam
36. The Secret (www.thesecret.tv)
37. An Inconvenient Truth
38. Pay it Forward

Appendix 8: Inspirational Books

1. 2150 A.D., by Thea Alexander
2. Another Heart in His Hand, by J. J. Gold
3. A Return to Love, by Marianne Williamson
4. Beloved, by Toni Morrison
5. Bridges to Heaven, by Jonathan Robinson
6. Bringers of the Dawn, by Barbara Marciniak
7. The Care of the Soul, by Thomas Moore
8. The Celestine Prophecy, by James Redfield
9. Creative Visualization, by Shakti Gawain
10. Feel the Fear and Do It Anyway, by Susan Jeffers
11. Healing Words, by Larry Dossey
12. Holy Bible
13. Hope for the Flowers, by Trina Paulus
14. I Know Why the Caged Bird Sings, by Maya Angelou
15. Illusions, by Richard Bach
16. In the Meantime, by Iyanla Vanzant
17. Jonathan Livingston Seagull, by Richard Bach
18. The Joy Luck Club, by Amy Tan
19. Men Are From Mars, Women Are From Venus: A Practical Guide for Improving Communication and Getting What You Want, by John Gray
20. Mutant Message Down Under, by Marlo Morgan
21. One Day My Soul Just Opened Up: 40 Days and 40 Nights, by Iyanla Vanzant
22. Oprah Winfrey: The Real Story, by George Mair
23. Out on a Limb, by Shirley MacLaine
24. The Prophet, by Kahlil Gibran
25. Real Magic, by Wayne Dyer
26. Starseed Transmissions, by Ken Carey
27. Think and Grow Rich, by Napoleon Hill
28. Way of the Peaceful Warrior, by Dan Millman
29. Woman, Thou Art Loosed! by T.D. Jakes
30. Awaken the Giant Within, by Anthony Robbins
31. The Book of Secrets, by Deepak Chopra, M.D.

Appendix 9: Inspirational Music

Happiness:
Baby I'm a Star - by Prince
Born to be Wild - by Steppenwolf
Celebrate Life - by Karl Anthony
Celebration - by Kool & the Gang
Don't Worry, Be Happy - by Bobbie McFerrin
Every Little Cell in My Body Is Happy - by Karl Anthony
Everybody Have Fun Tonight - by Wang Chung
Good Vibrations – by The Beach Boys
Songs of Love From Around the Planet – by Passion Planet
What a Feeling – by Irene Cara (Flashdance Soundtrack)

Fear:
Third Piano Concerto – by Sergey Vasil'yevich Rachmaninov
Faith – by George Michael
I'm Free – by Jon Secada
Nowhere to Run – by Martha & The Vandellas
Pray – by M.C. Hammer

Hurt:
Footloose – by Kenny Loggins (Footloose Soundtrack)
Get Over It – by The Eagles
Greatest Love of All – by Whitney Houston
Heard It Through the Grapevine – by Marvin Gaye
Kiss of Life – by Sade
What Is Love (Baby Don't Hurt Me) – by Haddaway

Anger:
Express Yourself – by Madonna
Hound Dog – by Elvis Presley
Jump – by Van Halen
Let's Go Crazy – by Prince
My Prerogative – by Bobby Brown
Put A Little Love in Your Heart – by Annie Lennox (Scrooged Soundtrack)

Frustration:
Bad – by Michael Jackson
Billie Jean – by Michael Jackson

I Want a New Drug – by Huey Lewis & The News
Wanna Be Starting Something – by Michael Jackson

Disappointment:
Don't Let the Sun Go Down on Me – by Elton John
Eye of the Tiger – by Survivor
Hero – by Mariah Carey
Higher Love – by Steve Winwood
Staying Alive – by The Bee Gees (Saturday Night Fever)
Tell It to My Heart – by Taylor Dane

Loneliness:
C'mon Ride the Train – by Quad City DJs
Dancing With Myself – by Billy Idol
Desperado – by The Eagles
I Want to Know What Love Is – by Foreigner
Love Shack – by The B-52s
Rhythm Nation – by Janet Jackson
We Built This City on Rock and Roll – by Jefferson Starship
I'm Gonna Be (500 Miles) – by The Proclaimers

Inadequacy:
Amazing Grace – by Various Artists
I'm Too Sexy – by Right Said Fred
Man in the Mirror – by Michael Jackson
Searching My Soul – by Vonda Shepard
Soul Provider – by Michael Bolton
U Can't Touch This – by M.C. Hammer
You Can Do Magic – by America
You Gotta Be – by Desiree

Feeling Overloaded (stressed):
2 Legit 2 Quit – by M.C. Hammer
Never Give Up on A Dream – by Rod Stewart
Push It – by Salt n' Peppa
Relax – by Frankie Goes to Hollywood

Self-pity:
Bust a Move – by Young M.C.
Get on Your Feet – by Gloria Estefan
I Feel Good – by Tony, Tone, Toni

I've Got the Power – by Snap
New Attitude – by Patti LaBelle
Vogue – by Madonna
What One Man Can Do – by John Denver

Table of Figures

Notes

[1] Fred P. Gallo and Harry Vincenzi, *Energy Tapping* (Oakland, CA: New Harbinger Publications, 2000).

[2] John Robbins, *The Food Revolution: How Your Diet Can Help Save Your Life and Our World* (York Beach, ME: Conari Press, 2001).

[3] George Howard Bell, *Textbook of Physiology and Biochemistry*, 4th ed. (New York: Williams and Wilkins, Ballantine, 1954).

[4] Dean Ornish, "The Patient as Your Partner: Patient Accountability and Compliance," a presentation given at the American College of Cardiology 53rd Annual Conference in New Orleans, March 2004.

[5] Responding to the D'Adamo Blood Type Diet, Dr. Stephan Bailey stated in the article "Eating According to Your Blood Type: A Bloody Bad Idea," published in the Tufts University *Health and Nutrition Letter* from August 1997, that "there is no anthropologic evidence whatsoever that all prehistoric people with a particular blood type ate the same diet."

[6] J. W. Helge, "Prolonged adaptation to fat-rich diet and training; effects on body fat stores and insulin resistance in man," International Journal of Obesity 26 (2002): 1118–1124.

[7] John Robbins, *The Food Revolution: How Your Diet Can Help Save Your Life and Our World* (York Beach, ME: Conari Press, 2001).

[8] "Obesity-Related Metabolic Disorders," *International Journal of Obesity* 19 (1995): 811.

[9] Cited in John Robbins's *The Food Revolution: How Your Diet Can Help Save Your Life and Our World* (York Beach, ME: Conari Press, 2001).

[10] "Fad Diets Versus Dietary Guidelines," American Institute for Cancer Research, 1999, http://www.aicr.org/faddiets.

[11] Dean Ornish, *Great Nutrition Debate*, February 14, 2000.

[12] Robert O. Young and Shelley Redford Young, *The pH Miracle: Balance Your Diet, Reclaim Your Health* (New York: Warner Books, 2002).

[13] Within the context of this book I will often use the term *allergy* but I really mean is a food reaction or a food sensitivity and not a classic food allergy.

[14] Elson M. Haas and Cameron Stauth, *The False Fat Diet: The Revolutionary 21-Day Program for Losing the Weight You Think Is Fat* (Ballantine Books, 2001).

[15] Ellen W. Cutler, *The Food Allergy Cure: A New Solution to Food Cravings, Obesity, Depression, Headaches, Arthritis, and Fatigue* (New York: Three Rivers Press/The Crown Publishing Group, 2003).

[16] Fred P. Gallo and Harry Vincenzi, *Energy Tapping* (Oakland, CA: New Harbinger Publications, 2000).

[17] Instead of giving all the primary bibliographic sources for this statement, I prefer to refer here to John Robbins's excellent book on this topic called *The Food Revolution: How Your Diet Can Help Save Your Life and Our World* (York Beach, ME: Conari Press, 2001).

[18] "Heart Disease and Stroke Statistics – 2005 Update," American Heart Association, www.americanheart.org/downloadable/heart/1105390918119HDSStats2005Update.pdf.

[19] "United States Cancer Statistics – 2002 Incidence and Mortality," http://www.cdc.gov/cancer/npcr/uscs/pdf/2002_USCS.pdf.

[20] "Overweight and Obesity: Health Consequences," U.S. Department of Health and Human Services, 2004, http://www.surgeongeneral.gov.

[21] BMI is a measure of weight in relation to height. To calculate your own BMI you can use the following formula: BMI = weight (kg)/height (m)2 or BMI = (weight (pounds)/height (inches)2 x 703. You can also use the easy tools available at www.SageEra.com. In adults, healthy weight means a BMI between 18.5 and 24.9. People with a BMI between 25.0 and 29.9 are considered overweight, and obesity is classified in three classes: Class I BMI 30.0–34.9, Class II BMI 35.0–39.9, Class III BMI >40.0.

[22] "Actual Causes for Death in the United States, 2000," U.S. National Center for Chronic Disease Prevention and Health Promotion, Chronic Disease Prevention Fact Sheet, 2000, http://www.cdc.gov/nccdphp/factsheets/death_causes2000.htm.

[23] "Actual Causes for Death in the United States, 2000," U.S. National Center for Chronic Disease Prevention and Health Promotion, Chronic Disease Prevention Fact Sheet, 2000, http://www.cdc.gov/nccdphp/factsheets/death_causes2000.htm.

[24] "Aim for a Healthy Weight: Information for Patients and the Public," U.S. National Heart, Lung and Blood Institute, 1999, http://www.nhlbi.nih.gov/health/public/heart/obesity/lose_wt/patmats.htm.

[25] "Statistics Related to Overweight and Obesity," U.S. National Institute of Diabetes & Digestive & Kidney Diseases, 1999–2000, http://www.niddk.nih.gov/health/nutrit/pubs/statobes.htm#preval.

[26] "Heart Disease and Stroke Statistics – 2005 Update," American Heart Association, http://www.americanheart.org/downloadable/heart/1105390918119HDSStats2005Update.pdf.

[27] Robert O. Young, *Energy Report with Anthony Robbins*, Parts 1–3, Interview by Tony Robbins, Living Health Program by Robbins Research International Inc., 1999.

[28] Innerlight is the name of Dr. Robert Young's alkalizing products set, which is based on his health restoring program called New Biology.

[29] Robert O. Young and Shelley Redford Young, *The pH Miracle for Weight Loss: Balance Your Body Chemistry, Achieve Your Ideal Weight* (New York: Warner Books, 2005).

[30] L. A. Frassetto et al., *American Journal of Clinical Nutrition* 68 (1998): 576–583.

[31] Tadataka Yamada, David H. Alpers, Neil Kaplowitz, Loren Laine, Chung Owyang, Don W. Powell, Textbook of Gastroenterology, Volume One, (New York: Lippincott Williams and Wilkins, 2003)

[32] B. A. Ames et al., "High-dose vitamin therapy stimulates variant enzymes with decreased coenzyme binding affinity (increased K(m)): relevance to genetic disease and polymorphisms," *American Journal of Clinical Nutrition* 75 (2002): 616–158.

[33] Gerard J. Tortora and Sandra R. Grabowski, *Principles of Anatomy and Physiology* (New Jersey: John Wiley and Sons, 2003).

[34] Robert O. Young and Shelley Redford Young, *The pH Miracle: Balance Your Diet, Reclaim Your Health* (New York: Warner Books, 2002).

35 F. Garcia-Contreras et al., "Cola beverage consumption induces bone mineralization reduction in ovariectomized rats", *Arch Med Res.* 31, no. 4 (2000): 360–5.

36 L. A. Frassetto et al., *American Journal of Clinical Nutrition* 68 (1998): 576–583.

37 V. Radosavlevic et al., "Fluid intake and bladder cancer. A case control study," *Neoplasma* 50, no. 3 (2003): 234–238.

38 Robert O. Young and Shelley Redford Young, *The pH Miracle for Weight Loss: Balance Your Body Chemistry, Achieve Your Ideal Weight* (New York: Warner Books, 2005).

39 Gerard J. Tortora and Sandra R. Grabowski, *Principles of Anatomy and Physiology* (New Jersey: John Wiley and Sons, 2003).

40 Richard Anderson, *Cleanse and Purify Thyself, Book I: The Cleanse* (Christobe Publishing, 2000).

41 Robert O. Young, E*nergy Report with Anthony Robbins*, Parts 1–3, Interview by Tony Robbins, Living Health Program by Robbins Research International Inc., 1999.

42 Robert O. Young and Shelley Redford Young, *The pH Miracle for Weight Loss: Balance Your Body Chemistry, Achieve Your Ideal Weight* (New York: Warner Books, 2005).

43 Robert O. Young and Shelley Redford Young, *The pH Miracle for Weight Loss: Balance Your Body Chemistry, Achieve Your Ideal Weight* (New York: Warner Books, 2005).

44 L. A. Frassetto et al., *American Journal of Clinical Nutrition* 68 (1998): 576–583.

45 Robert O. Young and Shelley Redford Young, *The pH Miracle for Weight Loss: Balance Your Body Chemistry, Achieve Your Ideal Weight* (New York: Warner Books, 2005).

46 L. A. Frassetto et al., *American Journal of Clinical Nutrition* 68 (1998): 576–583.

47 Robert O. Young and Shelley Redford Young, The pH Miracle for Weight Loss: Balance Your Body Chemistry, Achieve Your Ideal Weight (New York: Warner Books, 2005).

48 You can buy one of the best alkalizing water devices through http://www.hightechhealth.com/.

49 Bradford. B. Lowell and Bruce M. Spiegelman, "Towards a molecular understanding of adaptive thermogenesis," *Nature* April 2000: 652–660.

50 Northwest Georgia Gastroenterological Association, http://www.nwgagastro.com/education/yourdigest.asp.

51 Instead of giving all the primary bibliographic sources for this statement, I prefer to refer here to John Robbins's excellent book on this topic called *The Food Revolution: How Your Diet Can Help Save Your Life and Our World* (York Beach, ME: Conari Press, 2001).

52 K. S. Schaefer and S. E. Kegley, "Persistent toxic chemicals in the U.S. food supply," *Journal of Epidemiology and Community Health* 56, no. 11 (2002): 813–817.

53 Robert O. Young, *Energy Report with Anthony Robbins*, Parts 1–3, Interview by Tony Robbins, Living Health Program by Robbins Research International Inc., 1999.

54 M. Horowitz et al., "Life Event Questionnaires for Measuring Presumptive Stress," *Psychosomatic Medicine* 39, no. 6 (1977): 413–431.

55 T. H. Holmes and R. H. Rahe, "The social readjustment rating scale," *Journal of Psychosomatic Research* 11 (1967): 213–218.

56 M. Friedman and D. Ulmer, *Treating Type A Behavior and Your Heart* (New York: Alfred A. Knopf, 1984).

[57] J. Stout, "Amino acids and growth hormone manipulation," *Nutrition* 18, no. 8 (2002): 683–684.

[58] David Niven, *The 100 Simple Secrets of Happy People* (San Francisco: HarperCollins, 2000).

[59] David G. Myers, *The Pursuit of Happiness: Discovering the Pathway to Fulfillment, Well-Being, and Enduring Personal Joy* (New York: Quill, 1993).

[60] Udo Erasmus, *Fats That Heal, Fats That Kill: The Complete Guide to Fats, Oils, Cholesterol, and Human Health* (Burnaby, BC, Canada: Alive Books Publishing, 1993).

[61] I personally take and highly recommend the oil blend by Udo Erasmus, for I believe that it has every kind of essential oil the body needs and in the right combination. Having studied his work and met Dr. Erasmus in person, I trust that he provides the best possible products based on the most sound scientific research and knowledge.

[62] Ray Kurzweil and Terry Grossmann, Fantastic Voyage: Live Long Enough to Live Forever (New York: Rodale Books, 2004).

[63] J. I. Kreisberg and P. Y. Patel, "The effects of insulin, glucose, and diabetes on prostaglandin production by rat kidney glomeruli and cultured glomerular mesangial cells," *Prostaglandins Leukot Med.* 11, no. 4 (1983): 431–442.

[64] Nancy Appleton, *Lick the Sugar Habit* (Avery Publishing Group, 1996).

[65] Arthur Agatston, *The South Beach Diet: The Delicious, Doctor-Designed, Foolproof Plan for Fast and Healthy Weight Loss* (New York: Rodale Books, 2003).

[66] Ray Kurzweil and Terry Grossmann, *Fantastic Voyage: Live Long Enough to Live Forever* (New York: Rodale Books, 2004).

[67] Edward Howell and Victoras Kulvinskas, *Food Enzymes for Health and Longevity* (Twin Lakes, WI: Lotus Press, 1994).

[68] David Wolfe, *Eating for Beauty: For Women and Men: Introducing a Whole New Concept of Beauty, What It Is, and How You Can Achieve It* (Maul Brothers Publishers, 2002).

[69] Nancy F. Butte et al., "Nutrient Adequacy of Exclusive Breastfeeding for the Term Infant During the First Six Months of Life," World Health Organization, Geneva 2002.

[70] Ray Kurzweil and Terry Grossmann, *Fantastic Voyage: Live Long Enough to Live Forever* (New York: Rodale Books, 2004).

[71] Robert O. Young, "Health Talk for Weight Loss," Interview (Audio CD), San Diego, 2004.

[72] J. W. Helge, "Prolonged adaptation to fat-rich diet and training; effects on body fat stores and insulin resistance in man," *International Journal of Obesity* 26, no. 8 (2002): 1118–1124.

[73] Virginia Messina and Mark Messina, *The Dietitian's Guide to Vegetarian Diets* (Gaithersburg, MD: Aspen Publishers, 1996).

[74] Laimer et al., "Markers of chronic inflammation and obesity: a prospective study on the reversibility of this association in middle-aged women undergoing weight loss by surgical intervention," *International Journal of Obesity Related Metabolic Disorders*, May 2002.

[75] J. A. Varner et al., "Chronic administration of aluminum-fluoride or sodium-fluoride to rats in drinking water: alterations in neuronal and cerebrovascular integrity," *Brain Research* 784, nos. 1–2 (1998): 284–289.

[76] J. A. Varner et al., "Chronic administration of aluminum-fluoride or sodium-fluoride to rats in drinking water: alterations in neuronal and cerebrovascular integrity," *Brain Research* 784, nos. 1–2 (1998): 284–289.

[77] T. J. Woodruff et al., "Public health implications of 1990 air toxic concentrations across the United States," *Environmental Health Perspectives* 106, no. 5 (1998): 245–251.

[78] Patricia Bragg and Paul Bragg, *Water: The Shocking Truth That Can Save Your Life* (Santa Barbara, CA: Health Science, 1995).

[79] E. B. Rimm et al. "Prospective study of alcohol consumption and risk of coronary heart disease in men." *The Lancet* 338 (1991): 464–468.

[80] An American Academy of Pediatrics Medical Library article from January 6, 2004, shows that between 56 and 85 percent of school-age children consume at least one soft drink daily. This adds the equivalent of 10 teaspoons of sugar to their daily diet and contributes to their risk for obesity, diabetes, and other serious conditions.

[81] David S. Ludwig, Karen E. Peterson, and Steven L. Gortmacher, "Relationship Between Consumption of Sugar-Sweetener Drinks and Childhood Obesity: A Perspective, Observational Analysis," *The Lancet*, February 17, 2001.

[82] Neal Barnard , president of the Physicians Committee for Responsible Medicine, http://www.pcrm.org.

[83] On its website, the Northwest Georgia Gastroenterological Association says that "each month 44 percent of adults take antacids or other medicines to treat heartburn," http://www.nwgagastro.com/education/yourdigest.asp.

[84] For more information on healing immune disorders and allergies including food allergies, please refer to Ellen W. Cutler, *Winning the War Against Immune Disorders and Allergies: A Drug Free Cure for Allergies* (Independence, MO: Delmar Learning, 1998).

[85] In her book *The Food Allergy Cure: A New Solution to Food Cravings, Obesity, Depression, Headaches, Arthritis, and Fatigue*, Ellen Cutler discusses extensively how weight loss can be achieved with the appropriate enzymes.

[86] Bernard Jensen, *Doctor-Patient Handbook: Dealing with the Reversal Process and the Healing Crisis Through Eliminating Diets and Detoxification* (Bernard Jensen International, 1978).

[87] E. M. Castano et al., "Fibrillogenesis in Alzheimer's disease of amyloid beta peptides and Apo lipoprotein E." *Biochemical Journal* 306, pt. 2 (1995): 599–604.

[88] Paul M. Ridker et al., "C-Reactive Protein, the Metabolic Syndrome, and Risk of Incident Cardiovascular Events," *Circulation* 107 (2003): 391.

[89] Stuart P. Weisberg et al., "Obesity is associated with macrophage accumulation in adipose tissue," *Journal of Clinical Investigation* 112 (2003): 1796–1808.

[90] T. S. Church et al., "Reduction of C-Reactive protein levels through use of a multivitamin." *American Journal of Medicine* 115, no. 9 (2003): 702–707.

[91] Lithium orotate is my latest discovery in supplementation. I have achieved great success with it both personally and with my clients. I was introduced to it by my dear friend Dr. John Gray, the world-renowned author of the book *Men Are from Mars, Women Are from Venus*.

[92] H. A. Nieper, "The clinical application of lithium orotate," *Agressologie* 14, no. 6 (1973): 407–11.

[93] D. Mueller-Oerlinghausen et al., "Reduced mortality of manic-depressive patients in long-term lithium treatment, an international collaborative study by IGSLI," *Psychiatry Res.* 36 (1991): 329–331.

[94] F. K. Goodwin and K. R. Jamison, *Manic-Depressive Illness* (Oxford, England: Oxford University Press, 1990).

[95] H. A. Nieper, "The curative effect of a combination of Calcium-orotate and Lithium orotate on primary and secondary chronic hepatitis and primary and secondary liver cirrhosis," from a lecture at the International Academy of Preventive Medicine, Washington, DC, March 9, 1974.

[96] "Overweight and Obesity: At a Glance," U.S. Department of Health and Human Services, The Surgeon General Call to Action to Prevent and Decrease Overweight and Obesity, February 2004, http://www.surgeongeneral.gov.

[97] According to www.saveharry.com and "Soft Drink Markets in 174 Countries Worldwide Documented," *Beverage Marketing,* press release, June 15, 2001. People drink approximately 565 cans of soft drinks per capita per year. Each can contains 10 teaspoons of sugar. http://www.beveragemarketing.com/news2p.htm.

[98] John Robbins, *The Food Revolution: How Your Diet Can Help Save Your Life and Our World.* The annual medical cost directly attributed to meat consumption in the U.S. alone is $60–$120 billion.

[99] John Robbins, *The Food Revolution: How Your Diet Can Help Save Your Life and Our World.* Four percent of the world's population (in the U.S.) eats 23 percent of the total beef produced in the world.

[100] John Robbins, *The Food Revolution: How Your Diet Can Help Save Your Life and Our World.* In America, 70 percent of chickens and 90 percent of turkeys are sufficiently contaminated with Campylobacter to cause serious illness.

[101] In her insightful book, *Lick the Sugar Habit,* Dr. Nancy Appleton writes that the average American consumes at least 149 pounds of sugar per year.

[102] Walter M. Bortz, *Diabetes Danger: What 200 Million Americans at Risk Need to Know* (New York: SelectBooks, 2005).

[103] Walter M. Bortz, *Diabetes Danger: What 200 Million Americans at Risk Need to Know* (New York: SelectBooks, 2005).

[104] Walter M. Bortz, *Diabetes Danger: What 200 Million Americans at Risk Need to Know* (New York: SelectBooks, 2005).

[105] Robert Kubey and Mihaly Csikszentmihalyi, "Television Addiction Is No Metaphor," *Scientific American Special Edition* 14, no. 1 (2004).

[106] Deepak Chopra, *Ageless Body, Timeless Mind: The Quantum Alternative to Growing Old* (New York: Harmony Books, 1994); also available as audio tape.

[107] I. M. Lee, "Physical activity in women: how much is good enough?" *JAMA* 290, no. 10 (2003): 1377–1378.

[108] Elson Haas with Daniella Chace, *The New Detox Diet* (Berkeley, CA: Celestial Arts, 2004).

[109] Al Gore, *An Inconvenient Truth: The Planetary Emergency of Global Warming and What We Can Do About It* (New York: Rodale Press, 2006).

[110] G. L. Booth and E. E. Wang, "Preventive Health Care 2000 Update: Screening and management of hyperhomocysteinemia for the prevention of coronary artery disease events," The Canadian Task Force on Preventive Health Care, *CMAJ* 163, no.1 (2000): 21–29.

[111] T. J. Woodruff et al, "Public health implications of 1990 air toxics concentration across the United States," *Environmental Health Perspectives* 106, no. 5 (1998): 245–251.

112 J. A. Varner et al, "Chronic administration of aluminum fluoride or sodium-fluoride to rats in drinking water: alterations in neural and cerebrovascular integrity," *Brain Research* 784, nos. 1–2 (1998): 284–298.

113 G. Hyland, "The physiological and environmental effects of non-ionizing electromagnetic radiation," European Parliament Directorate General for Research, 2001.

114 K. S. Schafer and S. E. Kegley, " Persistent toxic chemicals in the U.S. food supply," *Journal of Epidemiology and Community Health* 56, no. 11 (2002): 813–817.

115 H. Lai and N. P. Singh, "Single- and double-strand DNA breaks in rat brain cells after acute exposure to radio frequency electromagnetic radiation." *International Journal of Radiation Biology* 69, no.4 (1996):513–521.

116 G. L. Booth and E. E. Wang, "Preventive Health Care 2000 Update: Screening and management of hyperhomocysteinemia for the prevention of coronary artery disease events," The Canadian Task Force on Preventive Health Care, CMAJ 163, no. 1 (2000): 21–29.

117 I would highly encourage you to buy Dr. Jensen's books and to follow his advice.

118 Bernard Jensen, *Dr. Jensen's Guide to Better Bowel Care: A Complete Program for Tissue Cleansing Through Bowel Management* (New York: Avery Penguin Putnam, 1998).

119 I personally define a fast as not eating anything but drinking water only. A cleanse entails for me drinking only juice or broth for a certain amount of time. I will leave it up to you to decide whether or not you want to join the debate over definitions of a cleanse versus a fast versus a detoxification. In this publication, I care more about providing immediate support to those seeking to lose weight and bring the body back into balance rather than entering a war on definitions. I have chosen the words "cleanse" and "detoxification" as general terms in order to explain how health and vitality can be easily restored through the elimination of wastes at all levels in the body.

120 There are several rejuvenation centers I would highly recommend for fasting. The first on my list would be the Hippocrates Institute, which, according to its website, www.hippocratesinst.org, states "The Institute's goal is to reawaken the total consciousness within ourselves and allow us to realize that good health and free will is every person's birthright, and that a life free of disease and needless pain is our human legacy. The Hippocrates philosophy is dedicated to the belief that a pure enzyme-rich diet, complemented by positive thinking and non-invasive therapies, are essential elements on the path to optimum health." Another institute I highly recommend is Dr. Gabriel Cousens's Tree of Life Center. I have also attended Tony Robbins's cleanse and life changing program called Life Mastery twice.

121 You can purchase pH paper in most health food stores or online through Micro Essential Laboratory, www.microessentiallab.com.

122 I would highly recommend the greens of David Wolfe's Nature's First Food and Dr. Udo Erasmus's Green Blend.

123 Robert O. Young and Shelley Redford Young, *The pH Miracle: Balance Your Diet, Reclaim Your Health* (New York: Warner Books, 2002).

124 I personally use a Needak rebounder.

125 Deepak Chopra and David Simon, *Grow Younger, Live Longer: Ten Steps to Reverse Aging* (New York: Three Rivers Press, 2002).

126 I use an enema at least once a week. If you can find any centers in your area, I would highly recommend taking two sets of five each of colon hydrotherapy per year.

[127] Dr. Herbert Ross is a certified acupuncturist and neuro-emotional therapist (NET). He is a personal chiropractor to motivational speaker Anthony Robbins and an internationally known authority on alternative and natural solutions to sleep disorders, as well as founder of the Aspen Sleep Institute in Colorado. Dr. Ross is coauthor of *Sleep Disorders: An Alternative Medicine Definitive Guide* (Lanham, MD: National Book Network, 2000).

[128] You can order a high-quality and easy-to-use enema kit from Health and Yoga at http://www.healthandyoga.com/html/product/enemaequipment.html.

[129] To view some of these creatures you can check out Dr. Anderson's website at http://www.cleanse.net.

[130] For more information, please refer to the books of Dr. Richard Anderson, *Cleanse and Purify Thyself, Book I: The Cleanse and Cleanse* and *Purify Thyself, Book II: Secrets of Radiant Health and Energy* (Christobe Publishing, 2000), as well as his website at http://www.cleanse.net.

[131] Tadataka Yamada et al., *Textbook of Gastroenterology*, 4th Ed., Vol. 1 (Philadelphia: Lippincott Williams & Wilkins, 2003).

[132] J. Rainer Poley, *Journal of Pediatric Gastroenterology and Nutrition* 7, no. 3 (1988): 386–94, http://www.cleanse.net/why_one_should_cleanse.HTM.

[133] Udo Erasmus, *Fats That Heal, Fats That Kill: The Complete Guide to Fats, Oils, Cholesterol and Human Health* (Burnaby, BC, Canada: Alive Books, 1993).

[134] Udo's Oil, named after its developer, Dr. Udo Erasmus, can be purchased in most health food stores or online.

[135] I have learned to prepare delicious gourmet raw food meals from the following books: *The Uncook Book: New Vegetarian Food for Life* (Regan Books, 1999) by Juliano Brotman with Erika Lenkert; *The Sunfood Cuisine: A Practical Guide to Raw Vegetarian Cuisine* (Maul Brothers Publishing, 2002) by Frederic Patenaude; and *The Raw Gourmet* (Burnaby, BC, Canada: Alive Books, 1999) by Nomi Shannon.

[136] Fred P. Gallo and Harry Vincenzi, *Energy Tapping* (Oakland, CA: New Harbinger Publications, 2000).

[137] Cloe Madanes, *Strategic Family Therapy* (The Jossey-Bass social and behavioral science series) (Indianapolis: Jossey-Bass, 1991).

[138] Deepak Chopra, *The Ultimate Deepak Chopra Collection*, CD Audio Program (Nightingale-Conant Corporation, 1998).

[139] Sogyal Rinpoche, *The Tibetan Book of Living and Dying*, (San Francisco: HarperSanFrancisco: 1994).

[140] http://www.hawking.org.uk/disable/dindex.html.

[141] I wrote this definition during a seminar I attended with Deepak Chopra in the Himalayas in January 2005.

[142] Wayne Dyer, *10 Secrets for Success and Inner Peace* (Carlsbad, CA: Hay House, 2002).

[143] Deepak Chopra, *The Soul of Healing Meditations*, CD Audio Program (Rasa Music, 2003).

[144] H. Friedman and S. Boothby-Kewley, "The Disease-Prone Personality: A Meta-Analytic View," *American Psychologist* 42 (1987).

[145] Daniel Goleman, *Emotional Intelligence: Why It Can Matter More Than IQ* (Bantam Books, 1995).

146 D. Wegner & J. Pennebaker, Eds., *Handbook of Mental Control* (Prentice-Hall, 1993).

147 Philip G. Zimbardo, *Psychology and Life* (HarperCollins Publishers, 1988).

148 Daniel Goleman, *Emotional Intelligence: Why It Can Matter More Than IQ* (Bantam Books, 1995).

149 J. Jacobi, *Complex Archetype Symbol in the Psychology of C. G. Jung* (Princeton University Press, 1959).

150 Philip G. Zimbardo, *Psychology and Life* (HarperCollins Publishers, 1988).

151 Stephen F. Davis and Joseph J. Palladino, *Psychology* (New Jersey: Prentice-Hall, 2005).

152 Daniel Goleman, *Emotional Intelligence: Why It Can Matter More Than IQ* (Bantam Books, 1995).

153 Mark Epstein, *Thoughts without a Thinker* (New York: Basic Books, 1995).

154 I would highly encourage you to attend all of Tony's events beginning with his first program called "Unleash the Power Within." In the meantime, I recommend reading his books. If you would rather hear him speak, make sure to get his outstanding program "Get the Edge" and/or "Personal Power," which is the most successful audio tape ever produced.

155 D. Wegner and J. Pennebaker, Eds., *Handbook of Mental Control* (Prentice-Hall, 1993).

156 C. Thoreson, "Stanford study on anger and second heart attacks," paper presented at the International Congress of Behavioral Medicine, Uppsala, Sweden, 1990.

157 D. Felten et al., "Noradrenergic and peptidergic innervation of lymphoid tissue," *Journal of Immunology*, 135 (1985): 755–765.

158 "Scientific Findings About Forgiveness," John Templeton Foundation, http://www.templeton.org/capabilities_2004/spirit02B.html.

159 Roger Walsh and Frances Vaughan, *Paths Beyond Ego: The Transpersonal Vision* (New Consciousness Reader) (Jeremy P. Tarcher, 1993).

160 D. Childre and Howard Martin, *The HeartMath Solution: The Institute of HeartMath's Revolutionary Program for Engaging the Power of the Heart's Intelligence* (San Francisco: HarperCollins, 2000).

161 D. Childre and D. Rozman, *Transforming Anxiety* (Oakland, CA: New Harbinger Publications, 2006).

162 R. Ader et al., *Psychoneuroimmunology* (Academic Press, 1990).

163 Steven Schwartz, *Abnormal Psychology: A Discovery Approach* (Mayfield Publishing Company, 2000)

164 D. Spiegel et al., "Effect of psychosocial treatment on survival of patients with metastatic breast cancer," *The Lancet* 2 (1989): 888–91.

165 Tony Robbins has been one of my most significant teachers for the past 17 years. Although I recommend all of his books and tapes I highly recommend experiencing him at one of his live seminars. They are highly powerful and enable most human beings to reach the next level of personal growth and development.

166 Compassionate communication combines elements of nonviolent communication (Marshall Rosenberg et al., *Nonviolent Communication: A Language of Life: Create Your Life, Your Relationships, and Your World in Harmony with Your Values* [Encinitas, CA: PuddleDancer Press, 2003]); relationship versus dominator communication (Dr. Riane Eisler, *The Power of Partnership: Seven Relationships That Will Change Your Life* [Novato, CA: New

World Library, 2003]); tonglen, the Tibetan Buddhist technique for transcending the pain of other people by breathing it in (Pema Chödrön, *When Things Fall Apart: Heart Advice for Difficult Times* [Boston: Shambhala Publications, 2000]); the work of David Hawkins (David Hawkins, *Power vs. Force: The Hidden Determinants of Human Behavior* [Carlsbad, CA: Hay House, 2002]); as well as teachings by Deepak Chopra and Tony Robbins.

[167] Michael Murphy and George Leonard, *The Life We Are Given: A Long-Term Program for Realizing the Potential of Body, Mind, Heart, and Soul* (Inner Work Book) (Jeremy P. Tarcher, 1995).

[168] D. Childre and Howard Martin, *The HeartMath Solution: The Institute of HeartMath's Revolutionary Program for Engaging the Power of the Heart's Intelligence* (San Francisco: HarperCollins, 2000).

[169] This is the powerful Tibetan Buddhist practice of tonglen. It is wonderfully described by both His Holiness the Dalai Lama in his writings as well as by Pema Chödrön in her marvelous book *When Things Fall Apart*.

[170] I have personally drawn great value from both the book and the seminar titled *Nonviolent Communication: A Language for Life* by Dr. Marshall Rosenberg as well as the book *Power vs. Force* by Dr. David Hawkins.

[171] For more details about the power of questions, please refer to Anthony Robbins' *PowerTalk: Learn to Use Power of Questions!* (Audio Cassette) (Audio Renaissance, 1992) by Anthony Robbins and Barbara De Angelis or Personal Power (CD set) (Sound Ideas, 2000).

[172] From Tony Robbins's "Unleash the Power Within" seminar.

[173] Thomas Merton, *Gandhi on Non-Violence* (New York: New Directions Publishing, 1965).

[174] If you are interested in further training in nonviolent communication, you can reach Wes Taylor through the Center for Nonviolent Communication at www.SageEra.com/WesTaylor.

[175] Daniel Goleman, *Emotional Intelligence: Why It Can Matter More Than IQ* (Bantam Books, 1995).

[176] I highly recommend all of Tony Robbins's seminars, including "Unleash the Power Within" and "Date with Destiny," in addition to his tape series *Get the Edge*™ and all the other programs he has developed.

[177] Deepak Chopra, *Magical Mind, Magical Body: Mastering the Mind/Body Connection for Perfect Health and Total Well-Being (Audio Program, Unabridged)* (Niles, IL: Nightingale-Conant Corporation, 2003).

[178] To plan my days, my weeks, and the rest of my life, I use Tony Robbins's Results Planning Method, which I find the best life management system available today.

[179] Every day we cultivate consciously the feeling of gratitude for life's gifts while realizing that every day above ground is a great day. In addition, we have an outcome each day. For instance, Monday we practice the Law of Giving. We learn how to give and to receive gracefully.

[180] I currently take Dr. Ellen Cutler's BioSet Probiotic but I have also had great results with Flora Grow from Arise and Shine.

[181] One of my preferred tapes is Deepak Chopra's *Everyday Immortality: A Concise Course in Spiritual Transformation* (Random House Audio Publishing Group, 1999).

[182] I use a loofah from Earth Therapeutics that you can get at any health food store, but a simple body brush would be just as good.

[183] I adopted this question many years ago from my teacher Wayne Dyer.

184 To help you with this process I highly recommend reading Napoleon Hills's book *Think and Grow Rich* (Fawcett Books, 1983); Tony Robbins's books *Unlimited Power: The New Science of Personal Achievement* (Free Press, 1997) and *Awaken the Giant Within: How to Take Immediate Control of Your Mental, Emotional, Physical and Financial* (Free Press, 1992). However, to jump-start the achieving of your dreams, attend Tony Robbins's "Unleash the Power Within" life seminar.

185 I highly recommend Deepak Chopra's *The Seven Spiritual Laws of Success: A Practical Guide to the Fulfillment of Your Dreams* (based on Creating Affluence) (San Rafael, CA: Amber-Allen Publishing, 1995); Tony Robbins's *Get the Edge* audio program (San Diego, CA: Guthy-Renker, 2000); Louise Hay's *Songs of Affirmation* (Chants and Meditations/Audio Cassette/207) (Carlsbad, CA: Hay House Audio Books, 1986); and Wayne Dyer's *101 Ways to Transform Your Life* (Carlsbad, CA: Hay House, 1995).

186 There are some outstanding greens and essential oils available out there. I personally use Udo's Oil and vary between Udo's Super Greens, Dr. Robert Young's InnerLight Greens, and David Wolfe's Superfood.

187 This could be made of low-sugar fruit blended with some overnight-soaked raw nuts, one pitted date, and an organic flavor extract such as orange, vanilla, or cinnamon.

188 There are some outstanding greens and essential oils that you can buy. I personally use Udo's oil and vary between Udo's Super Greens and David Wolfe's Superfood.

189 In his marvelous book, *A Theory of Everything: An Integral Vision for Business, Politics, Science, and Spirituality* (Boston: Shambhala Publications, 2001), Ken Wilber attributed this quote to Dr. Phillip Harter of Stanford University School of Medicine. However, I have not been able to confirm the source of it thus far.

Index

E

Edison, Thomas, xxxi, 167, 211
Eggs, 26, 29, 35, 45, 50, 97, 99, 111, 112, 118
Eisler, Riane, ii, xxix, 286
Emotional mastery, 12, 157–162, 175–176, 185, 216, 224
Emotions, 6, 9, 30, 33, 66, 110, 111, 116, 129, 154–159, 160–166, 171–174, 177–179, 184, 191–196, 201–206, 214, 224, 266
Enema, 106–108, 116, 118, 122, 284, 285
Energy psychology, iii, 10, 12, 119
Environment, 6–8, 30–31, 44, 52—53, 72, 91–93, 104–107, 118, 121–125, 133–138, 177–179, 183–185, 203, 213, 227
  acidic environment, 8, 26, 35, 48, 91–92, 100, 124
  food quality and the environment, 12, 44
  social environment, 7, 136
  spiritual environment 122
Enzymes, 9–10, 28, 32, 3–40, 44, 50–66, 91–92, 102, 111–116, 121–125, 198, 203–205, 209, 210, 215, 268, 279, 281, 282, 284
  enzyme inhibitors, 35
Erasmus, Udo, 29, 34, 40, 101, 281, 284, 285
Essential fatty acids (EFAs), 29–35, 55, 59, 61–62, 98, 100, 113, 115, 123, 208–210
  omega-3, omega-6, 34, 58–59, 115
Exfoliation and sweating, 103, 105

F

Faith, xxvii, 166, 201, 202, 272, 216, 278
Fasting (see also cleansing and detox), 97, 102, 106–222, 284

Fat (see also essential fatty acids), 114–125, 132–139, 174, 190–193, 197, 281, 285
  body fat, 24, 28, 278, 281
  burn fat, 12, 37, 80, 120
  false fat, 9, 17, 25, 111, 112, 119
  fats that heal and fats that kill, 33–40, 281
  high-fat 4, 5
  holding on to fat, 124
  omega-3, omega-6, 34, 58–59, 115
  too fat, 227
Fatigue, 4, 9, 12, 26, 50, 55–57, 75, 91, 96, 111, 116, 120, 121, 123, 278, 282
  chronic fatigue, 57
Fear (see also feelings and emotions), 132–138, 143, 150–157, 165, 170–180, 213–216, 220, 271, 272
  of overweight, 17
  of criticism, 110
Feelings, 129, 145, 154–166, 179, 180–184, 208, 217–219, 269
  dark feelings, 145
  destructive feelings, 143
  of gratitude, 13, 140–143, 146, 150, 162–166, 180, 201, 208–213, 222
Fiber, xxi, 7, 8, 28, 33–38, 45–46, 52, 59, 66, 125, 208
Fish, xxxiii, 29, 32, 41–44, 55–58, 63–655, 113, 196, 215
Flax seed, 35, 231, 253, 258
  oil, 29, 32–35, 65, 113, 123, 195–196, 231–259
Fluoride, 47, 91, 281, 284
Food, xxi–xxxv, 4–13, 25–73, 88, 90–129, 136–139, 146–148, 153, 157, 161, 173
  70/30 Rule, 65
  food allergy, 9, 42, 49, 110, 120, 171, 197
  food combining, 11, 33, 41–43, 146, 209–210, 214–216, 269, 275, 234, 255–258, 268, 270, 280–284

About the Author

A trained researcher and scientist, Mariana Boze-san was raised in communist Romania, where she learned to appreciate food early in life. After her emigration to Germany, she began struggling with overweight and lived as a yo-yo dieter for more than two decades. Sick and tired of being sick and fat, Bozesan gave up a successful high-tech career to heal and find a permanent solution to weight loss. For five years, she traveled around the world, did extensive research, and studied with renowned weight loss, health, and lifestyle experts, thereby uncovering the secrets of successful dieters. The Diet for a New

Life books and programs, which she subsequently developed, reveal her research results. As a vehicle for her new mission, Bozesan founded the SageEra Institute (www.SageEra.com), a socially conscious company that supports more than 30 charities worldwide. A consciousness leader, Mariana is now continuing to contribute to the awakening of the human spirit by showing that permanent weight success is only possible by addressing all areas of life including the physical, mental, emotional, and spiritual.

Educated at Stanford University and Karlsruhe University in Germany, Bozesan holds advanced degrees (MS, BS) in artificial intelligence, computer science, and mathematics. She is currently a Ph.D. student at the Institute of Transpersonal Psychology in Palo Alto, California, from which she also holds a Master's degree (MATS).

In addition, Bozesan has been an angel investor since 1995. She is an early member of the Munich Business Angel Network and an ongoing investor in high-tech companies and medical devices. Moreover, she has invested in Business Angels and VC funds in Silicon Valley and Europe, including The Angels

Forum in Palo Alto and EarlyBird Venture Capital in Munich, Germany. Her specialty in investing is Consciousness Leadership. A serial entrepreneur, Bozesan is co-founder, President and CEO of Infobahn Romania SRL and Infobahn International GmbH. Before Infobahn, Bozesan worked for Oracle Corporation, where she was Director of Business Development for Europe, the Middle East and Africa. Based at Oracle headquarters in Redwood Shores, California, Bozesan also served as Global Alliance Marketing Director for Hewlett-Packard. Bozesan also worked for Digital Equipment Corporation now Hewlett-Packard, where she was Open Networks Marketing Manager based in Paris, France and Marketing Manager for Artificial Intelligence (AI) in Munich, Germany.

An humanitarian at heart, Bozesan served as a board member of The International Museum of Women in San Francisco, California, is member of the Founders Council of The Chopra Foundation, advisory board member of The Spiritual Alliance to Stop Intimate Violence (SAIV), and the President and Founder of The Bozesan Foundation. The Bozesan Foundation is a privately held philanthropic organization, which contributes to the education of young people in Africa, China, India, and in former communist countries.

An inspiring public speaker, Bozesan has made several TV and radio appearances, and has been interviewed by international magazines such as *Cosmopolitan, Marie Claire,* and *Capital.* She lives with her family in a three-generation household in the San Francisco Bay Area and in Bavaria, Germany.